DEAR
AUSTRALIAN

DEAR AUSTRALIAN

An anthology based on a
selection of the most
memorable letters to

THE AUSTRALIAN
1964-1981

researched and edited by
PHIL PEARMAN
Letters Editor of *The Australian*

Lansdowne Press
Sydney Auckland London New York

DEDICATION

SOME 40,000 readers of *The Australian* have had their views published in the nation's national daily newspaper since it first appeared in July, 1964. Their views record the many changing attitudes of Australians, from the 60s to the 80s, and made possible the publication of this anthology. *Dear Australian* is dedicated to those who cared enough to have their say.

Published by Lansdowne Press, Sydney
a division of RPLA Pty Limited
176 South Creek Road, Dee Why West, N.S.W., Australia, 2099.
First published 1982.

©Copyright Phil Pearman 1982.
Designed by Phil Pearman
Produced in Australia by the Publisher
Typeset in Australia.
Printed by Tien Mah Litho Printing Co. (Pte) Ltd.
2 Jalan Jentena, Jurong Town, Singapore 2261 .

National Library of Australia Cataloguing-in-Publication Data.

Dear Australian.

Collection of letters to The Australian.
Includes index.
ISBN 0 7018 1618 X.

I. Australian letters. I Pearman, Phil.
II. Australian (Sydney, N.S.W.).

A826'.308

Contents

The Editor,
GPO Box 4162,
Sydney,
NSW 2001

Dear Australian,

This anthology has been in the making for 18 years, since The Australian began publishing in July, 1964, quickly followed by the first letter for publication, giving their verdicts on the new national daily newspaper.

Those correspondents became the forerunners of some 40,000 letters published in The Australian to date. These views combine to make a record of the attitudes of Australians to the tumultuous changes in lifestyle over the last two decades. The period under review coincides with the maturing of Australia; in many ways, the letters presented in this book show a nation come of age.

Dear Australian is a unique social history, unique because it is based on the comments of some 680 correspondents from all walks of life and political persuasions; in effect, they have kept a finger on the national pulse during the changes.

For some, the anthology will be a nostalgic reminder of a golden age, as one correspondent puts it, paying tribute to Sir Robert Menzies, for others, the letters will point the way to much more assertive Australia, perhaps towards a republic.

Dear Australian says a great deal about the level of debate in The Australian's letters page and about the correspondents who have made this book possible. Day by day, they have monitored the mood of the nation and in so doing they have given us this entertaining and valuable social history. Dear Australian is a tribute to them.

PHIL PEARMAN
Letters Editor

ACKNOWLEDGEMENTS

I would like to thank News Limited for the full co-operation extended to me during research and preparation for this anthology, in particular the library staff.

My thanks also go to the cartoonists, Bruce Petty, Larry Pickering and Bill Mitchell, for allowing me to reproduce some of their deft strokes over the years and so complement the letters in this book.

And I want to thank Rosemary, who did so much in so many ways to help make *Dear Australian* a reality, and Vanessa, Angela, Mark and Dominic who all helped in their own ways.

Introduction

THE process of selecting letters for publication is like fossicking; you can strike a streak of literary gold in the first letter, or it may take a week or so to discover. A golden example is this letter, published in *The Australian* in August, 1981:

> *ENGLAND having managed to retain the Ashes, I seek the courtesy of your columns to inform those very many of my Australian friends who now owe me a bottle of something, that if they wish I shall be happy to roll over each and every bet as double or quits on England still retaining the Ashes at the conclusion of the next series between us, to be played in Australia.*
>
> *I suggest this in part to avoid a possible dislocation of Australian liquor supplies were all my creditors to meet their obligations simultaneously; and in part because of a shortage of storage space at home, space which I will ensure is more than doubled for when it will be needed in 1982-83.*

JOHN MASON
British High Commissioner
Canberra

Under the dust of the files containing the letters published in *The Australian* since July, 1964, there glittered a treasure chest of views to be explored, the anger, wit, pessimism and optimism of a young nation stirring through changing, turbulent times.

Thus the idea for *Dear Australian* came about.

What started as an entertainment, an anthology looking nostalgically at our recent past, developed into a unique social history, a view of Australia like no other, as seen through the eyes of a wide cross section of Australians.

Day by day, month by month, year by year, the letters built into a fascinating jigsaw of Australian moods and attitudes. The research was helped by the fact that the period under review only went back to 1964, making the events covered within the memory of most people who read this book, giving them the added benefit of hindsight to flavor their enjoyment.

The period covered — July, 1964 to Christmas, 1981 — coincides with the time when Australia changed, maturing from the relatively innocent days of the early 60s to the turbulence of the 70s and early 80s. The research was a daunting task; some 40,000 letters had to be examined, mostly with reading aids because the material had been reduced for filing purposes — in effect Australia put under a magnifying glass.

The emphasis on change in lifestyle meant that the subjects for selection fell into place. Each section is arranged in chronological order so that the reader can trace the changing moods over the years.

This changing attitude is highlighted in the sections titled The Permissive Society, Censorship, Drugs, Homosexuals, The Great Debates, which among other things looks back in anger to the bitterness of the Vietnam war and the execution of Ronald Ryan, the last man hanged in Australia, the controversies over the contraceptive pill and the White Australia Policy, and the anxieties concerning abortion and divorce.

Nowhere are the changes more pronounced than in the issues affecting women — Working Wives and Women's Rights, covering the rise of feminism.

The Cost of Living looks at the changes that inflation brought about and the way it affected the lives of pensioners.

These Changing Times notes the changes in social habits caused by the introduction of decimal currency, daylight saving, the metric system and the growth of the computer lifestyle.

The political letters date from the era of Menzies and Calwell and include the shock death of Prime Minister Harold Holt, the rise of Whitlam and Gorton, the euphoria of Labor's victory at the polls in 1972, the uproar over Whitlam's sacking in 1975, the enraged aftermath for Sir John Kerr and the death of Menzies.

From The Heart looks at the best of the open letters over the last two decades; like the letter from Simon Townsend in 1968 written from a cell in army barracks and explaining why he used the side of a coin to scratch on the wall, "Wars will cease when men refuse to fight;" or the emotional tribute that Tracey Wickham's father paid to his champion daughter in 1980.

That's Entertainment recalls the rebirth of Australian movies, the coming of color TV and the ABC's critics have their say.

On the lighter side, the love/hate relationship with the Poms, the royal family, Joh Bjelke-Petersen, Max Harris and cartoonists Bruce Petty and Larry Pickering are recalled.

In This Sporting Life, Tony Greig and Jack Fingleton salute Melbourne on the success of the Centenary Test in 1977; letters record the uproar over Greg Chappell's underarm bowling decision against New Zealand and later over the Dennis Lillee kicking incident; and Cyril Pearl sparks a response by complaining about the spread of the menace from the south, Australian Rules.

Australiana is covered with sections that look at the States and the Sydney versus Melbourne rivalry; the plight of Aborigines in the 60s, 70s and 80s; the call for Waltzing Matilda to be named as the national anthem; the agony and ecstasy of reactions as the Opera House took shape; Henry Lawson's drinking habits are dissected; the rise in strikes and the spread of the dole are condemned over the years; moves for Christian unity are recalled as well as calls from migrants for a better deal; the role of the RSL and the need for Anzac Day are examined along with letters clashing over repeated demands for a republic.

The book is laced throughout with PS letters, capturing some of Australia's wit over the last two decades, such as:

> *I TAKE issue with your editorial, Whitlam the Great? (3/12) regarding Mr Whitlam's lack of humility. He has learned humility and is now perfect — he is the first to admit it.*

> **I. B. NANKERVIS**
> Pymble, NSW

> *I AM afraid Ms Jenny MacLeod got it wrong in her letter last Friday when she saw Mr Whitlam's sacking as the action of a banana republic. It is, in fact, the action of a banana monarchy.*

> **DONALD HORNE**
> Woollahra, NSW

The book is dotted with familiar names, some put together in the Celebrity section, it is left to Joan Sutherland to end this anthology with a fervent call for unity to the "Promised Land".

Thus the pages are turned back to the way we were. It is only a short step back to 1964, yet for some readers it will seem like a giant step back to a saner, more orderly world, while other readers will see it as even greater stride back to a dark age.

Whatever your attitude, *Dear Australian* will tap many memories as the 684 correspondents have their say over the years. Together, they paint a fascinating picture.

For the record

DEAR Australian contains the views of 684 correspondents made up as follows: NSW (296), Victoria (162), Queensland (86), South Australia (43), A.C.T. (37), Tasmania (29), Western Australia (14), Overseas (11) and the Northern Territory (6).

Some 40,000 letters have been published in *The Australian* from its inception in July, 1964, to the end of research for this anthology, Christmas 1981. The figures show that more letters are now being published, in line with *The Australian*'s expansion of space to allow more readers to express their views. For example, the total number of letters published in 1965 was 2017; in 1973 it was 2063; in 1980 it was 2939, but by 1981 the total number of views published had risen to 3335.

The figures show up the recent exodus of Victorians to live in Queensland: Victorian correspondents led Queensland from 1964 to 1978, but in 1979 Queenslanders had more letters published compared with Victorians and the gap widened considerably in 1980 and 1981.

NSW correspondents contributed by far the greatest number of letters, 16,793, followed by, in order: Victoria, Queensland, South Australia, A.C.T., Tasmania, Western Australia, Overseas and the Northern Territory.

In the beginning

The Australian made its debut on July 15, 1964. The first edition was a sell-out. From coast to coast, the public took a good look at Australia's new national daily, then reached for their pens . . .

First the good news . .

THE *Australian* has got off to a flying start and one anticipates the high standard achieved will be maintained. The arrangement of news items is excellent with an equally excellent editorial. A fine newpaper indeed.
E. C. BELLCHAMBERS
Brighton-le-Sands, NSW

CONGRATULATIONS on the first issue of *The Australian* and this is no mere empty compliment.

What a pleasure it was to read those sane and informative columns of foreign news and comment, so different from the stuff we have been getting about Goldwater (dismissed as a hopeless reactionary without a scintilla of evidence being furnished to let the reader form his own opinion) and about Sukarno and Subandrio, Verwoerd and the Tunku. If *The Australian* goes on as it has begun, it's sure to be a success.
JOHN E. WEBB
Manly, NSW

CONGRATULATIONS on the birth of your new baby. Isn't he big? And like every fond mother you are full of expectation, thinking he might be a leader in Australia one day. We sincerely hope he is.
ROBERT S. GALLIMORE
Collaroy, NSW
27/7/64

THESE letters were included in The Australian's first letters page on Monday July 20, 1964.

. . . then the bad news

THE *Australian* is a real flop and unless several radical changes are made I cannot see it becoming a profitable venture, but, in fact, folding up altogether before very long. No doubt today's sales will probably be your best. I am sadly disappointed as I was hoping for a highly competitive newspaper.
H. BRUCHERA
Balmain, NSW

I HAVE just bought my first copy of *The Australian*.

The only reason that it is not my last is that it must improve — it couldn't get worse. *The Australian* — a pretentious title, but a proud one; a real challenge. But a misnomer. The Mainlander yes, *The Australian* No.

There is a difference, you know. Tasmania. The only recognition of the existence of a third of a million people is in the south-east corner of the weather map.
ROBERT CARR
Hobart

Pandering to superstition

I WAS disappointed to see this fine modern newspaper pandering to the age-old superstition of printing horoscopes. True, the column was headed For Those Who Trust, but if it must be included as a selling gimmick, a better title would be, For Amusement Only.

Professor Bok of Mount Stromlo has put Australia in the forefront of astronomical research and it behoves all responsible people to take care that they do nothing which could encourage gullible people to continue thinking along pre-scientific lines.

Otherwise, I compliment this new venture.
L. M. BEADNELL
East Malvern, Vic

Beginning

Stimulating

INCREDIBLE! A daily newspaper in this country with no clinical report on star footballer Joe Nerk's sore toe? No pictorial pandering to the chosen race — the teenagers? No pictures of slobbering babies, puppies or adolescent extroverts? No pearls of wisdom from some ancient journalist and his Bartlett's Familiar Quotations?

Wonderful! Sincere congratulations on your first issue! Your paper is a refreshing stimulating change from the sensationalism.

This is an exciting day; a new line of mass communication has been established in our community. May *The Australian* grow in stature with each new edition and abide by its tenets to "speak fearlessly, criticise, not be influenced and praise the individual, and advance the national welfare."

DAVID BRENNAN
Camberwell, Vic
20/7/64

Sneer, smear

AS a proud, bloody, but unbowed member of the Australian Labor Party, I welcome *The Australian*, not because I believe it will be pro-Labor, but because I believe it will be impartial.

One's political beliefs can never be made ready for the irresponsibly vindictive slashings of vitriolic pens — but they should at all times stand ready for the scrutiny of informed and impartial comment.

If *The Australian* gives this, in a society already dangerously inured to the grim technique of political sneer and smear, it will always be a welcome visitor in our house.

IAN LASRY
Brighton, Vic
20/7/64

The first was the last

THE first number of *The Australian* declared that the new paper would be neutral and not support any political parties in Australia.

Believing you, I started to buy *The Australian*. The first was the last I bought. In your references to the result of elections of the A.L.P. Victorian executive (Black Week For A.L.P. and other articles), you showed your true color.

The Australian is just one more paper supporting the Liberal Party.

T. A. LOBB
Mitcham, Vic
5/8/64

WITH the publication of *The Australian* this country has taken a great step forward. Now Mr Calwell and his nasty gang will be flayed mercilessly from coast to coast.

Keep up the good work and the next step forward this country will take will be through the door to disaster.

BARRY TURNER
Wagga, NSW
5/8/64

Arthur Calwell

IT is unfortunate that biased Labor supporters and uninformed and misguided neutralists should criticise your paper for a so-called Liberal view. It should be obvious to free-thinking Australians that, at present, the Liberal outlook is the one "radical," detached, honest and independent "party."

Thus it is inevitable that a newspaper, which promised a neutral political view, should coincidently agree with Liberal policy.

R. F. L. PEIME
Lawes, Qld
13/8/64

Oops . . . sorry, wrong number

MAY I offer my congratulations on the first issue of your paper. I particularly welcome the coverage given to international news. However, on ringing the number given as your Hobart correspondent, I was surprised to find myself speaking to the barman at one of Hobart's hotels, The Man at the Wheel. I feel that whatever his off-duty activities may be, your man in Hobart is not, in fact, The Man at the Wheel.

ADRIAN GIBSON
Federal Member for Denison, Tas
20/7/64

PS

THIS is what I have been waiting for for 10 years — no emotionalism, no sensationalism, just evaluated news. If you're not sure, don't print it; if you print it, I'll accept it as fact; if I find you out, I'll cancel my subscription.

STUART HALEY
Greenwich, NSW
27/7/64

These changing times

Dollars or royals?

MY sympathies lie with Bernard Robinson in his letter (July 29) opposing "dollar" as the name of our new decimal currency. South Africa and Sierra Leone in their recent changeover to decimal currency chose distinctive names; our effort to copy a powerful ally is shameful.

American films and magazines have been dominating our thinking for years and it is almost a rarity to find a British or Australian film on TV.

During the controversy between the "royal" and the "dollar", the daily press plugged hard for the dollar. Under these circumstances, most people found it easier to fall into line than to think about another name.

G. DUDLEY
Oakleigh, Vic
14/8/64

PS

HAVING read the pamphlet, Notes on Decimal Currency, issued with the approval of the Australian Inter-Bank Decimal Currency Committee, I am able to suggest a very simple solution to the difficulties there described, connected with a change of currency. We should forget the whole thing.

BOB BOASE
Carlton, Vic
11/8/64

Why prices will rise

MR Boase's comments on decimal currency (22/9) are valid, but there is a further reason why prices will inflate: the lowest coin in circulation will rise in value by 240 per cent, that is from one halfpenny to one cent (1.2 pence). This is because the dollar is to be equated to the present 10/-.

If the dollar were to be valued as equal to 5/- (incidentally as it is now understood to be by anyone using Australian slang) then the lowest coin, one cent, would be worth 0.6 pence — a comparatively insignificant rise.

To give examples: The cost of milk rises today by one half penny a pint. With the advent of the proposed decimal currency, the least it can rise will be one cent or 1.2 pence per pint. A fivepenny postage stamp will cost five cents or sixpence. (It would be unthinkable that it would cost four cents or 4.8 pence!).

If, however, the dollar were to be worth 5/- instead of 10/-, milk could rise by 0.6 pence, fivepenny stamps would cost nine cents (or 5.4 pence) and there would be no rise at all in anything now costing threepence as this would exactly equal five cents.

J. RICHARDS
Balwyn, Vic
1/10/64

PEOPLE who are not in favor of the dollar should cease looking at the past and realise that public opinion is in favor of the dollar. We know that most people of Britain like the name royal. We know, too, that they are not interested in the progress of Australia.

K. KEESMAN
Geelong West, Vic
28/8/64

Decimal currency

C will stand for Chaos Day

YOUR editorial of December 23 is to be commended for drawing attention to the tremendous problems yet to be solved before the proposed Australian dollar currency can be introduced.

I disagree most emphatically with the Associated Chambers of Commerce of Australia, which stated that work is well under way for a smooth transition to decimal currency on Changeover Day — C-Day. The ACCA has obviously been reading too much Decimal Currency Board bally-hoo.

C-Day will definitely be most appropriately called Chaos Day unless some really commonsense decisions are made soon, as to date nothing worthwhile has been achieved.

There is certain to be a grave shortage of decimal coins for some months after C-Day and the proposed public education program is an insult to the mentality of the Australian citizen.

Your closing point that there is a possibility of making "a major mess of introducing the decimal system in our business accounting" is more than true, but you have overlooked the really vital point.

Business accounting has been in decimal form for decades, all published financial information is in whole (decimally recorded) pounds and thousands of businesses record shillings and pence for costing and other accounting purposes as decimal fractions of our pound.

With some commonsense practical planning, instead of the present theoretical nonsense, a £-based decimal currency could be introduced with no dual-currency confusion and at a fraction of the cost of the proposed inadequate dollar system

If the ACCA is so sure of satisfactory dollar progress, perhaps it can tell the business community where the essential thousands of skilled temporary technicians are coming from to convert the 500,000 business machines (it now takes two weeks to have a typewriter urgently repaired), and also what would happen if war broke out soon after C-Day, with banks unable to record in £.s.d. and the rest of the business community unable to do otherwise.

R. W. PARRY
Melbourne
8/1/65

How will housewives cope?

IT is February 1966 and a housewife purchases an item at the local self-service store with a price-tag reading "2/10 or 28c."

She tenders one dollar and the girl cashier (after apologising for having run short of the new currency) gives her 35c and 3/8 as change.

In the expert opinion of Dollar Bill — that cute little fellow with all the answers:

HOW long will it take the cashier to calculate the correct amount of change to be paid in this case?

HOW long will it take the housewife to verify that she has, in fact, been given the correct change?

The fact that other shoppers will be waiting patiently (?) in line while such little dramas are being played out — and there will be a lot of them — may seem of trivial importance to Dollar Bill.

But when translated into terms of slower store traffic, lost man-hours and the danger of losing the customer's goodwill, such little dramas take on a more ominous aspect.

This is not to be construed as a criticism of the plan to adopt a decimal currency system. Such a move is long overdue and it is to be hoped that our weights and measures will soon follow suit.

However, the proposal that the "old" and "new" currencies be permitted to run concurrently for two years not only encourages such confusion as shown above, but also encourages people to continue thinking in terms of £.s.d., which is most undesirable.

Even at the cost of postponing the introduction of decimal currency until adequate supplies can be minted, it would be far more practical to establish a firm "cut-off date" for £.s.d., after which all retail transactions would be conducted in dollars and cents only.

Although this would oblige people holding old currency to change their money at a bank prior to making any purchases, surely this slight inconvenience would be worthwhile?

I have personally witnessed such a currency conversion and can positively state a firm date for changeover is vastly preferable to the existing "tapering-off" proposal.

ROBERT A. ROBINSON
Berwick, Vic
10/5/65

Decimal currency

Depressed by the dollar designs

LIKE many another, I have been depressed by the designs released for our new dollar currency.

The idea seems to have been to celebrate this country's past achievements in the persons of worthies drawn from various fields of enterprise.

The arts are represented by a certain Mr Henry Lawson, who wrote a few readable short stories.

I can think of dozens of potential rivals, just as second rate and just as unknown, both inside and outside this country.

Why advertise our lack of a viable native literature?

The representative of the sciences is Mr Hargrave, who flew kites many years ago; and thus, to the chauvinist, qualifies as a pioneer of aviation.

Talk about the Russians gratuitously claiming precedence!

Among the remaining assorted bunch of scowling pioneers appears Mr Greenway, who designed charming churches, some of which still stand and delight the eye.

In my own view, he is the only one who merits houseroom — probably a small corner on the half-dollar bill!

If we must advertise our achievements, why not those which are manifest and indisputable? Dawn Fraser for the 1 dollar, Herb Elliot on the 2 dollar, Ron Clarke on the 5 dollar.

If the images fade, we can easily change the designs.

If we wish to be less ephemeral, let's stick to the native fauna.

Echidna and other charming creatures run rampant over our new coins; why not over the new notes also?

After all, appearances are that this country is stricly for the birds!

R. W. JONES
Downer, A.C.T.
17/1/66

First conversion

I REFER to an article in Martin Collins' page (9/7). Reference is made to Petersville Ltd, Clayton, Victoria, as the first company to convert to decimal currency — "a claim hardly likely to be doubted."

Trans-Australia Airlines has processed all payrolls in decimal currency since July 1 for its 700 employees in Queensland. The gross and net payroll and all deductions are computed in decimal currency and the "advice to payee" slip in the pay envelope shows all amounts in the new currency, with a conversion of the net pay into £.s.d. for checking of the contents.

This changeover was not a surprise to our staff. The TAA decimal currency change-over committee has been training staff in the advantages of the new currency for six months so they will be able to render service to the travelling public by answering their decimal currency problems expertly.

E. D. ELPHINSTONE
Chairman
Decimal Currency
Committee
Trans-Australia Airlines
Brisbane
29/7/65

Decimal confusion

IT is quite a long time past C-Day and decimal currency is now an inescapable fact of Australian life.

Everyone in the community has experienced some difficulty in making the mental adjustment to this major change, but how little have we been helped by the retail trade!

Retailers in this matter seem determined to emulate King Canute.

As an example, I conducted a private survey of the advertisements published in a Sydney newspaper last Sunday. My sample comprised 19 advertisements.

In these advertisements prices were quoted as follows: pounds only, 7; dual currency, pounds first, 6; dual currency, dollars first, 5; dollars only, 1.

It should surely be obvious that this practice is only delaying the "mental" conversion of the public and unduly prolonging the period of confusion.

Perhaps the national press could co-operate by refusing to accept advertisements which give prominence to pounds rather than dollars.

D. M. CARMENT
Clifton Gardens, NSW
14/7/66

> **PS**
>
> *IT is becoming more evident that a $5 bill is needed now decimal currency has had a chance to function and I would like to suggest that Sir John Monash be represented on this note. Sir John was a great Australian and a worthy figure to be represented on this, a much needed note in the community.*
>
> **R. POMFRETT**
> Booval, Qld
> *1/7/66*

These changing times

Tasmania says yes

WHY don't you squares on the mainland follow the lead of Tasmania and get with it on this daylight saving lark?

It's great! You ask the mums and dads and the teenagers.

Of course, we did have a bit of opposition at first from the farmers.

One said he worked all the hours of daylight anyhow and he did not want another thrust upon him!

A water conservationist voiced his fears that the "extra" hour of sunshine would evaporate the hydro storage lakes and yet another moaner feared that the extra hour of sunshine would burn up the grass in his paddocks!

I guess you have your share of amazing personalities who can visualise a 25-hour day, but thank goodness they are in a minority.

(Mrs) A. M. BETTS
Launceston, Tas
12/10/67

Queensland says no

THE attitude of Mrs Betts of Tasmania (Letters, 12/10) to daylight saving is strongly reminiscent of the fox that lost its tail.

It tried to talk every other animal into getting rid of its tail, too.

Down there in the Apple Isle they're stuck with daylight saving, an old wartime bugbear, and have to put up with it . . . and kid themselves they like it, by cripes!

Up here in tropical Queensland, we don't want it — it's just an extra hour of afternoon summer heat.

Try enjoying a hot tea in what amounts to late afternoon, in blazing sunshine!

We kicked it last time; why resurrect a dead horse?

Daylight saving? Ugh!

R. CARSON GOLD
Deagon, Qld
20/10/67

PS

WHEN I woke this morning the sun was shining and the birds were singing. Thank goodness, daylight saving is over.

N. STYLES
Eastwood, NSW
2/3/72

Fair go on daylight

ACCORDING to the Victorian and Queensland ministers at the daylight saving conference, most citizens in their States "are satisfied with the present arrangements."

Are they unaware that while Australians tend to placidly accept preservation of the status quo on most matters, they are capable of enthusiastically adopting beneficial changes once they have been introduced?

Why should we be deprived of that extra hour of daylight for leisure and relaxation on summer evenings, so widely enjoyed in most of the advanced countries of the world? If the ministers' real reason is that farmers wouldn't like daylight saving, why don't we hear more of farmer resistance in those countries where the practice now exists.

I suspect that any local farmer resistance may be due more to ignorance and extreme conservatism than to any sustainable objection, and consider that, as far as daylight saving is concerned, another great Australian tradition, of "giving it a go," should be honored.

(Prof) R. O. SLATYER
Forrest, A.C.T.
18/12/69

Daylight saving

A trial will show it is acceptable

ANOTHER summer has now passed with the mainland States being denied the advantages of daylight saving.

A vigorous campaign last summer generated unprecedented publicity and interest in the issue — so much so that the State governments decided to have a meeting on the matter on December 10 last.

The outcome of this meeting was rather nebulous and, apart from a statement by Sir Henry Bolte that he could be interested in discussing the possibility of daylight saving with NSW, not a word has been said since then.

The success of the idea, if it hadn't already been proved in all other industrialised countries in the world for periods exceeding 50 years, has been demonstrated conclusively in Tasmania for three summers and now in Thredbo Alpine village.

Yet our State governments have been procrastinating and vacillating on the issue for 25 years. Unless action is taken promptly, we will again be told that it will be too late to do anything for next summer.

The advocates of daylight saving do not ask that the practice be foisted on an unwilling public, as happens with much government legislation. We simply want an opportunity of demonstrating by a trial period that daylight saving is acceptable and practical in this country.

NSW and Victoria can indeed introduce it without the other States' co-operation, so we look to the two governments concerned to grasp the nettle and make a firm decision on this issue.

L. M. WILSON
Pymble, NSW
6/4/70

Hideous

NOW is the winter of my discontent soon to be made hideous summer by this sun of daylight saving.

I'll lose my long cool mornings and be given long hot evenings in return.

I will be told that any sacrifice will be all worthwhile because, as a result, families are frolicking at the beach in some never-ending midsummer's idyll.

In truth, the kids are watching TV as usual and mum is getting tea ready as usual.

The only difference is that dad arrives home boozed in daylight instead of after dark.

For the sake of dad's dignity, may I have my long mornings back please?

I. T. MAYNARD
Neutral Bay, NSW
24/10/81

Archaic

SO Queensland's Premier, Mr Bjelke-Petersen, may not adopt daylight saving time again?

This State has been a hundred years behind the rest of the Commonwealth all along; another hour more or less won't make any difference!

All the States are likely to adopt sex education, abortion reform, homosexual legislation and other social reforms long before poor archaic Queensland.

(Mrs) R. WEBB
Mt Gravatt, Qld
10/2/72

It's over, thank goodness

THANK goodness summer-time is over for another six months. Now, in order to get to work on time, I won't have to get up in the dark each morning.

For a while I won't have to sweat it out on 30deg afternoons that seem never-ending. Now I need not eat my evening meal, or watch the news on TV, while the sun is still blazing fiercely.

The incidence of skin cancer in Australia is one of the highest in the world. Why should the NSW Government, through daylight saving, encourage people to spend more time in strong sunlight and thus probably increase the risk of their contracting skin cancer?

Queensland, wisely won't have a bar of daylight saving. Watch a Queenslander out in the country. He probably wears a wide-brimmed hat to protect him from the sun's rays.

In summer, many parts of NSW are as hot as many parts of Queensland. Please let us live through the heat of next summer without the agony of summer-time.

Those who want another hour of daylight may rise 60 minutes earlier.

HAROLD J. POLLOCK
Sydney
13/3/74

PS

ALL I can say about the NSW crowd is that if they voted a Labor Government into office, they deserve daylight saving.

IMELDA STEWART
Southport, Qld
14/5/76

These changing times

How the shoppers will fare

THE headline Metric Threat To Prices and the associated statement attributed to Mr E. W. Barr in *The Australian* (11/4) will convey to many readers an erroneous impression that unless "corrective action is taken" to change the proposals for the contents of packaged goods under metric conversion, the cost of living will be increased because of significant price rises.

The actual position is that as packaged goods are converted to metric quantities, the housewife might find herself buying goods in slightly different sized packages, but this does not mean that her housekeeping bills need rise, nor, incidentally, does it mean that the average weight of her shopping basket will change.

What it does mean is that the size of some of the containers she will purchase will be a little larger than they used to be, so will last longer.

If she pays 10 per cent more for a 500g tin of jam, it should be because she is getting 10 per cent more jam, which will presumably last 10 per cent longer. Where she would have bought over a period 10 tins of jam, she will now only buy nine.

For goods which are usually consumed at one sitting, there could indeed be a 10 per cent increase in the quantity and hence in the cost of that portion of the meal. For some, the increased quantity would mean there was too much and a smaller can would be purchased.

For other families, the present can is less than would ideally be suitable, so some extra material at a proportionate increase in price would be welcome.

The "natural" sizes in which goods are packed are a function of the system of units being used. In the imperial system such values as 8oz, 12oz and 1lb are favored sizes because they allow relatively easy price comparisons with one another and with competing brands or products.

These are not necessarily the best sizes for the purchaser; they simply represent a range of rounded imperial sizes from which the purchaser selects that nearest to his requirements.

In a metric environment, an equivalent range of sizes suitable for easy price comparisons has such values as 250g, 375g and 500g. It happens that these are each 10 per cent bigger than the "corresponding" imperial sizes.

For liquids the "natural" imperial sizes of 10 and 20 fl oz may be replaced by metric sizes of 250 and 500ml, which are each 1 per cent less than the corresponding imperial size.

Under the metric system to which we are converting, the half kilogram will generally replace the pound as a basic quantity, a place it already holds in metric countries of long standing.

To cling to 450g as a "replacement" for the pound would be to perpetuate in a disguised form the old system when we should be aiming at adopting values which our children and children's children will find natural and which will facilitate easy assessment of prices.

A. F. A. HARPER
St Leonards, NSW
(The writer is an executive member of the Metric Conversion Board.)
21/4/72

PS

R. W. PARRY (20/1) has pointed out that the translators of the Good News Bible have made a number of errors when metricising cubits, spans etc. No wonder membership of churches is falling, given its lack of success in conversion.
HILARY POWER
ROD POWER
Beecroft, NSW
26/1/77

Metrics

It's mumbo jumbo!

HOW much longer are the people of this country to be expected to suffer this metrication mumbo jumbo in silence?

I am sure I speak for the vast "silent majority" when I say that we are fed-up with and strongly opposed to the introduction of the metric system. We are weary of trying to work out the temperature by dividing the Celsius figure by 5, multiplying by 9 and adding 32; the racing enthusiasts are thoroughly bamboozled by weights in kilograms and race distances in metres; and why should soft-drink bottles be labelled 900ml instead of 32 fl oz?

If the trading community wishes to adopt the metric system for its dealings with metric countries, let them do so by all means, but why foist it all on us? We neither want it nor understand it. In any case, neither the previous Liberal-Country Party Government nor the present Labor Government ever asked the people its wishes in the matter, so the mandate was never given for this metric madness.

I would therefore call upon the new Government either to reverse this policy, or at least to hold a plebiscite to ascertain the wishes of the people, or else I call upon the long-suffering public of this land to raise their voices in protest and make their wishes known. Let us inundate our parliamentary representatives with letters of protest.

Let us form anti-metric committees to fight this unnecessary burden on our way of life. Let those who live near any office of the Metric Conversion Board go to that office and make their protests heard loud and clear. After all, if the confusion is bad enough now, with just a few changes, think of what it will be like later.

I suppose that all this Europe-is-best nonsense, which really inspired metrication, will have us driving on the right hand side of the road before long, though heaven forbid.

N. W. RUSSELL
North Rockhampton, Qld
12/1/73

No justice

A MAN got a knighthood for directing Australia's conversion to decimal currency; but events have shown, as many had feared, that the seeds of national inflation were then sown.

The loss of those two pennies in each shilling was the beginning of a chapter of spiralling costs and was fostered by traders taking advantage of public confusion about the new currency by adding a bit more to their prices.

Further nurtured by the introduction of the metric system, the main principle of which seems to be smaller quantities for higher prices, inflation goes on without check. And for the present economic mess nobody but governments is to blame.

My standard packet of rolled oats for porridge reveals a two-inch empty space at the top. My former 2oz packet of cigarette tobacco would last three days; now the 50g packet lasts barely two and the price has just about doubled.

And so on, horribly to infinitude. There aint no justice in the world at all.

M. SHARLAND
Sandy Bay, Tas
1/8/74

A shapely 92-60-90

MR K. Grover (30/12) should not confuse the issue by suggesting that 35mph be converted to 16m/s. Nowhere in the metric countries is this the case, not on the roads, anyway.

Speeds of cars are in kilometres per hour (kmh) and so are all road signs and speedometers; m/s is used in the sciences.

By the same token, incidentally, the popular unit of length is the centimetre (cm) and not the millimetre (mm) as I have seen seriously suggested by some authority on conversion.

Although the millimetre is part of the 1000-scale (1km equals 1000m; 1m equals 1000mm; 1mm equals 1000-microns, etc.), in everyday life one uses the centimetre (1m equals 100cm).

As a unit, the cm is nearest to the inch so that the mental adaptation from inch to cm is not a too difficult one (1 inch equals about 2.5cm).

So, for a shapely metric girl, it is 92-60-90 (cm) and not 920-600-900 (mm).

H. JAEHRLING
Mt Waverley, Vic
8/1/71

PS

WITH all due respect to the much admired Spike Milligan (The Australian, 13/6), he didn't know how tall he was BEFORE metrics. He was, in fact, 5 feet, not 5 foot!

K. SAUNDERS
North Balwyn, Vic
19/6/80

METRICATE Halfpenny!

RITA DENHOLM
San Isadore, NSW
9/3/77

Metrics

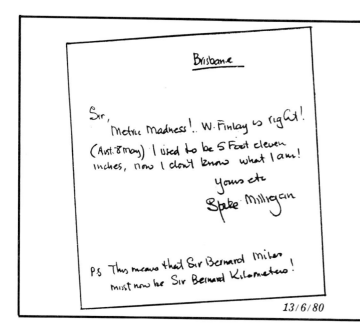

Brisbane

Sir,

Metric Madness!.. W. Finlay is right!
(Aust. 8 may) I used to be 5 Foot eleven
inches, now I don't know what I am!

Yours etc

Spike Milligan

P.S This means that Sir Bernard Miles,
must now be Sir Bernard Kilometers!

13/6/80

A rule of thumb

I WAS interested in the argument by P. K. Cooke (*The Australian*, 4/12) that the old measurements are based on reality because his thumb is one inch across.

Although manufactured in 1907-08, I seem to be designed more on the metric system. My little finger nail is exactly 1cm across.

The width of my middle finger is 2cm. The span of my first two fingers and the width of my palm are both 10cm. The span of my thumb and middle finger is 20cm and my navel is exactly one metre from the floor.

(Dr) H. H. MACEY
Floreat Park, WA
10/12/79

Acquiring a feel for it

SANDRA Jobson has actually found the secret of mastering the metric system (13/2) which she feels is giving her, and others, trouble.

As she suggests, she will develop an idea of all the metric measurements she will normally use simply by relating them to familiar items.

Ms Jobson's mother used the same method to determine concepts of imperial weights and measures and in time will develop similar metric concepts. It's surprising how infrequently we need to use exact measures.

In our own good time and as more facets of our daily activities are converted, we will acquire a "feel" for the new measurements, developing our own personal guidelines through transaction and "doing" experiences.

For example, a 5c piece is about 1mm thick, an 18c stamp is 2cm wide, a metre is a long pace, and it's 1000km from Brisbane to Sydney.

The mass or weight of a 20c piece is about 10g, a litre carton of milk has a mass of about 1kg, a standard petrol drum (44 gallons) contains 200 litres and a hectare is about the area of a soccer or rugby field (not two swimming pools, as Ms Jobson says).

Metrication in Australia is by no means "bogged down." The process of learning metrics is a gradual one. That is why overall conversion has been programmed to take about 10 years.

The greatest impact on the individual is occurring now. But by simple comparisons of the kind suggested by Ms Jobson and those above, most people will find the difficulties more imagined than real.

GAVIN HANDLEY
St Leonards, NSW

(Mr Handley is the Metric Conversion Board's Public Relations Director.)
25/1/76

Here's hoping

I WHOLEHEARTEDLY agree with Mr Hanlan (Letters, 9/9) and am pleased that somebody intelligent is prepared to show up the metric system for what it is.

I, too, demand that we return to the days of hope and glory when we knew what we were talking about and knew with certainty that 12 inches made one foot, 16½ feet one rod and 5940 feet one mile.

When 16 ounces made one pint and 20 of them made one pound (unless it was 240 pennies). When 43560 square yards made one acre and 24¾ cubic feet made one perch of stone. When 64/64th made one inch, men were men and women stayed in the kitchen.

So hoping for a return to sanity and the imperial system, I remain,

PAUL O. PODGORNIK
Drummoyne, NSW
20/9/81

These changing times

I REFER to the article (June 28) by your computer correspondent, Cedric Allen.

Mr Allen stated that the universities of Australia have become the object of criticism because of their failure to provide an adequate stream of commercial data-processing programmers, although they had been provided with the computers to teach them.

The situation at the University of Sydney is so far from this description that some comment is necessary.

The University of Sydney has acquired and is now

Preparing the way

operating two computers; and the bulk of funds for these came from private donations secured largely by the efforts of Professors H. Messel and J. M. Bennett, of the School of Physics.

They were primarily obtained to provide computing services for the research activities of the university, an entirely legitimate aim for which they are now only barely adequate.

Although funds have from time to time been sought for the extension of these facilities to allow a broad-based teaching program, these representations have been almost wholly unsuccessful.

However, because the university recognises the extreme importance of education to data processing, a substantial proportion of the time of the computers and staff of the computing department has been devoted to teaching purposes.

The first call on our teaching facilities has been in-
Continued next page

Computers

From previous page

evitably to provide the computing experience which is absolutely necessary for the adequate education of engineers, physicists and other graduates in existing disciplines.

Even so, the department has provided courses on computing available to persons outside the university.

At no stage has the university been provided with a computer for teaching purposes.

We hope, in fact, to expand our teaching activities in the coming year, but this will only be possible because of the donation to the university of a 7040-1401 system by IBM Australia Pty. Ltd.

Even so, we will be severely handicapped by the fact that the university, because of the many equally legitimate demands on its slender resources, has been able to provide a computing staff establishment only barely adequate to our present activities.

Thus, at Sydney, at least, the situation is that the university has never received any significant assistance towards the education of commercial data-processing staff and has had to find computing facilities even for its existing courses largely from non-government funds.

However, it has bent over backwards to do what it could in data-processing education in the face of continued official apathy to the problem.

It may interest you to know that over the past 12 years we have put some 2000 students through our courses, in spite of the lack of aid and certainly not because of it.

Where would EDP be in Australia today were it not for this?

C. S. WALLACE
School of Physics,
University of Sydney.
1/7/66

Automatic farmers

YOUR feature, The Farmer Is Beginning To Use Computers Now (Computer Supplement, May 17), is correct in its anticipation that computers will find a ready acceptance among Australian farmers.

In fact, Australian farmers may already be ahead of those in the United States in this respect.

Genetic calculations on computers are commonplace in research and on a commercial basis in the chicken business at least.

Most stock-feed formulas are worked out on computers and many local farmers are no strangers to the use of computers in financial and management studies.

Several years ago, a bank in NSW requested of a farmer client some involved information concerning a proposed loan.

Expressing surprise at the alacrity with which the details were supplied, it received the bland answer, "Oh, we put it through the computer!"

Resource-allocation problems of the nature described in the feature have been tackled on a research basis in Australian universities since at least 1958; and farmers can now arrange for the inexpensive calculation of involved linear programs, best-bet fodder reserves,

gross-margins analysis and more elaborate problems.

Burgeoning farm-management research laboratories have been established at two universities to my knowledge — New England and Western Australia.

One of these, the University of New England, processed data for 301 farms in the eight months to June 30, 1965, and expects to handle some 700 records in the present year on a custom basis for farmers in co-operation with professional farm-management advisers.

In terms of number of farmer clients, the University of New England Farm Management Service Centre is probably the largest in the world.

The University of Iowa has in the past been a generous host to many Australian agricultural scientists who would strive to emulate the renown of its distinguished staff.

Equally fervently, these Australians would like to match its research endowments — the combined budgets of the two university centres mentioned would be at most 5 per cent of the mouth-watering $800,000 mentioned in your feature.

E. J. WARING
Canberra
27/5/66

Lack of foresight

WE ARE constantly informed through the columns of your paper and others that the age of automation is almost upon us.

In the United States, positive steps have been taken to counter the problems that will arise from this advance of science.

Under the Manpower Re-

development and Training Act of 1962, organisations whose members are affected by automation may obtain grants through the Federal Government Manpower Administration to retrain those people affected.

This country, however, in typical fashion will probably
Continued next page

Computers

How to get your own back

PETER Ryan (8/6) rightly takes issue with the Kafka-esque computerisation and de-personalisation of society, but he must now ponder fighting back.

I will be happy, on request, to let him have access to my De'Lisle Defilement Kit for Computers. It consists of two items; a tiny but powerful alnico bar magnet and a simple gatekeeper's punch.

Across the foot of each computer communication, Peter will find a line of magnetised characters to the order of the alphabets of lost Aztec civilisations. These can be erased, singly or severally, by gently stroking with the magnet. Such erasings will cause computers at worst to stall into the somnolence of malfunction, but at best to regurgitate transistors and micro-circuit wafers into their "out" baskets.

This degaussing ploy is recommended for perpetration on all communications beginning "You are directed . ." or "First and final . ."

For computer communications beginning "Congratulations, you have already won . . ." and "You, as a member of an executive demographic group . . .," it is suggested that the shape of an asymmetrical rhomboid be outlined in the area containing punched holes. The gatekeeper's punch should then be employed to add an additional hole at each corner of the rhomboid.

Such an augmented card has been known to blow all fuses for blocks around its processing computer (it is alleged in International Computer Defilement circles that the Great New York Blackout started this way).

The minimum result from hole-defilement (but perhaps the more desirable) is that all book and record club and easy credit offers will be consigned to a garbled version of your name, c/o The Father Divine Mission, Upper Zambesi.

GORDON DE'LISLE
Brighton, Vic
16/6/70

From previous page

allow automation to overtake us before doing anything about it.

This is not entirely the fault of the Federal Government; the trade unions have also shown a lack of foresight.

Instead of agitating for action by the technical-training establishments in this country, they have done little or nothing except bemoan the fact that people are going to be displaced.

In the past we have been left behind by progress (mechanisation of the coal-mining industry is an example).

Automation will cause hardship to many more people than the introduction of machinery to the mines did.

This is Australia's chance to show that we are really the progressive and technically minded nation that Mr Holt frequently tells us his party has made us.

R. G. WITTRIEN
Glenbrook, NSW
7/2/67

Irreplacable tea lady

I WAS interested in your article, And Out Goes Tea Lady (25/2).

As the effect of higher wages is felt more on the upper management level, surely a more rational alternative to the retrenchment of the tea lady would be a judicious pruning of the expensive executive tree. After all, one could employ 10 tea ladies at $70 a week for the same cost as one $35,000-a-year executive.

Machines, of course, should never replace the tea lady.

By no stretch of the imagination can a machine-made cup of tea or coffee replace the personal touch of the lady with her delicate gradations of tea, hot water, sugar and milk (milk, mind you, not whitener!).

Are we to accept the mechanical second or third best? I am sure our "more educated" have better respect for the finer things of life.

JOHN GRAHAM
Mulgrave, Vic
12/3/74

PS

WE are living in a a great age. It should be called the era of the computer errors. Last year we were in the telephone directory; this year we are not listed. When I queried the matter, the answer was familiar: "Sorry, it's the computer."

(Mrs) R. SAUER
Castlecrag, NSW
25/7/75

Computers

What kind of society will it be?

I HAVE followed with interest your series on The Computer Holocaust, which has to some extent collated and emphasised trends which have been noticeable throughout the period of my life . . . some 66 years.

The indicators have been there for a long time, but hitherto whenever people have spoken of them, they have been dismissed as by-products of vivid imaginations such as those of Verne, Wells, Orwell or Asimov and so on . . . fantasies to be airily dismissed by hard-headed pragmatists who made up our governments and so-called leadership groups.

Now 1984 is a mere half a dozen years away and the fantasies are seen to be realities which are pressing hard upon us.

While I appreciate your putting the picture quite succinctly before us, I trust that you will not let the matter rest there but keep up a constant pressure upon our leaders and upon the general readership of *The Australian* for a serious and purposeful seminar in order to plan, as far as it is possible, the kind of society which must emerge as the new technology develops.

For instance, while we may rejoice at the prospect of extended leisure . . . two or three working days per week — maybe even less . . . and while we may talk of education for leisure, just how will that leisure be funded? Indeed, how will living itself be funded?

Leisure without means is poverty of a serious kind; and means postulates some sort of income.

Do we assume . . . dare we assume . . . that the wealth produced by the new technology is to be centralised and then equitably distributed? Or does the present structure persist, with the owners of the means of production claiming a "traditional" right to the first fruits, while those who have become unemployable are allowed a "dole"?

Our politicians, our unionists . . . all of us have not yet really examined the situation. Mr Hawke calls upon Mr Fraser to convene an objective conference . . . free from party politics; what is the likelihood of a character such as that of our Prime Minister grasping the urgency of the matter?

E. C. SAVAGE
Windang, NSW
24/8/78

THE concern of employees of Telecom that job opportunities will be restricted as a consequence of computers, directs attention to the need to examine the social effects of increasingly sophisticated technology.

There are now 350,000 Australians registered for work and an estimated 150,000 who have dropped out of the workforce as a consequence of unemployment. The Borrie Report on Population predicts an increase of 500,000 in the numbers of people of workforce age in the next four years.

The prospect of providing one million jobs by increasing consumer demand becomes more unlikely as each year of economic recession drags on.

Those people who are in a position to spend seem increasingly reluctant to do so judging by the steady increase in savings bank deposits.

The sinister implications

At the lower end of the income ladder, unemployment beneficiaries and their dependents have added some 350,000 people to those previously living on or below Professor Henderson's poverty line. These Australians are clearly unable to increase their consumption of goods and services either to help themselves or as a response to the call of all politicians for patriotic spending.

Against this dismal background, technologically created unemployment has sinister implications, especially if there is no attempt to share its benefits with the displaced and the unemployed.

Once-only redundancy payments are really only conscience money to the immediate victims. The long-term benefits of technology are largely retained by manufacturers or suppliers of services and the skilled employees who control the machines and computers.

In the past, technology has released large numbers of people from long hours, low pay and excessively hard work, but beyond a point, which we have not tried to identify, technology makes men and women its victims unless there is a fairer distribution of its benefits.

The Telecom dispute has immense social implications for the future of work in Australia. It should be the subject of a major investigation of the social and also the energy consequences of excessive reliance on advanced technology.

DAVID SCOTT
Executive Director
Brotherhood of St Laurence
Melbourne
13/10/77

The permissive society

── The agony of it all ──

IT is with sadness that I read such railings against censorship as appeared in R. F. Brissenden's review of The Other Victorians on January 20.

May I, as one who has devoted a lifetime to the searching out of printed filth and to the protection of the innocent, speak out boldly?

We, who not only support our leaders' wise provisions to prevent the pollution of this country, but carry them into practice, do not do this for ourselves.

Most of us, God knows, have been corrupted long ago; it is for the young, to keep them in their innocence, that we have labored.

To speak personally, in a lifetime's work I have seen (and impounded) material that would send a man mad.

How many of your readers, who would support the academic "liberalism" of your reviewer, have actually felt the blood pounding to their heads, the trembling of their hands, the shortening of their breath, all the painful excitement that pornography would induce in them if they were permitted to see it?

I can remember, sir, that as a young man and new to the job (fresh from a good church school), I was often obsessed and unhealthily excited for days after by some lewd transparency discovered in the baggage of a traveller returning from Japan.

And even now, though retired and soon to be a grandfather, I can still feel that throbbing, blinding excitement when I look again at some of my souvenirs — even though I may have studied them a thousand times before.

I would describe myself as a normal, average family man, sir, but the inner agonies I was subjected to by this filth, the distractions it caused to my devotion to my wife and the corrupting influence it exerted on my colleagues should provide sufficient argument against your reviewer's stand.

For if we, now mature and one would hope inured against their vile charms, should still be disturbed by "frank" films and provocative advertisements for feminine undergarments, how can the young (whose blood is more tempestuous than ours) cope with real pornography?

JAMES FLANAGHAN (Ret.)
Jolimont, Vic
9/2/68

Mini-skirts

I REFER to the current short-skirt controversy at the Postmaster-General's Department.

I am compelled to record the fiercest possible agitation aimed directly at these rigid, inflexible mini-minded gentlemen.

The retaliatory measures taken to dissuade their staff from wearing the mini-skirt typify the conservatism that is perpetuated in our government institutions.

Does the shorter skirt contravene any section of our Constitution?

If it were not so absurdly ludicrous, it would be the most hilarious conflict of the decade.

To dictate a mode of dress is surely not within the PMG's realm of responsibility, let alone the reasoned height (above knee level) of skirts.

Please, Mr Hulme, could you advise your subordinates to kindly stick to their cables?

GEORGE ANTHONY CORBAN
Croydon Park, NSW
26/7/66

Lolita off

THERE is, I think, a need for a daily paper which can reasonably be put in the hands of adolescents to keep them informed of the significant happenings in the world at large.

However I found your article, Lolita And The Chinese Scholar, distinctly "off beam." Doubtless it was amusing to the sophisticates who regard the problems of illicit sex lightly, but considering the possible harm to the thinking of a considerable number of young Australians, whose parents are still struggling to raise them with a Christian-based morality, wouldn't it be better to let the former find their amusement elsewhere?

M. TREZISE
Box Hill, Vic
25/7/64

Permissive

The pollution of our culture

IT is sad watching the Australian progressives demanding free access to pornography as a human right — students selling pornography in the union, for instance.

How strange to see it a political issue, the demand for toleration of this anti-human cultural material.

Gordon Hawkins (8/9) refers to the situation in Denmark. He does not say that the Danes are making something like $20 million a year by exporting this stuff to Germany and America. When a leading public figure was recently exposed as having taken part in sex films, a newspaper there said he was to be praised for having helped solve his country's economic problems.

Le Monde of Paris recently reported that a young woman in Denmark had made a name for herself, and a great deal of money, by performing in public with stallions and dogs. The Society for the Prevention of Cruelty to Animals there was hoping to secure legislation to protect animals from degradation in stage and screen sex shows. No one there apparently thinks of seeking protection for human beings in this way.

A new form of prostitution has grown up, whereby "performers" are sought, for the crudest of shows, for money — and all this is on the increase, and by no means dying away. Now in New York, apparently, you can pay to watch pornographic films being made.

I believe I am a progressive and I am here in Australia to help reform English teaching, to make it possible for children to find the human qualities in themselves — towards a more human society.

After writing three books on culture and symbolism, I have come to the conclusion that pornography — and I would include a great deal that appears on film today, in books and in magazines — is destructively anti-human and spreads hate abroad. In this, it is complementary to the hatred that culminates in war. It degrades man's image of himself and makes desperate, but false, solutions to the problem of life more likely.

It is perplexing for me to see Australians wanting to roll in the filth like everyone else — believing that this is a "right" of the adult which their Government will not allow them to have.

Surely there are better ways of expending one's energy — and, as far as pornography is concerned, aren't we better off without this form of erosion of our sense of the dignity and value of ourselves?

DAVID HOLBROOK
Queenscliff, NSW
15/9/70

Who are the most moral?

THE Reverend Alan Walker, discussing the censorship on ABC television, comments that he would "hate to see us like Denmark."

Current Australian morality includes involvement in Vietnam, kangaroo massacre to feed cats and dogs, a road toll that looks like My Lai, a share market which is an international nasty joke, school boys dabbling on the stock exchange, a predatory and avaricious attitude towards our natural resources (the Reef, Aboriginal tribal grounds) and a miserly, selfish approach to education, health and social welfare.

In Denmark, there is only one school class as large as 28; in Sweden, 30 is the legal limit. In Scandinavia, the road toll is low, deserted wives living on social scraps are virtually unknown, people cannot enrich themselves overnight at the expense of others or the country, minorities (such as the Lapps) are treated generously and the aged are not left abandoned in sordid loneliness (and, for the record, Sweden does NOT have the highest suicide rate and hasn't had for very many years).

More directly on the Danish censorship, Dr Hendrick Hoffmeyer, a leading Danish psychiatrist, says: "There is no scientific evidence to show that pornography encourages crime. It is also worth noting that in Denmark and Sweden, where restrictions have been removed, the ratio of sexual crime is dropping."

And to quote Erik Manniche, a lecturer at the Sociological Institute of Copenhagen: "Many male tourists come to Denmark expecting to find women available everywhere, but they are usually disappointed. In this country, the payment of money for sex, or the classical background for seduction — false promises, pressure or abuse of a form of dependence — are considered much more immoral."

Which is the more moral society?

(Mrs) MARGARET MORTIMER
Richmond, Vic
26/2/70

Permissive

Oh! Calcutta!

MANY people, in quite properly declaring their disapproval of Oh! Calcutta!, or what they imagine Oh! Calcutta! to be, overstep the mark by demanding that it be banned.

The essential and distinctive principle of a liberal society, and one to which the Council for Civil Liberties is naturally committed, is that citizens must be allowed to make their own moral choices insofar as these do not violate the rights and liberties of others. This applies especially in the area of taste and public decency.

It is immaterial whether it is a majority or a minority, or the good or the bad, that wishes to do the suppressing. Thus a Christian majority has no more right to ban Oh! Calcutta! than an anti-Christian majority has to ban the Bible, though plenty of people, in fact, abuse their powers.

It is perfectly proper for individuals to fulminate from the pulpit, or to distribute pamphlets, or to advertise against what they consider to be immoral.

They may persuade or convince others to boycott, or ignore what they find immoral and if it is a commercial enterprise and their standards are widely shared, they may kill it by their scorn and their absence.

But it is here that their legitimate power ends, as long as they can reasonably avoid the performance, i.e. Oh! Calcutta! is different in a hall and as a public display in the streets.

If the performance is discreet and not imposed upon people, the adult citizen must himself decide what he will view.

Suppression, bannings and witch-hunts are likely to do far more damage to society, by removing the individual's freedom of choice.

To impose Christian or any other morality is to deprive people of their freedom and therefore of their humanity, while to affirm their freedom does not imply approval of all the different things that they may choose.

J. B. JONES
Adelaide

(The writer is president of the South Australian Council for Civil Liberties.)
1/3/71

Thomas Keneally

Four-letter exercise

IT was my husband's bad, or good, fortune to have had a novel of his issued by Penguin Books the day after the issue of Portnoy's Complaint.

As far as I know, my husband's novel did not sell 75,000 copies on its first day of issue, this failure being partially due, I feel, to the indifference of the Chief Secretary and the police to local writers.

Though my husband is not a pornographer of any standing and has failed to be banned even in Ireland, he did manage to use a four-letter word participally in his last novel, and should surely be given credit as a trier.

I suggest, therefore, a pornography tariff for the native-born Australian writer, by which, for example, one four-letter word written by an Australian is worth at least four imported four-letter words.

Only by some such means can the local writer become subject to that brand of official attention which will guarantee him a large sale.

JUDITH KENEALLY
Epping, NSW
9/9/70

No! Calcutta!

I CANNOT understand the South Australian Government's attitude in permitting Oh! Calcutta! to be shown in Adelaide before obtaining the approval of the electors of this State.

After all, the Government went to the people for their approval in connection with late shopping and the Government found it necessary to have a royal commission into the moratorium.

Does the Government not think that Oh! Calcutta! is an important issue?

I am sure that the majority of the South Australian adults and electors would not have a production like Oh! Calcutta! in their city.

In my opinion the whole show is just nudity and promiscuity and I believe it will do no good for the morals of the young citizens of this State.

What is the LCL Opposition doing about it?

GEORGE BASISOVS
Dulwich, SA
16/2/71

Permissive

Gnawing at our morals

I DO not really know how other States are placed lately, but I am sorry to say it seems that if any State is heading downhill it is South Australia.

Almost daily, we find yet another case of gnawing at our moral fibre by some additional form of depravity — it seems to me.

On March 28, television viewers witnessed many minutes of dancing by a girl with no bra. Imagine what this would do to the minds of male teenagers and young children.

And here are a few more "quicksanders" that indicate where we are blindly and depravedly heading:

1. Two sex shops allowed to operate in Adelaide recently.
2. Obvious turning-a-blind-eye (so far) to magazines containing crudities.
3. Portnoy's Complaint allowed into SA in 1970, or thereabouts.
4. Highest illegitimacy rate and highest number of illegitimate births in SA's history (despite the pill).
5. A 100 per cent increase in under-18 drunken drivers during July-December last compared with the previous half-year.
6. A new high in marriage breakdowns.
7. Record outbreak of youthful suicides.
8. Juvenile delinquency in 1971 well above 1970.
9. High abortion figure since legalisation bent things a bit.

Other States would have some of this — but as much?

W. N. WREFORD
Henley Beach, SA
6/4/72

Sex shops and crime

RECENT reports indicate that attempts in various States to set up sex shops selling pornographic books, films and other materials have produced a fairly predictable police and governmental crackdown.

Leaving aside questions of taste, religion or morality, it is commonly argued by those who advocate the repression of pornography that its liberalisation would lead to an increase in sex crimes; that pornography "causes" sexual offences.

In a book entitled Law and Order in Australia, to be published by Angus and Robertson later this month, we have reviewed the more important recent evidence relating to the connection between pornography and sex crimes.

We have said there: "Our conclusion . . . is that it is very likely that exposure to pornography does not cause an increase in delinquent or criminal behavior; on the contrary, it is probable that exposure to pornography causes a decrease in the incidence of certain sexual offences, in particular offences against female children.

"It would certainly be paradoxical if . . . in maintaining the status quo of strict censorship, one of the costs is to be that the possibility of reducing the incidence of sex crimes against children should be overlooked."

G. D. WOODS
P. G. WARD
Sydney, NSW
(The writers are associated with the Sydney University Institute of Criminology.)
24/4/72

Buffoonery

THE Festival of Light is an attempt to convince the media and the politicians that the majority of people in the community oppose the gradual and long overdue increase in tolerance towards the sexual behavior of other people, and the interest shown by some people in sex as portrayed in books and films.

Being short on reasoned argument and reliable information to justify their fear of this new tolerance, the festival organisation cannot afford to engage in open debate to show that it has the support of sensible people, but prefers instead to manufacture this impression by enticing the public to its meetings with irrelevant offers of kite-flying, choirs and pop groups for the young.

The need to resort to ploys of this kind is a manifestation of the weakness of their real support in the community.

Consequently, the Humanist Society of South Australia speaks out for those people who feel intimidated by the Festival of Light, who fear that, against all sense and reason, this step backwards just might succeed.

The Humanists advise both the media and the politicians not to be fooled by the festival's combination of bombast and buffoonery.

No matter how many people this shameful waste of the church's money is able to muster at these meetings, they will not be representative of the mass of open-minded Australians. Rather, they will be representative of an age that ended with the death of Oliver Cromwell.

PETER WOOLCOCK
Norwood, SA
(The writer is president of the SA Humanist Society.)
9/10/73

Permissive

A perishing society?

IN reply to Michael Glass's letter (13/10), I do not believe the recent election result was a vote for "permissiveness," as many people of all parties know that any government's task is made much harder when moral values and individual responsibilities are swept aside.

A glance through any daily newspaper makes it evident that all governments are grappling with the ill-effects of permissiveness, and indeed moral issues have become the dominant ones for politicians of all creeds

In a speech made at Harvard University in the U.S. on 8/6/78, the Russian author, Alexander Solzhenitsyn, said: "In the West, man's sense of responsibility to God and society grows dimmer and dimmer . . . a total liberation occurred from the moral heritage of Christian centuries, with their great reserves of mercy and sacrifice . . ."

He concludes that Western society could well be a "perishing society" and that "our lives will have to change if we want to save life from self-destruction."

As recently as 9/10/78, in an article in *The Australian*, Dr Herman Kahn states that "you (Australia) need more of the Protestant work ethic, the Confucian ethic — some damned ethic."

Consequently, it is not only the so-called "bigoted" clergy who try to sound a warning, and stress that what is needed is not more of each person doing his or her own thing, but a renewed (or a new?) sense of responsibility and self-discipline in all of us.

(Mrs) MARIE McCARTNEY
Eastwood, NSW
20/10/78

Alexander Solzhenitsyn

Virginity

BENEATH all the glitter of John Hallows' Forum article is sadly an old and decrepit argument that should have been buried long ago. Mr Hallows says that because many people do something, it is okay: a vast number of young unmarried women are no longer virgins, ergo we should accept premarital sex as the standard of right behavior.

It is a style of argument I suspect the Lockheed executives may have used. Most or many policiticans and public servants in certain countries take bribes and are not honest, ergo that is the standard that Lockheed needs to accept.

Many Germans joined the Nazi Party on the same basis. Most people (Hallows' sane men?) were supporting Hitler, ergo National Socialism is the way of life to accept.

Mr Hallows has tried to con us with slipshod thinking in asserting that many or most automatically means right; it was not true with the nazis; it is not true with Lockheed; and I do not believe it is true with premarital sex.

BRIAN LIGHTOWLER
Indooroopilly, Qld
22/9/76

Unbridled

AS a member of the older generation, and so presumably a square or old hat, it nevertheless makes me sad to read that Virginity Takes Back Seat, *The Australian* (17/8), and that most people agree with sex before marriage.

What has happened to our moral standards when young boys and girls can sleep around with anyone they choose? In our day, we called that promiscuous and immoral. Much value was placed on restraint, control and purity before marriage.

But today, according to most people, sexual permissiveness is no longer a sin. I opt out to belong to the minority group and call it a very grave sin indeed. Look what happened to Sodom and Gomorrah where all sorts of sexual licences were allowed. Those cities were destroyed.

I sincerely hope my grandsons and grand-daughters will be virgins when they go to the altar — if indeed there is any altar left to go to.

Judging by the godlessness of the setting up of the false idol sex, there probably won't be any religion left, only the sickly subject of sex, sex, sex. No wonder there are so many sex crimes when it is the fashion for sex to be unbridled.

MARGARET BARCLAY
Glenelg, SA
29/8/79

Just sorry

I'M also an oldie, but I don't take the same disapproving view as Margaret Barclay, (Letters, 29/8) of the sexual permissiveness of our younger generation. I'm just sorry I was born too early to join in the fun.

PEGGY BOOTH
Valentine, NSW
5/9/79

Censorship

THE TRIAL OF LADY CHATTERLEY

Bad books for the young

MR W. D. Richardson, A.C.T. Public Librarian, deserves support for withdrawing the books of Blyton, Crompton and Johns from the Canberra Public Libraries.

No children's library of responsibility would stock these authors and no Children's Book Council elsewhere in Australia promotes these books.

The Blyton and Biggles books, in particular, are the products of impoverished style, stultified imaginations, continuously repeating the same plot, the same characters, the same impossibilities, the same trivia.

I have known girls of 14 in England who had read nothing but Blyton from the age of seven and were incapable of reading anything above a nine-year-old level of reading difficulty, conception of ideas, or character insight.

The oft-lauded moral values of Blyton books are lost amidst a plethora of pettiness, nastiness in child relations, name-calling, contempt of everyone and all things non-British and of the police; suburban values are portrayed in their most banal aspects, non-conformity and intelligence are jeered at and snobbery and condescension to servants and inferred social inferiors is frequent.

In a vintage year, Miss Blyton earns £40,000 and is the best seller in Britain, next to the Bible.

A readability test of Blyton along with some more creative writers for children, all popular, puts Alison Uttley with the Little Grey Rabbit series, Edward Ardizzone's Little Tim books well ahead of the Noddy books in reading ease.

The Public Library of South Australia has excluded these three authors from its collections since the late 1940s.

BARBARA BUICK
Hazelwood Park, SA
22/8/64

Censorship

I CONGRATULATE you on your front page story (24/7) on the ban imposed on the Ian Fleming thriller, The Spy Who Loved Me.

I hope you will give more prominence to this case in your continued campaign against the follies of Australian censorship, as the full facts behind this particular instance reveal the clandestine nature of many bans. In view of the current vogue for James Bond books and films, this would be opportune strategy.

The Spy Who Loved Me was published in England in 1962. The ban in Australia must have been imposed in this same year, as it is the practice for the Fleming thrillers to be published in Australia only a few weeks after publication in London.

However, The Spy Who Loved Me does not appear

The ban on 007

on the list of prohibited books published in the Commonwealth Gazette for August, 1963 (the last full list published). Although this list admits to being incomplete (though it contains 190 titles!), it seems as though The Spy was not referred to the Literature Censhorship Board (under Regulation 4a of the Customs Regulations), but was seized by Customs officials on their own initiative.

You are not quite the first people to spotlight this ban (Donald Horne mentions it in The Lucky Country), but I know from conversations with Fleming fans in this country that this book is

virtually unknown in Australia, thus showing the effectiveness of this secretive banning.

It should be noted that in two NSW newspapers and periodicals which recently published extracts from Kingsley Amis' The 007 Dossier, The Spy Who Loved Me was included in a list of Bond thrillers, but there was no mention of the Australian ban!

Even more significant, perhaps, was the item in our local paper in Armidale some weeks back which printed a report of the banning of The Spy Who Loved Me in South Africa without admitting the Australian ban. Ignorance is bliss?

(Dr) BARRY BALDWIN
Lecturer in Ancient History
University of New England
Armidale, NSW
2/8/65

Warm, sensitive Catcher

ASSUMING your correspondent, Mr Ayles (23/9) doesn't have his tongue in his cheek when he makes his hysterical outburst against "such filth as Catcher in the Rye," perhaps he is just the man I've been seeking for years.

I'd like someone to explain to me what it is that even the narrowest-minded prude could object to in this warm and sensitive novel, once banned in this country.

Usually when a book is banned, no matter how exasperated one may be with those who guard our morals, their thinking is obvious — they consider there are too many four-letter words, too much sex, too much blasphemy, or too much criticism of established institutions within the pages of the offending work.

A sad and sorry viewpoint,

perhaps, but at least you can fathom the reason for the banning. In the case of Catcher in the Rye, however, none of these things applies.

In fact, the word "purity," used both as the wowser would use it and in its wider and nobler application, was never more applicable to a book than in this instance!

G. CURRAN
Hornsby, NSW
29/9/65

PS

IT seems that the censorship allows Australian TV to show black women dancing bare-breasted, but not white women. Would anyone care to explain the philosophy behind this color bar?

DAVID R. BEAN
Killara, NSW
3/7/68

Four-letter comedy

AT the farewell dinner of the Federal Parliament in Canberra in his honor, Lord De L'Isle, the Governor-General, a connoisseur of fine literature, referred to the so-called four-letter words.

He said censorship was "all part of our comedy here" and only helped the Minister of Customs and Excise to extend his bookshelves.

This message, not recognised by *The Australian*, was referring to the censorship of certain literature in this country, which is beyond description.

What a message in 1965. Fantastic!

PETER BRIX
Sydney
11/5/65

Censorship

The sexualisation of life

YOU look forward in your editorial of May 27 to "a more broad-minded approach to the question of censorship."

May I point out that broad-mindedness of this kind has led to severe reactions abroad?

For example, in Germany this year, 400 physicians (including nearly a hundred gynaecologists and 45 professors) signed a memorandum to the Federal Ministry of Health on "the sexualisation of public life." These authorities stated that "one-sided and selfish misuse (of sex) degrades and destroys the human personality and the community." Such "one-sided misuse" of sex would undoubtedly be encouraged by the type of "prominent books and magazines" which Senator Anderson is at present keeping out of this country.

The same group of German physicians condemned: "The unrestrained propagandistic exploitation of the female body and of sexual allurements for advertising purposes, and for all kinds of unscrupulous profit-making in business, the theatre, films, television, illustrated magazines, books etc."

In America, the New York Academy of Medicine last year "urged President Johnson to utilise the FBI in gathering facts about salacious literature and co-ordinating a fight against it." The academy went on to condemn smut-peddlers for intensifying a problem with "deep going socio-medical implications for the entire nation."

It is quite certain that "a more broad-minded approach" to censorship in this country will offend countless mothers and fathers who are already deeply concerned at the threat to the mental and moral health of their children presented by so many books and magazines that are freely circulating in Australia.

J. A. PHILLIPS, SJ
Corpus Christi College
Glen Waverley, Vic
3/6/65

'Dirty book'

MRS Schmid states that protests against Lady Chatterley's Lover are voiced by men (9/6). She would like the book republished here for the enlightenment of Australian women.

I should like to quote against Lady Chatterley a person who was both a woman and a literary critic of unquestioned ability: Dame Edith Sitwell.

In her recently published autobiography, Taken Care Of, Dame Edith describes the work as "a very dirty and completely worthless book, of no literary importance."

After quoting a specimen of Mr Mellors' talk, Dame Edith goes on:

"Nobody seems to have thrashed Mr Mellors, which was what he deserved; and this unutterably filthy, cruel and smelly speech has been, apparently, accepted by the more idiotic of the British public as being a fine example of the working man's frank splendid mode of expression. No decent working man, no decent man of any class, would have uttered it."

(Miss) CHRISTINA MISELL
Librarian
North Balwyn, Vic
16/6/65

'Don Juan' was censored

ON obtaining the current issue of an English women's magazine (Nova), we were amazed and extremely annoyed to find that an article, The Don Juan Syndrome — Men With Compulsive Sexual Appetites, by Alma Birk, JP, had been torn out by the Australian censors.

Alma Birk is the associate editor of the magazine and has written articles on such controversial subjects as divorce, marriage, the American suburban housewife etc.

We consider this magazine a leader in its field, if only because it attempts to treat women as intelligent beings by consideration of such topics as Vietnam.

Thus we were angry at this censorship which seems to force women back into the kitchen to read unrealistic romances and do their cookery, cleaning etc.

Is it that the censors wish to revert to the time when, cowering in horror, women were told of "the birds and bees" on their wedding night; when women's sexual appetites were supposedly negligible and no attempt was made to understand those of men?

CAROL Y. NIMMO
JUDITH S. NIMMO
Taringa, Qld
8/9/66

┌ PS ─

I TURN to you in desperation for advice. While overseas I read Tropic of Capricorn (unbelievable). My Life and Loves (so detailed) and de Sade's Justine (in French). I am a simple girl and very upset, since, on arrival in London two weeks hence, I shall be unable to resist seeing Ulysses. Please tell me: Is the Minister for Customs empowered to impound my head?

A. S. NEWMAN
Roseville, NSW
15/5/67

Censorship

Who is more mature?

WE would like to draw attention to a statement reported in *The Australian* by Dr Delamothe, Queensland Minister for Justice.

Defending censorship, he said there was a need for the Government to protect immature minds — "the very young . . . and also those adults in our community with adolescent minds."

In other words, some adults are more adult than others. We seem to have heard that argument before — in George Orwell's *Animal Farm*, from Napoleon and his pigs.

In which category does the Minister for Justice place us? Presumably we are among the immature — since we are not allowed to import works of such authors as T. E. Lawrence, Steven Marcus, Henry Miller, Simone de Beauvoir and Jean Genet. Presumably also, the various boards of censors are among the ranks of the mature, since they have to examine these works before forbidding them to us.

We will accept the minister's argument the day he proves that his mind and the minds of his censorious friends are more mature than ours. So far the evidence proferred does not seem very substantial.

Incidentially, Dr Delamothe brushes aside the objection "that censorship is wrong" and excludes this "bald statement" from the category of "good reasons for making any change." One would think the argument from justice should carry more weight with a Minister for Justice.

BILL HAYDEN
MHR for Oxley
Qld
15/7/68

Unladylike Love Story

ONCE again the Australian censors have come to the rescue of that elusive spectre, "public morals," with their scissors, bips and artistic sensitivity.

It appears that Love Story *(The Australian, 18/3)* is to undergo possible butchery for Ali McGraw's unladylike expressions. Having seen the film in the U.S., I wonder how such an acclaimed and uplifting no-bed-scene, no-violence film can be held up, while the everyday Hollywood trash comes through with flying colors.

The Australian obviously was in no danger of defying the law by publishing the word "bullshit."

Perhaps the censors could put quivering pen to paper and draw up an exhaustive list of obscenities for automatic censorship. In this way, censorship would not be left to the haphazard day-to-day standards of a small group of people, but would be objective and unambiguous.

Ironically, "those words" which *The Australian* (or any newspaper) would never publish are avoided in the film.

ELISABETH BIRD
Sydney
23/3/71

How awful!

I HAVE just seen the film Clockwork Orange. How ghastly!

This was most certainly not a film as we knew films in past years. No coherent story, no account of the success of a good cause, no warm smiles or warming story.

It was just a cavalcade of bashings, murder, rape, nudity — full frontal nudity, viciously exposed by male marauders. Clothes ripped from distracted women. An old man confronted and beaten. Awful!

I would urge the mature, decent citizen to see this film, especially the family man and woman concerned for the welfare of their daughter, for young womanhood which, as American author Harold Bell Wright, of more kindly times, said, represents "riches which the nation can ill afford to squander."

And, having seen Clockwork Orange, then say they don't want censorship.

T. FELMASTER
Yarraville, Vic
17/4/73

PS

THE Australian reported (20/2) that Last Tango in Paris had been passed uncut by the Film Censorship Board and your film critic suggests that this could be an example of Australian nationalism and independence. What a yardstick! If this type of film continues to gain acceptance, someone may well soon be writing about "The Mucky Country."

PAT NEASEY
Sandy Bay, Tas
5/3/73

Drugs

The dangers of marijuana

FIRST Michael English and now Michael Dover (7/10) have aired their naive opinions in your columns about the merits of smoking marijuana.

W. R. Bradney (27/9) set forth arguments against its use in rather stringent moral terms, but the possibility of physical, social and economic side effects have been neglected.

I would like to consider these factors — basing my comments on observations made while living for many years in the Mexican-American section of Los Angeles.

Marijuana is as scarce in the United States as the police can make it, but due to the large mobile population there is still some available.

Marijuana smoking in itself can be as relatively harmless as smoking normal cigarettes or drinking alcoholic beverages. As in many other things, it is the frequency of usage which is significant.

Individuals who find it necessary to take refuge in steady marijuana smoking certainly suffer, but alcoholics and heavy smokers have their difficulties, too.

The real difference with marijuana lies in the potentiality of escalating the addiction into a more expensive and dangerous habit. An alcoholic can only increase his intake; he doesn't move on to radically more damaging drugs.

Dope pushers rely on marijuana to get customers for their more highly priced wares. Most of the inmates of Synanon House, a self-cure hospital for drug addicts in Santa Monica, California, started with marijuana and were subsequently hooked on heroin.

Once on the "H" (which has happened to some very aware and intelligent people), the addict finds that his resources are no longer adequate to furnish his body with the narcotics which it craves.

The addict desperate for a fix will do anything to obtain the needed money.

Often he becomes a pusher himself and has a real incentive to hook others on narcotics, so that he can support his own habit.

Marijuana smoking can certainly have unpleasant effects. Over-indulgence in marijuana, as with alcohol, can bring on mental, physical and economic disability.

Total disintegration of the personality can result from the use of heroin as the natural next step after marijuana — and the climb back to a normal life is long and hard.

NORMAN K. SANDERS
Sandy Bay, Tas
8/11/65

The dangers in scare tactics

ONE of the more justifiable charges made against opponents of drug-use for pleasure and recreation is that, in their resort to scare tactics, they often make statements that are half-truths, or plainly wrong.

As these, when made by persons in positions of influence or authority, are later quoted as accurate expressions of fact, it becomes all the more important to ensure that errors are corrected.

The Minister for Customs is reported as saying *(The Australian,* 5/9): "More young people . . . die from drugs in the U.S. every day than from any other cause." Taken within the context of his speech, most listeners would assume that these deaths are the result of drug abuse.

In 1968 — the most recent year available to me from W.H.O. sources — the most frequent causes of death for persons aged 15-24 were accidents, heart disease, cancer, suicide and homicide.

Of 23,012 accidental deaths, 16,543 were due to road crashes and of the remainder only 481 were due to poisons, which would include accidental drug overdose. Suicide accounted for 2353 and homicide 3357 deaths.

Even if one assumed that all suicides were due to drug overdose, one is still nowhere near the number of deaths due to car crashes. It is most unlikely that in the subsequent three to four years accidental drug deaths have increased 47 times to overtake the toll of accidental deaths.

Continued next page

Drugs

Dangers in scare tactics

From previous page

In fact, in 1968 there were 3000 deaths in all age groups due to accidental poisoning by solids and liquids; 229 of these were caused by narcotic drugs, 120 by aspirin and 926 by sedatives and hypnotics.

On the face of this data, it does not appear that drugs are the principal cause of death in young persons, even though I have no wish to minimise the risk of fatalities caused directly or indirectly by misuse of drugs such as heroin, amphetamines and hallucinogens.

Marijuana, in terms of lethal dose, is some 5000 times safer than alcohol. Hence one would have to smoke about 800 marijuana cigarettes over a few hours to reach the lethal level — something that could be done with less trouble by drinking a bottle of whisky.

It is a sobering thought.
F. A. WHITLOCK
Brisbane
12/9/74

(The writer is Professor of Psychological Medicine at the University of Queensland)

Mackay warns over sentences

EXACTLY a year ago, a crop of marijuana worth $250,000 was discovered growing, carefully concealed, on a farm at Tharbogang, near Griffith, NSW.

Three weeks later, three acres, worth $150,000, were found at Hanwood together with a quantity of refined hemp ready for consignment to the drug market.

Fines imposed on the two growers were $250 and $500 respectively. Jail sentences were suspended on the ground that they had "previous unblemished records" and were considereed "unlikely to do it again". Both growers were adults.

On January 31, the Griffith Area News reported a Leeton trial where youths received jail sentences and fines of $900, $600 and $300 for smoking the end-products of the growers. Charges are also being heard against Leeton juveniles for smoking marijuana.

The contrast between these two judgments is alarming. It seems that crime, carefully organised and planned for profit, can be defended successfully, but that the end victim of the crime becomes the criminal.

Perhaps the discretion left in the hands of indiviual judges and magistrates in cases of this kind is too great when such disparity can result.

I have written to the NSW Attorney-General asking for a full review of this situation. Would any readers sharing my concern care to do the same?
DONALD B. MACKAY
Griffith, NSW
10/2/75
AUTHOR'S FOOTNOTE: Mr Mackay, the anti-drug campaigner, vanished in 1977 after leaving a hotel in Griffith, NSW. It is believed he was murdered for his campaign against drug trafficking, but no trace of his body has been found.

Babies drugged to keep quiet

ONE hears a good deal about the drug problem. Most of the fuss is about teenagers and their marijuana or middle-aged women and their sedatives and pain-killers.

I have recently become aware of a drug abuse which seems to me far more sinister; this is the practice of giving young babies tranquillisers and sedatives when their natural boisterousness is inconvenient.

I know of one mother who gives her infant son phenobarb every night to ensure that he sleeps. I suspect that these practices are widespread.

The teenagers are probably hurting no one by smoking their pot. The middle-aged women are usually hurting only themselves by their dependence on aspirin or whatever.

The ill-advised mothers and their doctors may be causing irreparable damage to the next generation.
MARITA BUSHELL
Highbury, SA
31/1/74

Homosexuals

Lonely, bitter and humiliated

AS a homosexual and, I feel, a responsible member of the community at large, I welcome the Attorney-General, Mr Hughes' attempt to promote rational discussion on the subject of deviation.

Unfortunately, I can see the collective Mrs Grundys of the country rising, pens poised, at the thought of approximately 550,000 Australians of all ages and walks of life being given a place in the community, which is supposedly theirs from birth.

Excuse the bitterness I feel. Australia is the country that I think of as my homeland, but my friends and I have at one time or another lost our jobs and our careers, been ostracised socially, subjected to police harassment, jail, have paid bribes to police and been subject to vicious beatings and blackmail because of our deviation.

It all sounds rather dramatic and over-stated, but as an average homosexual (is there really such a thing?) who is not particularly overt about his predilection, nor fierce in his denial of it, the above details are never far from my thoughts.

Changing the law will not help the loneliness, the bitterness and the humiliation that many feel, but it is the beginning of a re-education program that in generations to come may lead to greater awareness and understanding. I hope the law can be relaxed if not changed completely.

But I cannot blame anyone for the lack of compassion from the man in the street; he just does not know and he is not told. With all the research and fact-finding going on, no one has thought to disseminate the accumulated information throughout the country.

So ignorance breeds intolerance and the cycle is repeated year after year.

Far from trying to justify my behavior to an antagonistic community, I have learned to live with myself, learned to accept things as they come. However, there are many who still struggle with guilt-ridden consciences and who attempt basically futile cure treatments; understanding can help these people.

If this plea is emotional, it is only because homosexuality is still one of those subjects that generates only subjective and not, as Mr Hughes hopes, rational discussion.

HOMOSEXUAL
Pyrmont, NSW
10/6/70

PS

I NEVER thought I would live to see the day when an archbishop and so-called intelligent students of a university would favor homosexuality. To my way of thinking as an ordinary working individual, the men who indulge in this neurotic and hideous pastime should be publicly ostracised by all decent people.

THE GADFLY
Brisbane
8/8/64

Shocked

A HEADLINE in *The Australian* stated Dr Woods Agrees With Legalised Homosexuality.

Presuming Dr Woods was correctly quoted, this must be one of the most distressing statements made by a leading churchman.

We are not surprised when men in leading positions, who hold a pagan philosophy, demand that the perversion be condoned and legalised. We are profoundly shocked, however, when a leading churchman also agrees to this.

F. G. COONEY
Murrumbeena, Vic
8/8/64

Condemned

TO WHAT end does Archbishop Woods want homosexuality legalised? Holy Scripture condemns roundly all irregular sexual practices and one would expect Dr Woods to subscribe to such views.

If he argues that we should do evil that good may come, he is again anti-scriptural.

ISABEL McLENNAN
North Melbourne, Vic
4/8/64

Too smug

ISABEL McLennan (4/8) objects to the idea of homosexuality being legalised on the ground that it is contrary to Holy Scripture. What has Holy Scripture to do with legislation designed for a secular society?

One of the most irritating things about religious bodies and their adherents is the smug assumption that they are the sole repositories of all moral wisdom.

L. R. MELVILLE
Coogee, NSW
8/8/64

Homosexuals

This cancerous growth

MR Peter Brebner of Acceptance (5/4) defends homosexuality and urges the Festival of Light to do something about the prostitution and strip shows of Kings Cross and R-rated pornographic films.

We certainly share his concern over these decadent, depraved aspects of our society. We devote a major proportion of our resources to cleaning up both heterosexual and homosexual prostitution and pornography.

The gift of natural heterosexual sex is from God; the deviations, perversions and unnatural behavior such as sodomy are the "work of the devil" as suggested by Mr Brebner (Genesis 18/19).

Your readers should note:

1. That there is no official Catholic organisation for homosexuals, nor is Acceptance recognised in any way by the Church.

In fact the most recent Vatican Statement on homosexuality states: "At the present time, there are those who, basing themselves on observations in the psychological order, have begun to judge indulgently and even to excuse completely, homosexual relations between certain people. This they do in opposition to the constant teaching of the Magisterium and to the moral sense of the Christian people.

"In Sacred Scripture, they are condemned as a serious depravity and even presented as the sad consequence of rejecting God. This judgment of scripture does not, of course, permit us to conclude that all those who suffer from this anomaly are personally responsible for it, but it does attest to the fact that homosexual acts are in-

The Rev Fred Nile

trinsically disordered and can in no case be approved of."

(Reference Declaration On Certain Questions concerning Sexual Ethics, para 8, pages 7/8.)

2. That homosexuals, who are sexually immature and have not progressd to the normal and natural heterosexual state of sexual development, can and are being helped and adjusted to normality.

3. Most experts reject the fallacious homosexual arguments used in Mr Brebner's letter, i.e. only 4 per cent are homosexually orientated and only 4 per cent of that 4 per cent may be irreversible. The Australian public must reject those gross exaggerations which claim that 5 per cent, 10 per cent and even 20 per cent of our population are homosexual!

4. It is pseudo-religious organisations such as Acceptance which have revealed their "hysterical ignorance and prejudices" concerning homosexual-sodomy by rejecting the plain teaching of the Bible and the Church. Romans 1: 26-27: "So that even their women turned against God's natural plan for them and indulged in sex sin with each other. And the men, instead of having a

normal sex relationship with women, burned with lust for each other, men doing shameful things with other men and, as a result, getting paid within their own souls with the penalty they so richly deserved." They fully deserve the judgment of Christ concerning anyone who causes a child to stumble in moral or spiritual terms (Matthew 18: 6-7).

5. Our FOL campaign is based on compassion — the principle of child-care, not child-abuse!

Finally the Festival of Light position has been fully supported in a recent statement by seven leading Jewish organisations in the U.S. which urged Americans to help fight "the cancerous growth and increasing power of the homosexual revolt in America."

In their joint statement they said:

"For the past decade, religious Jewish Americans have watched with increasing outrage the cancerous growth and increasing power of the homosexual revolt in America.

"This moral rot has reached the point where the security and very existence of our republic is in peril — faced as we are by internal as well as external enemies, who have said they will bury us.

"We call upon our fellow Americans to join us in doing battle against this dangerous movement, which threatens to undermine our educational system, our political system and our national morale."

(Rev) FRED NILE
National Co-ordinator
The Australian Festival of
Light
Sydney
12/4/78

Homosexuals

The compassionate view

THE Rev Fred Nile of the Festival of Light quotes at length from Pope Paul's recent document on Sexual Ethics, but he fails to include an important section. The document reads (par 8):

"A distinction is drawn, and it seems with some reason, between homosexuals whose tendency . . . is transitory, or at least not incurable, and homosexuals who are definitively such because of some kind of innate instinct or a pathological constitution judged to be incurable."

While falling far short of what we would hope for, this at least faces the facts of the situation, unlike Mr Nile, whose claim that only 4 per cent of 4 per cent are irreversibly homosexual cannot be taken seriously!

The document continues: "In the pastoral field, these homosexuals (i.e. the second 'constitutional' category) must certainly be treated with understanding and sustained in the hope of overcoming their personal difficulties and their inability to fit into society." This is a far more compassionate stand than Mr Nile's, whose "pastoral care" would include electric-shock and nausea-drug aversion "therapy."

Acceptance, which Mr Nile seeks to discredit as not being an "official Catholic organisation" (no more or less official than any charismatic prayer group), is largely in the business of pastoral care. We run, in Sydney, a telephone counselling service which deals with people and their problems as they are, without any pre-conceived notions as to what they "should" be. (This service, which received 205 calls in the week ending 13/4/78, is in association with Lifeline and we speak to their trainee counsellors each year).

We provide Mass each week in an atmosphere of mutual care and support. We also have discussions, theatre parties, barbecues where people can meet in a social situation. Not all our members, of course, are Catholic. We are open to everyone.

While we would appreciate a change in the Church's official attitudes, we are grateful for the support we do receive in providing pastoral care for this substantial portion of God's people.

(Brother) PETER
BREBNER
Acceptance
Darlinghurst, NSW
25/4/78

Gay teachers fight bigotry

THE NSW Gay Teachers and Students Group has been criticised on account of educational material on homosexuality that is being prepared for schools. It must be stated that this material is being prepared by two teachers who made a submission to the Schools Commission. There has been no grant to the NSW Gay Teachers and Students Group.

Accurate information about homosexuality is greatly needed in schools. Late last year, the group received a letter from a student which said: ". . . as I am only 16 and gay, I experience problems every day about my sexuality. Problems of losing friends and general persecution. I would strongly support the teaching of homosexual awareness in my school . . ."

The Schools Commission is to be commended for recognising the need to break down the ignorance and bigotry surrounding the subject of homosexuality.

As the dangers of anti-homosexual bigotry are more appreciated, things are improving. Parents are now speaking up for their gay children, making representations to such bodies as the NSW Privacy Committee on their behalf.

The work of the Gay Counselling Service and Parents and Friends of Gays are becoming better known and appreciated. The NSW Gay Teachers and Students Group can also be contacted.

MICHAEL GLASS
On behalf of the group
Kingsgrove, NSW
5/3/81

PS

MS Joanna Beaumont (The Australian, 26/10) and Tony Cook (The Australian, 13/10) miss the whole point about homosexual teachers. I certainly do not want to deprive anyone of his fetishes, but I just cannot accept that homosexual teachers have a right to indoctrinate other people's children, in a captive audience situation, with their own perversions, especially as they now flaunt the fact that they are homosexual 24 hours a day.

DAN O'DONNELL
North Brisbane, Qld
3/11/77

Brickbats

Dreary intellectualism

WHILE I feel that *The Australian* is doing much to elevate journalism in this country from the morass in which it welters, I must endorse Jonathan Black's comments (4/10) on the unvaried heaviness of the content material.

No doubt a newspaper, like a nation or an individual, has to endure the painful process of growing up, in which case let us hope in the case of *The Australian* a period of adequate adolescence has now been passed!

Your efforts to maintain high quality and provoke critical thought are admirable, but intellectualism alone is a dreary diet.

A measure of maturity must necessarily include a capacity for humor and what can best be described as a certain lightness of touch.

The occasional, oft-maligned "human interest" story would not, I feel sure, cause any charges of journalistic chicanery to be levelled; perhaps even without resorting to tabloid tactics, a soupcon of glamor might also be included and thereby serve to lighten the gloom of contemporary affairs!

In the words of the French — "Courage, mes braves!"

(Mrs) IRENE MALLAL
Tea Tree Gully, SA
12/10/65

Phantom of the opera

THERE is a story of an opera conductor who dreamt that the roof had fallen in. He awoke to find that he was conducting the last act of Samson and Delilah and the roof had, in fact, fallen in. The authenticity of this story has never been confirmed, but there are a number of true stories in which the conductor has mounted the rostrum and commenced the concert to find that the orchestra was playing a different overture from the one he had anticipated.

I had, hitherto, deemed myself fortunate that no such catastrophe had befallen me, but I must confess my experience of last Tuesday over-shadowed any disaster suffered by conductors

in the past. It would appear that I conducted an entire performance of The Yeomen of the Guard at the Regent Theatre, Sydney on November 28 and was totally unaware that I had done so until I read the review of the performance in your newspaper two days later.

WILLIAM REID
Director of Music
Elizabethan Orchestra
Sydney
8/12/78

Frances Kelly replies: It was the Australian Opera's nightmare. The printed program stated that the conductor was William Reid, no announcement was made to the contrary and who was I to argue? I couldn't even see him in the pit from my seat.

Deplorable

THIS association of women deplores the recent innovation in your newspaper — i.e. of printing photographs of women's fashions.

Many of our members became subscribers to your paper because they welcomed the presentation of news without the rubbish of the so-called women's section.

We sincerely hope that you do not intend to follow this stupid practice of thinking that women are only interested in recipes and clothes, etc.

L. G. WOODCOCK
President
United Association of
Women
Sydney
10/2/65

Appeasers!

AS you have failed to condemn Mr Kaunda of Zambia for his irresponsible calls for bloodshed and violence against his quite peaceful neighbor, Rhodesia, I go on record publicly, if you have the courage, to brand *The Australian* as a newspaper of appeasement and racial discrimination — against our own white, British race.

ALBERT W. MEHLERT
Secretary
Hands Off Rhodesia
Committee
Corinda, Qld
1/6/66

PS

CONGRATULATIONS on your publication of the guide to candidates (1/12). A whole page of straightforward information on political matters. How did you manage it?

EILEEN PRICE
University of New England
Armidale, NSW
5/12/75

Brickbats

Touch of hysteria over the news

AS one who had a hand in the founding of *The Australian* 15 years ago (we had such high hopes, remember, of articulating a sane, healthy and creative nationalism!), I am saddened by the belligerent nationalism you are at this time purveying.

Like the Prime Minister, who has taken to acting beyond himself, you seem to be out to rouse passions in a situation that needs calmness and to speed the drift from detente to confrontation. On any assessment, this cannot be in our genuine interest.

Over the last week or so, there has been a touch of hysteria in both your handling of the news and your comment on it. Day-to-day headlines, like U.S. Youth Facing Military Draft, Carter Warns He Is Ready For War, U.S. War Material For China etc are contributing to a crescendo of alarm that in the circumstances is false.

It is bad enough that Malcolm Fraser, that quixotic schoolboy, should choose to act like Billy Hughes and Bert Evatt rolled into one — even though the world knows by now that Australian leaders talk bigger than they act.

But that your paper, of whose influence on public opinion you are justly proud, should do its best to bolster his platform with public alarm is, I believe, a sad service to your treasured objectivity.

In your editorial Bully For The Bulletin (24/1), you indeed suggested you would not mind assuming the mantle of the jingoistic old Bulletin which nurtured all the ocker nationalism that was latent in late 19th-century Australia.

"This is a great country," you proclaimed, "and it will be even greater when we all march together, and not to the beat of different drums."

That martial ring notwithstanding, I and most of your friends will not spring to the salute. Diversity, not bumptious conformity, must remain our nation's moral strength.

As for Afghanistan, which did not exist for us until the day before yesterday, you might well consider what Professor Macmahon Ball and most of our foreign service professionals believe to be our best policy in a dismaying situation — that recent events should not push us towards belligerent confrontation, but towards harder efforts to find peaceful settlements.

There has been much reference to elections in the U.S. and Australia as an element in the West's reactions to Afghanistan. I trust they may be discounted. Far more relevant, I suggest, is the prospect of an "election" in the Kremlin. Do we want a hawk in power there when Brezhnev goes? Such spiteful tit-for-tats as boycotting the Olympics might well be seen in that light.

A century ago we were building fortresses on the headlands of our harbors to hold the Russians off. A century ago the British were waging war in Afghanistan to prevent the Russians advancing to the Persian Gulf and General Roberts was writing: "The less the Afghans see of us, the less they dislike us. Should the Russians in future years attempt to conquer Afghanistan we should have a better chance of attaching Afghans to our interest if we avoid all interference with them."

Just a thought for the times, and a plea for your return to realities.

DOUGLAS BRASS
Mt Eliza, Vic
1/2/80

Downright nauseating

I WAS one of the first local subscribers to *The Australian* and enjoyed the paper, particularly during its first years when its thought-provoking articles and commentaries surpassed those of the old lady, The Sydney Morning Herald.

During those years, to read *The Australian* meant to obtain positive stimulus, deeper understanding and broadening of outlook.

The high ideals which *The Australian* held now seem to have been replaced by the desire to become a commercially successful enterprise, even if this can only be achieved by an appeal to baser human instincts.

The Australian has changed from being uplifting to downright nauseating. I regret this change and have now cancelled my subscription.

HARRY HEITMEYER
Maitland, NSW
24/3/76

PS

I REFER to the leading article in The Australian (15/11). Isn't the use of "for we Australians" reminiscent of Mrs Everage's "excuse I?"
(Prof) LEONARD B. HARROP
University of NSW
Sydney
19/11/65

Bouquets

Don't forget the migrants

AUSTRALIAN newspapers seem to cater for almost everyone – the under 21, the medical hypochondriac, the horse-lover and the cricket fan. The only group which seems to be forgotten is the 1,000,000 new settlers who came within the last 20 years to this country.

For us, the world is not concentrated between New York, London and Canberra. We are hungry for news from the whole world, particularly Europe.

Why should we be forced to buy a two-month-old French or German newspaper for 5/– if we want to find out what really happens.

News digested and doc-tored by a U.S. State Department inspired journalist is not sufficient.

Hundreds of new settlers I know personally have stopped buying newspapers because they are bored with the perennial prowler story and bare-topped woman.

We are watching with interest *The Australian*. Are you going to follow the proud tradition of The Times, Manchester Guardian, Le Monde, Zuricher Zeitung and others, or has there been another parochial mouse born?

FRED GARWACKI
Auburn, NSW
7/8/64

A status symbol

MAY I congratulate you on what I consider an excellent paper, one that every Australian and expatriate may well be proud of. To be seen with a copy of *The Australian* on the university campus is regarded as an intellectual symbol.

TUNKU ABDUL AZIZ
Editor of Togatus
University of Tasmania
Hobart
30/7/64

Australian Christmas

I WANT to applaud the initiative of your newspaper in really being "Australian" this Christmas.

The wonderful record albums honoring our immortals, Henry Lawson and Mary Gilmore, besides remembering our first people, the Aboriginals, are worthy assets to all Australian music and poetry lovers.

In a period when our rich cultural history runs the risk of being swamped by the very weight of imported "culture," it is heartening to find such actions as your own being undertaken.

I (and I am sure I speak for many, many thousands of unionists and other Australians) wish to congratulate you on the production of these albums, which will give enjoyable hours to people throughout our country.

J. B. MUNDEY
Secretary
Australian Builders
Laborers Federation
NSW Branch, Sydney
17/12/68

Seeing red over the map

To me, your paper is a ray of sunshine in our otherwise dull and conformist society. To date you have melted the ice, as far as daily papers are concerned, by encouraging open discussion on topics which chill the hearts and minds of our conservative establishment, whether of the right or left.

However, you are inviting further simulated bulk subscription cancellations, accompanied by the usual outraged cries, by publishing (on Page One, mind you) a map of Australia colored RED!

As I love your paper, Dear Editor, could you arrange to have my copy printed in blue and overstamped with a thistle?

LEAH ANDREW
Ashburton, Vic
1/2/65

For speed readers . . .

MY New Year's resolution: To let you know how much I enjoy reading your paper. My only complaint; too many articles of interest, consequently it takes too much time. So, to solve the problem, I am going to take a speed-reading course. Please keep up the high standard of your paper.

W. N. J. VREEKEN
Bankstown, NSW
12/1/67

Bouquets

The bright spot on Saturdays

IT'S Saturday morning on Tamborine Mountain, a beautiful haven . . . but this must be our sixth successive weekend of rain and wind and mist, and our third cyclone (or non-cyclone) for the week.

But there's a bright spot, as always on Saturday: *The Australian* is delivered, rolled up in thick newspaper, at 7.30 am. A mar-vellous service; congratulations to everyone concerned.

I've been back in Australia for five years after spending about a third of my life in Britain etc and used to read The Times of London. *The Australian* fills a gap for me. I am most appreciative of its coverage and today's was an excellent paper.

I send various cuttings to my Australian brothers overseas — one is Assistant Bishop of Coventry, England, and the other retired from Westminster Abbey to Canada. They appreciate them very much.

This is just to record my appreciation.

(Miss) M. E. McKIE
Eagle Heights, Qld
24/3/76

Editorial on farms was a breath of fresh air

YOUR editorial (29/7) reads like a breath of fresh air.

At last a responsible daily newspaper is putting the message to city people about the plight of the farmer.

Australian farmers are contributing far more than their share in return for what they are receiving.

Your newspaper is to be congratulated for giving a more balanced outlook to the present farming situation, of which the National Country Party has been trying to tell Australians for years, but for which it has been ridiculed incessantly for pork-barrel politics.

J. D. ANTHONY
Deputy Prime Minister
Leader of the
National Country Party
Canberra
2/8/77

A Machiavellian touch

I WAS amused to see that *The Australian* has lost a subscriber in Mr Whiffin (Letters, 13/10) because he is offended by Whitlam's column.

I detect a fine Machiavellian hand here — by shoving Gough down our throats daily along with the bacon and eggs *The Australian* is ensuring that the most apathetic voters will be scared to the polls today to vote Liberal. The same hand is no doubt responsible for the scare headlines of the past week with the same end in view.

Mr Whiffin, don't give up your subscription to *The Australian* — what now will you read? There is no other newspaper on this continent.

ROSEMARY KITCHIN
Southport, Qld
18/10/80

┌─ PS ─

CONGRATULATIONS on your Vietnam peace issue. With a lifetime knowledge of the press of the world capitals, I class The Australian among the leading 10 dailies. I await my copy of Le Monde with confidence. The Guardian has come back to something like it was under Scott. Allowing charitably for kindly treatment of the U.S., you have given your readers a picture of what will go down in history as an example of calculated atrocity paralleled only by the nazi multiple genocide of World War II.

D. NORMAN
Balgowlah Heights, NSW
1/2/73

THE first New Year of your outstanding paper — accept hearty congratulations. May it survive to celebrate its century.

ALICE WALKER
Epping, NSW
1/1/65

This sporting life
Cricket

Thanks for the memory

BEFORE leaving Australia, I would like to express through your newspaper the appreciation of the touring MCC team of the magnificent organisation and of crowd participation in the Centenary Test.

It takes considerably more than 22 players to make a great game of cricket and the organisation of the Victorian Cricket Association, the crowd, the sponsorship of Benson and Hedges, Qantas, TAA and the Melbourne Hilton, the media's response and the many other individuals and organisations that participated played a major part in the game's success.

The very concept of a Centenary Test and the bringing together of past players was in itself brilliant and, thankfully, the game lived up to the true concept of a Test match between our two countries.

Naturally, we were disappointed at the final outcome, as it is always great to win. In retrospect, however, there were no real losers, as the game of cricket itself was without doubt the ultimate winner.

To Greg Chappell and his team, our congratulations and we look forward eagerly to our clashes in England in the coming season.

Finally, a big word of thanks to the Melbourne people who were quite magnificent and created the atmosphere which certainly helped players to give of their best, and added so much to the game's success.

Thanks, Melbourne, for an unforgettable experience.

TONY GREIG
Sydney
28/3/77

. . . and thanks again

MAY I say "heartiest congratulations" on your cricket edition and say it does justice to this incredible gathering in Melbourne, which has to be seen and experienced to be believed. That in itself is the highest praise I can give and I congratulate all who had a finger in the "pie."

May I single out your cricket buff, Murray Hedgcock, of London, who has excelled himself in taking us so vividly down the years of cricket. His research, and I know from actual experience what hard work that can be, is truly remarkable.

I have six copies of Saturday's issue, as I consider in the years to come it will be priceless and a museum possession.

This Test is amazing; to see one's old enemies at whom one used to glower and mutter, and to enjoy their company and talk is pleasure of the highest order. One takes one's hat off to Hans Ebeling whose idea it was, formed, as so many thought, up in the inaccessible clouds of fantasy.

JACK FINGLETON
Melbourne
15/3/77

Menzies and the Tests

I TRUST that before Don Whitington's entertaining book, The Rulers, reaches its second edition, he will correct his statement (5/9) that after 1946 Sir Robert Menzies began appearing regularly at Test matches.

It would be more accurate to say that after 1946, the Australian public (and Don Whitington) became aware that Sir Robert often watched cricket.

During the thirties, he watched first class cricket in Australia and England frequently, as did the late John Curtin. The only difference was that when Mr Curtin went to Adelaide Oval on a Saturday afternoon, his press secretary, Don Rogers, tipped off newspaper photographers to shoot "the boss." Mr Menzies went down unheralded and unphotographed.

It may also be news to many people that during his overseas trips in the thirties, Mr Menzies did some writing on cricket.

Before going to bed each night, he wrote a diary letter to his children describing what he had seen that day. These happenings, no doubt, included his visits to cricket matches in England.

JOHN K. TULLOH
Adelaide
16/9/64

Sport — Cricket

Synthetic broadcasts

IT was by sheer chance that I heard about and looked at Norman May's program televised by the ABC last Tuesday night tracing the development of cricket broadcasting in Australia.

As I had been personally responsible for devising, organising, naming and describing the original "synthetic" cricket radio broadcasts in 1934, when the Australian cricket team was in England, I felt some surprise that Mr May had made no attempt to seek information from me to ensure historical accuracy.

The general impression left with those who saw May's program must have been that the synthetic broadcasts began with Alan McGilvray in 1938.

I am a great admirer of Mr McGilvray as a very experienced and outstanding cricket broadcaster, but May was manifestly unfair to several who preceded him. There was Mel Morris, the ABC's Victorian sporting supervisor of that day, who shared with me the pioneering synthetic broadcasts of 1934. He did not rate a mention in May's program, nor did Dion Wheeler, brilliant in the use of effects for the synthetic broadcasts whose skill others later copied but never equalled.

Even worse, May totally ignored the second series of synthetic broadcasts when the Australians toured South Africa in 1936: these were provided by A. N. "Huck" Finlay, later the ABC's assistant general manager, and Mel Morris. That tour was two years before the third (1938) series on which May's program was focused.

By the way, the 1938 film showing that the synthetic broadcasts were created in the studio was made solely for publicity purposes — not to convince listeners that the broadcasts were not coming direct from England. After the 1934 and 1936 series listeners were well aware that the broadcasts were based on cables sent from the venue concerned.

It is true that, following the first of the 1934 broadcasts, I had to settle many bets about whether I was broadcasting from England or from Sydney: some listeners had missed the announcement that the broadcast descriptions were being re-created in the studio.

CHARLES MOSES
Darling Point, NSW
1/9/80

Sportsmanlike gesture

I WOULD suggest Ian Botham's final ball to Australian skipper, Greg Chappell, in the second and deciding England v Australia Test match, will be warmly remembered by cricket fans long after Dennis Lillee's boorishness is forgotten.

It was a sportsmanlike gesture by Botham, no mean competitor himself, to try and help Chappell achieve a deserved century.

One wonders whether Lillee would have extended such generosity to English skipper Mike Brearley were the situation reversed?

PETER BARNES
Ballarat, Vic
15/1/80

PS

FULL marks to Rodney Marsh on his suggestions for reducing the risks of bumpers in cricket. But surely his plan for protective head and chest gear deals with the affliction and not its cause? The remedy is to ban the bumper — to legislate so that a ball which does not pitch beyond a line drawn on the pitch is ruled a no-ball and the fielding side is debited two, or even four runs.

W. H. BICKLEY
Chapel Hill, Qld
26/12/75

WHO else is tired of seeing our gum-chewing cricketers going into girlish huddles complete with hugs and hand-holding? Good heavens, we will soon be seeing our opening batsmen go out holding hands!

J. MUNRO
Surfers Paradise, Qld
9/8/77

VERILY did we gnash our teeth and mouth a silent curse at the pretender who has introduced to our game not only white balls and colored bats, but huge towers to blot out the sun. One of these monstrosities will occasionally cast a shadow over our sacred strip at the SCG. Sir, this is not cricket. We must dig in, fight for our principles and have this tower dismantled. As the ultimate protest we may be forced to cancel the whole season. We are insulted by the proposal that we start at 10 am rather than 11 am. Dr Grace would turn in his grave.

T. D. TRUMBULL
Cremorne, NSW
25/11/78

Sport — Cricket

Constructive or destructive?

I READ Colin Tatz' article in *The Weekend Australian* (21-22/2) with interest. The worst thing with cricket this season has been the negative attitude by almost all Australian journalists. They have missed the point.

There are two types of sport — major and minor. Major sport has appeal for a mass audience, whereas minor sport, such as hockey, appeals only to a small number of devotees. Modern cricket, with all its faults, now appeals to a wide audience (as the gate takings this season indicate).

The conservative nostalgic journalists like Mr Tatz and Bill O'Reilly are the devotees and they resent — perhaps subconsciously — the influence on their sport of a wider audience. Major sport is generally professional and professionalism means change. Not all change is necessarily good, but some change is inevitable with a major professional sport.

Serious journalists in Australia and the UK would serve their papers, their readers and the sport better if they devoted space to making constructive suggestions as to how cricket — still in its transitional phase since the great schism of 1977 — should be organised in the next few years.

Instead, they bemoan every difference, real or imagined, between today's game and the way they remembered it in the past — a rose-tinted memory that does not include the bodyline series, the pelting of John Snow with beer cans in the early 1970s and the suggestions that the Old Trafford wicket was specially prepared for Jim Laker's 19 wickets in a Test match.

Ironically, if Mr Tatz has his way and the clock is put back, then he, Bill O'Reilly and the others who believe that 1980/81 has been the worst season ever, will shortly be unemployed, as there is little worthwhile journalistic work for the devotees of a minor sport.

ANDREW CARO
Formerly Managing Director
World Series Cricket
Pymble, NSW
26/2/81

That underarm incident

IN what I hope may be the last word on the Chappell affair, I would like to offer a word of advice to the hundreds of armchair cricket experts who have put pen to paper or fingers to the Remington keyboard to castigate Australia's captain.

Having pored over countless pages of Letters to the Editor in newspapers throughout the country, I have been struck by a total ignorance of the laws of the game by those who have been "disgusted," "ashamed," "horrified" by Chappell ordering the last ball to be bowled underarm in Melbourne last Sunday.

A majority of correspondents stated categorically that "New Zealand could not have won the match and were most unlikely to tie"

I HOPE all true cricket lovers in Australia will join with me in apologising to the New Zealand cricket team for the disgusting way in which Sunday's one-day international ended. Greg Chappell's decision to instruct his bowler to underarm the last delivery must be the greatest blot on Australian cricket.
RICHARD JAMES ELSON
Somerset, Tas
6/2/81

with seven runs wanted for victory and six to even the scores.

What seems to have escaped these patriotic "experts" is the fact that New Zealand had every chance to win the match, although needing seven runs off the last ball.

Had Trevor Chappell bowled a no-ball, then one would have been added to the score and a six off the next ball would have brought victory to the Kiwis.

Similarly, a succession of no-balls would have narrowed the margin of runs required, so victory was never at any time impossible.

While Chappell did not break any law of the game framed at the time, a little knowledge and cool-headedness by letter-writing pundits would have done much to put the Australian captain's decision in its rightful perspective under the circumstances.

HARRY DAVIS
Taringa East, Qld
5/2/81

Sport — Cricket

Kicking incident sparks outrage

SO Dennis Lillee has made the headlines again. Ian Chappell, Greg Chappell and Lillee have all, at one time or another, committed acts on the cricket field which have had the lead-bottomed troglodytes who run cricket, or, in the case of sporting commentators, think they run cricket, howling with horror. However, these cricketers are simply reformers, who actions result in the game being looked at critically. As a result of their actions many changes have been effected to the game which have made it a more colorful, interesting and better sport.

BARRY O'FARRELL
Canberra

FOLLOWING Dennis Lillee's disgraceful exhibition during play, he will, if quick enough, be able to finish his cricket season and step straight into rugby league — his scuffles wouldn't seem out of place there!

TOM FAITHFULL
Moree, NSW

TWO of Australia's most illustrious players have been involved in distasteful incidents in successive seasons. No player, no matter how accomplished or venerated, is greater than the game itself. Lillee's reputation as a great fast bowler was enhanced during the Perth Test, but his fame as a sportsman was diminished.

KENNETH HOPE
Rostrevor, SA

HOW can a sophisticated international cricketer be "provoked" into kicking a fellow player in public? Obvious conclusion that standards of behavior have reached an all-time low

would be the understatement of the century.

MICHAEL EISDELL
Paddington, NSW

MITCHELL, the cartoonist, foretold uncannily on Monday the ensuing Lillee behavior later in the day. Unfortunately, Mitchell, the artist, drew Lillee's head far too small.

J. DARLING
Burnie. Tas

WOW, the unsporting Match of the Century: Lillee v McEnroe!

LARRY FOLEY
Townsville, Qld

WHAT a pity the prima donna didn't have his tin bat with him. This time he could have thrown it again — at Miandad!

H. HICKLING
Jamboree Heights, Qld

I UNDERSTAND that Lillee's testimonial year campaign is not going too well and I had ideas of forwarding money to the fund, but I'm glad I didn't — I would have had to cancel the cheque immediately.

BARRY PAGE
Hill End, Qld

ALL these letters on the kicking incident appeared 20/11/81

Double or quits?

ENGLAND having managed to retain the Ashes, I seek the courtesy of your columns to inform those very many of my Australian friends, who now owe me a bottle of something, that if they wish I shall be happy to roll over each and every bet as double or quits on England still retaining the Ashes at the conclusion of the next series between us, to be played in Australia.

I suggest this in part to avoid a possible dislocation of Australian liquor supplies, were all my creditors to meet their obligations simultaneously: and in part because of a shortage of storage space at home, space which I will ensure is more than doubled for when it will be needed in 1982-83.

JOHN MASON
British High Commissioner
Canberra
21/8/81

Sport — Australian Rules

The menace from the south

IN the 1890s, the vine louse, politely known as phylloxera, threatened to exterminate Australia's vineyards.

The pest spread from Victoria to NSW where it was checked by control measures.

In the 1900s, another pest, prickly pear, spread through part of NSW. Again, it was checked by control measures — in this case, the voracious little insect, cactoblastis.

Today, another pest (some-times described as a fever and sometimes as a religion) threatens NSW — the curious Victorian aberration known as Australian Rules. It crossed the Murray many years ago, but now it has crossed the Murrumbidgee and before long, unless vigorous measures are invoked, the cry of "Up there Cazaly!" will resound through Sydney, from kindergarten to campus.

To protest against the northern spread of this pest, and to emphasise the urgent need for control, I propose to visit Melbourne on the day of the so-called "grand final," and at an appropriate time and place, to burn an oval football (22¼in by 29½in) as a fiery and symbolic gesture.

CYRIL PEARL
Paddington, NSW
14/9/72

If you can't beat 'em . .

THERE seems to be little doubt that Cyril Pearl had his tongue wedged firmly in his cheek when he penned his waspish critique in *The Australian* (14/9).

However, this attack on our national game of football, garbed as it was in the robes of flippancy, did contain the undertones of desperation that must have assailed both King Canute and the opponents of Commonwealth Federation.

I wish to inform Cyril that this "pest menace from the south" was, in fact, conceived and nurtured at Sydney University. Taken to Melbourne in early childhood, it grew into the healthy giant of today — dominant in Victoria, South Australia, Western Australia, Tasmania and the Riverina, while enjoying increasing popularity in Sydney and Queensland.

The principal reason for the success of the code has been the emphasis on club rivalry as distinct from the concentration of rugby league on the international scene. The wisdom of this policy is apparent today in the stark contrast of the robust prosperity of rules and the waxen pallor of league which has declined into a jet set gaggle of clattering slot machines, overpaid players and corpulent club manag-ers with a backdrop of rust-ing turnstiles and their redundant attendants.

The hierarchy, seeking to bolster their sagging regime, have injected rules innovations such as the Page method of finals and the replacement of players. It seems certain that the successful five-team finals of rules will be adopted by league.

Now, Cyril, should you desire to do something of a symbolical nature, do as the man said: If you can't beat 'em, join 'em.

JOE SMITH
Paradise Beach, NSW
27/9/72

It's better than pushing drugs

I GREATLY regret that my old friend Cyril Pearl (Letters, 14/9), a man of great personal and intellectual qualities, should have succumbed to the insidious modern mania for destroying anything regarded as foreign, objectionable, or difficult to understand.

Burning a football may sound an amusing way to register a protest, but there are people in the community who may take Mr Pearl seriously, and consider he is set-ting them an example of commendable behavior. How big a step is it from burning a football to burning a book, as Hitler did; or burning human beings, as napalm has in Vietnam and as Hitler did also?

Probably the 120,000 who attend Melbourne's Grand Final could be better engaged, but at least they're not pushing drugs in sleazy Paddington pubs or organising gang bangs at rock festivals.

Perhaps it illustrates the feeling of utter futility of the average Australian that people of sensitivity and sensibility can find no better way to protest than to burn a football — which, after all, is a thing of some beauty.

(To dispel any doubts, I should admit I shall be at the Grand Final in Melbourne. I have not missed for 20 years.)

DON WHITINGTON
Mosman, NSW
4/10/72

Sport — Coaching, The Springboks

The making of a modern champion

THE sports doctor with "considerable professional experience with sportsmen and women", to whom John Hallows referred *(The Australian, 8/1)*, has no doubts as to why records, particularly swimming records, are broken.

Your readers are exhorted not to listen to what the coaches say, but to believe that the breaking of records is due to nothing more than the fact that, like Mount Everest, the record "is there" to break.

Of course there must be the motivation, the incentive, of the record. However, surely your readers would not believe that this alone is enough to explain the staggering improvements seen in sports where the stopwatch and measure of distance are the criteria. Surely there are many advances in the MEANS of making these gains.

Take the sport I know best after coaching for more than 25 years — swimming.

There have been tremendous changes in training and coaching methods.

Are we to believe that advances in methods of training and in techniques are of much less importance than the fact that there is a record to break? The doctor you quote says, in effect, that swimmers today may as well go back to training only during the summertime, swim about 200 miles a year instead of the 1500 miles many record holders cover, do not bother about starting young in learning efficient techniques etc.

From his argument, it would follow that performances would continue to improve with far less application of science and effort of the coaches and athletes. The important thing would be the time there to beat.

May I point out that today's runners and swimmers, compared with only a few years ago, are covering hundreds of more miles in their preparation. In swimming we have come to recognise efficient technique and we know that we can only produce the champion if we start coaching the boy or girl in a regular systematic way, at least before puberty when the growth spurt starts.

If I coached our swimmers today as I did 10 or 15 years ago, very few would make even the qualifying times for State championships. Talent and incentive of records is no help without regular, hard training and systematic coaching of technique.

Surely the doctor cannot be serious when he says that he does not believe that "record breaking has anything to do with improved diet, training, or swimming methods."

I wonder what our sports doctor knows about the difference in training methods and coaching techniques between today and say 1956 when Shane Gould (a girl of great natural talent and a product of modern training methods) would have easily defeated Murray Rose to win the Olympic 400 and 1500 metres mens' championships?

His lecture on this should be interesting.

FORBES CARLILE
Ryde, NSW
12/1/72

A Mockery

MAY I bid a welcome to all the South African rugby players; you come here as representatives of your country.

However, please excuse me from attending your games; this is a pleasure I must deny myself and I want to tell you why.

To me, the term "representative" conveys that those selected come not only as envoys of their people, but are truly representative of them. This is a quality you lack because your eligibility for selection demands that you be "white" as defined by your discriminatory racial legislation.

I have tried hard to convince myself that it is possible to separate sport from politics and that football is purely "sport."

But try as I might, I cannot bring myself to cheer you on and forget that you have knowingly allowed yourselves to be chosen on principles of selection which are not only contrary to all the rules of sport and sportsmanship, but are abhorrent to all decent, right-minded citizens. You make a mockery of Hamlet's
What a piece of work is man;
How noble in reason,
How infinite in faculties.

I will not boo you, or hiss, or throw tomatoes; I will just stay away and mourn man's continuing inhumanity to man.

I hope your stay out here will be a happy one; I bear you no personal ill-will. It is, after all, far easier to become a football hero than a martyr in a seemingly hopeless cause — how hopeless became clear to me on my recent visit to your country.

P. GERBER
St Lucia, Qld
24/6/74

Celebrity

Mrs Everage peeved

I WAS peeved to read a letter printed in your magazine on May 2, which was written by a Mr Francis Lymburner.

In it, he refers to myself as Mrs Everidge. Norm's family name is Everage and I will thank Mr Lymburner to get his facts right.

He also talks about a Mr Robert Hughes, whoever he may be, and compares his views to mine, saying they are "of 50 years ago."

This is another fib, since 50 years ago I was only a hop in my father's glass of ale and even today I still have my own teeth.

I also take exception to Mr Lymburner's references to London's "homosexual underground."

While I was in the old country I travelled on the tube regularly and although it was far from spotless down there, I never once witnessed "an incident."

Why must people be so unnecessary?

EDNA MAY EVERAGE
Humoresque Street
Moonee Ponds, Vic
14/5/68

Theatre scene

I FEEL I must correct some statements published as a result of an interview a reporter of your paper, Mr Max Hollingsworth, had with me on Friday, May 2, the night of my departure from Australia.

1. I did not, repeat NOT, say that Australia was a cultural desert. When asked if I despaired of the cultural scene in Australia, I said that at the present moment, theatrically, there was no such thing compared with

┌Moon in perspective┐

AT the risk of being drowned out in the roar of the Saturn V engines, may I say why I do not think the imminent moon landing is to be lauded as "the greatest event in the history of mankind."

Perhaps on an astronomical scale — in man's relation to the universe — it is a most significant step. But this is only a tiny and rather unimportant part of our world.

I object to the money apportioned to the space program and to the priority it's given over other matters meriting scientific investigation. What we gain by it compared with what we might have gained from a similar effort and expenditure is insignificant.

Why must we race to the moon, as if it's a scientist's utopia, when we know so very little about our own world?

Far more important and neglected still is the study of life — what it is, how it begins, what intelligence is etc. Here is enough challenge to keep an army of scientists occupied. Yet these questions are virtually abandoned to philosophers.

Even about man himself we know so little. Instead of having become the major well-ordered discipline that it should be, psychology is still in its infant stage, plagued by masses of conflicting theories.

This imbalance of knowledge has now become critical. Complacently, we watch as the human race multiplies so indiscriminately as to endanger not only itself but all living things; while it pours its wastes and pollution into any convenient reservoir; while it disrupts the balance of nature, substituting a makeshift one of its own.

The greatest event in the history of mankind will come only when it learns that if it can not understand itself, then it must control itself.

ANTHONY CUTLER
Government House
Sydney, NSW
17/7/69

other countries with larger financial aid to the theatre and larger populations.

2. When asked what I considered to be a serious fault with the theatre scene in Australia, I said that too many people in control could not hold equivalent positions overseas and, therefore, did not invite top-flight experts to come to Australia, whereas in my case it was possible for me to do so.

3. I did not, as Mr Hollingsworth presumed, intend any jibe at the Council for the Arts and its chairman, Dr Coombs, with whom I have worked in the closest cooperation and without

whom the Australian Ballet would not exist.

I really did not think it necessary to point out that my interest in the Australian Ballet and the theatre in Australia as a whole are the major interests in my life, however much any attempt is made to make it appear otherwise. By my association with the theatre in Australia, which I hope will continue for many years, I believe that actions speak louder than words.

(Sir) ROBERT HELPMANN
London
22/5/69

Celebrity

TV royalty

I SPILT my champagne when I opened *The Australian* (25/7) and saw a picture of myself with the caption, "forgotten," underneath.

You had better inform the various TV networks that I am now passe, for they are still blindly offering me contracts at the rate of about two a week.

By the way, in my day, to be "king" you had to have the top-rating live television show in Victoria. If this still applies, Mike Walsh is now the royal one in that he outrates Mr Hannan by a healthy margin, according to the last three episodes of the Anderson analysis.

Just for the record, the average IMT rating so far this year amounts to the kind of double figure that I would have been called in to the front office for a "Please explain."

GRAHAM KENNEDY
Frankston, Vic
31/7/70

Our Glad

I AM writing to thank you for the excellent coverage you gave (10/4) to my 79th birthday and the launching of my book, My Life of Song.

The newspaper stories, radio and television reports gave me great pleasure and proved that I have not been forgotten since leaving the stage.

Would you be kind enough to publish this letter to the editor, in which I would like to thank all those people who sent me tributes, telegrams and letters on my birthday, and who wished me well with my book.

Their thoughts for me are greatly appreciated and the warmth of their greetings will always make me happy.

GLADYS MONCRIEFF
Isle of Capri. Qld
5/5/71

─Who will black up?─

I WAS scandalised to read of the ban imposed by the Federal Government on the colored American entertainer, Dick Gregory. This confusion of politics with show business is as absurd as the distinction certain foolish nations draw between politics and sport. However, since Mr Gregory is to be denied his visa, a replacement must be found, and found quickly.

Surely there must be at least one brilliant and versatile Australian comedian and entertainer ready and willing to black-up and attack Australia's foreign policy for a mere fraction of Dick Gregory's fee? If there be such a man, let him step forth and proclaim himself.

BARRY HUMPHRIES
Melbourne
8/9/70

Humorless generation

IN response to a letter of mine (8/9), in which I ironically suggested that an alternative figure be chosen to replace the hapless Dick Gregory, I received a polite phone call from one of the moratorium organisers kindly inviting me to attend:

Had not illness, heightened by agoraphobia, made this impossible, I feel bound to state exactly what I would have felt obliged to say if I had addressed the dissenting multitude.

First of all, I do not think that mini-Woodstocks, or dreary mobs freaking out to noisy dance music have got anything whatsoever to do with world peace.

I do not think that the most deeply conventional and humorless generation Australia has ever produced is likely to change our foreign policy by forming itself into a rabble only slightly less terrifying than the military rabble it affects to despise. And although it is not the purpose of this particular sit-in, but most assuredly a side issue, I do not believe that the legalisation of boring and highly chunderous marijuana ciggies has got

anything to do with civil rights or pacifism (though it has got a lot to do with inertia), any more than I think nudist colonies have got anything to do with democracy.

Furthermore, I do not believe that the hiring of a professional American rabble-rouser would have been at all likely to lend even a bogus air of seriousness to the naughty cavortings of a fundamentally apolitical mob of mindless moratorium mimics.

Last, in so far as I have any political views myself, I would be forced to announce, through the din of rock and the stench of pot, that I am as strongly opposed to communist imperialism in the Near and Far East as I am to the equally frightening imperialism of popgroup touts and cynical dope pedlars exploiting a mob of scatter-brained kids, trendy oldies, naive housewives and tedious Woodstock copycats, united perhaps in one single emotion:

Deadly, excruciating, Australian boredom.

BARRY HUMPHRIES
Melbourne
14/9/70

Celebrity

Requiem for Wakelin

MAY I, through the columns of your newspaper, pay respect to the late Roland Wakelin?

His place in the history of Australian art is now fully documented. With Roi de Maistre and Grace Cossington Smith, he was one of those pioneers who introduced to the younger painters of his time the precepts of Post-Impressionism and enlarged our parochial horizon.

To achieve this took courage and tenacity, and in our antipodean climate of the day approximated to Whistler's throwing of a pot of paint at the public's face. Like Whistler, however, he made his point and he helped to emancipate both painters and society's view of art.

That is now history: his work and the courage of his opinions form part of the fabric which we wear today.

To this we pay tribute.

His encouragement to younger painters, his kindness and his modesty made Wake a respected and loved friend. The fact that he lived in his long life through a period of unacceptance to a period of honored acceptance merely added to his dry and perceptive humor.

I will remember Wake at the opening of his large retrospective exhibition at the New South Wales Gallery. Surrounded by the examples of a life's work, I could not refrain from saying to him how very good it all looked.

He chuckled as only he could and replied: "You don't know how difficult it was to realise some of these pictures; painting is never easy."

RUSSELL DRYSDALE
Kildare Heights, NSW
7/6/71

We must wake up

EVERY Australian who feels pride and glories in the heritage of his country should read the September issue of Walkabout.

It draws attention to aspects of Australian behavior which should jolt us all out of our increasing apathy about what really goes on behind the glossy facade that we know of life in our cities.

We must wake up before it is too late to save our heritage. Train the youth of today to appreciate and protect the unique flora and fauna of this great land.

It is already a cynicism to see our coat of arms; our Qantas airline with the emblazoned figure of the

kangaroo on the tail of its planes; our young Olympic girl swimming champions holding aloft toy kangaroos to the TV millions; presenting a gold kangaroo pin to the Duke of Edinburgh. Everything to do with ecology and conservation should become of primary interest to us all today, not tomorrow.

This is not a sentimental outburst, but a plea to all Australians who wish to continue to feel pride and not shame about a situation that is worsening rapidly daily.

JOAN HAMMOND
Geelong, Vic
11/9/72

PS

I HAD given up trying to think of a worthy candidate for Australian of the Year 1976 when I was reminded of John Sinclair, the courageous conservationist who, in the face of political indifference and hostility in his home town of Maryborough, did more than anybody to save the miraculous Fraser Island from being sold off as sand — a great Australian.
PATRICK WHITE
Centennial Park, NSW
21/12/76

I TOOK exception to Mr Lapsley's description (21/5) of my living arrangements, which made me sound like a "mummy's boy." My parents occupy the top unit and my family the bottom. There are other points I would like to rectify, but mummy wants to use the pen.

Love, GARRY McDONALD
(You know, the bloke who plays Norman Gunstan, TV star)
Bellevue Hill, NSW
26/5/77

AS I twirled the knob of my radio set, I passed through a plethora of hypothyroid disc jockeys who conveyor-belted their way through the Top 30, leaving an indelible blank on my mind, and I suddenly realised that without ABC radio, Australians would be totally ignorant of the existence of classical music and literature via the airwaves.

SPIKE MILLIGAN
Woy Woy, NSW
18/11/77

Celebrity

The state of the theatre

MY opinions on the theatre scene in this country seem to have had such a depressing effect on so many concerned with the theatre that I would be grateful if you could publish this letter.

I am an actor. My opinions are personal, emotional and therefore suspect, I am neither a prophet, oracle, administrator nor expert of theatre, but unfortunately my views have been read as such.

This seems to me an example of a tendency nowadays, in a growing section of the Australian community, towards self-criticism and indeed condemnation.

This tendency may be a good thing; at least it opposes the smug "I'm all right, Jack" attitude. Success, in this country particularly, becomes more closely allied to material values every day.

I was last here 16 years ago. The most striking thing that has happened since then is the vast increase of money allocated to the theatre. State governments are now as concerned with arts centres as small countries are with their airlines.

The strongest aspect of Australian theatre is production design. The weakest is direction in production and administration. There are at least two critics of the first rank.

There are more actors and more of the better ones (I include women in the term actor). There are enough, indeed, for a single company of importance. But how and under whose direction (we have an administrator) do you assemble this company, and where?

In this respect, parochialism, jealousies and rivalry work against such a national concept. It seems, therefore, that a national company is unrealistic at this time.

Now to the real basis of theatre anywhere, anytime: the playwrights. Again, there is vastly more indigenous writing than 16 years ago. But with it has come an aspect difficult to deal with, yet understandable. It is, generally, a strong definitive attitude in the playwright.

But is the director or the actor so much better at his job than the writer at his? No. So that in production, he fights every alteration and every cut, and sometimes even ideas.

Patrick White's plays interest me enormously, but I should think them vastly difficult to produce and act. But they should be produced, nonetheless, with Buzo, Elliott and the others and given at least the production afforded to the Albatross. They are not great plays, but some are very good — The Removalist, for example; and the playwright is the soil in which theatre grows.

I heard Harry Miller say that the new play must be nurtured like a new-born babe and I agree. But too often the production is a hasty caesarian in an ill-equipped theatre.

So what is to be done? A little at a time and with vast patience.

Much greater encouragement of writers is essential. The actors, meanwhile, clamor for directors, who are essential to them for training and experience; but the actor can now exist independently of the new writers, on the sustenance of great plays already existing.

More and larger grants for writers, directors, actors are needed and an Arts Council-inspired international exchange system for reciprocal work and study on a yearly basis.

Of course, the subject cannot be dealt with fully in a letter of this kind; but I felt strongly moved to counter the doom-and-disaster impression I seem to have given up to now.

LEO McKERN
Melbourne
11/4/72

-PS

I'M not surprised about the return of migrants to their original countries. Having emigrated to Australia in 1946, tried to integrate happily as an Australian and always considered Australia to be my country, I find myself referred to in Miss Katharine Brisbane's column (5/8) as a "foreigner." It is not encouraging.

GORDON CHATER
Paddington, NSW
16/8/72

I REALLY don't know what Gordon Chater (Letters,

16/8) is beefing about in being mentioned in Katharine Brisbane's article (5/8) on Australian actors — at least he scored a place. I didn't win a guernsey even among the also-rans or hopefuls. It looks like a snap refresher course at NIDA for the old Noel, or perhaps a quick bash at the classics at the Old Tote, or the Rockdale Music Society — I'm easy.

NOEL FERRIER
Woollahra, NSW
31/8/72

Celebrity

Warren who?

IN your profile of Sir Robert Helpmann (*The Australian, Weekend Magazine,* July 29-30), he is quoted as saying:

"I would have liked to open with a monumental Shakespeare with King Lear. But Alf Garnett and the Queensland Theatre Company got in first."

For Sir Robert's information, Alf Garnett is a fictitious character like Noddy or Snow White. King Lear was played by myself and certainly not by Alf Garnett. I am an actor, who dresses up and camps about being other people. I shall be doing it at the Seymour Centre in September this year with the Queensland Theatre Company pretending to be King Lear, then in November I shall pretend to be Alf Garnett at the Mayfair Theatre in Sydney. They are quite different of course.

Could I extend an invitation through your columns to Sir Robert to pop in and have a look. He can't fail to notice the difference.

As King Lear, I wear hairy old clothes and have a hairy face and head. For Alf Garnett I wear a bald wig.

I thought it important that the future supremo of the Old Tote should know the difference between fact and fiction and I do hope that when he meets Lord Olivier he does not refer to him as Archie Rice.

WARREN MITCHELL
North Sydney, NSW
4/8/78

Warren Mitchell as Alf Garnett . .

. . and King Lear

Great gloom

REPERCUSSIONS of Mr Fraser's rule in Australia reach out to this country and bring a great gloom upon thinking people who are concerned about the quality of life in the future for our children and our children's children.

It's all too clear he's only concerned with the money-making qualities of uranium and a complete ignoramus on the sociological and ecological disasters that will follow in its wake.

First, for the Aborigines on whose land the desecration of mining will take place and (b) the legislation which was passed on Foreign Proceedings (Prohibition of Certain Evidence) Act, 1976. If ever there was a clamp on the freedom of speech, this piece of legislation must be top of the list. It gives complete dictatorial power to the Attorney-General and muzzles the citizen in the street.

Secrecy is what will eventually bring down a democratic government — it brought down Nixon, it will bring down Fraser.

SPIKE MILLIGAN
London

P.S. The cricket over here right now is beaut.
29/6/77

Our Joan

IT is the function of your theatre critic surely to appraise the performance he attends, not to pine wistfully for other fare. In disparaging the choice of The Merry Widow as a suitable vehicle for your great opera star, he ignores the thousands who like myself loathe and detest grand opera and were stunned into delight by the knowledge that we were going to watch and hear the wonderful tunes sung by Miss Sutherland.

In all the years I have been coming here, I have never seen anything in this always unpredictable country that so warmed my heart or filled me with admiration as this production.

Of course it must have cost a fortune, of course the money could have been spent on other projects — it always can — but to those like myself lucky enough to be there, it was a once-in-a-lifetime experience and they are almost always expensive.

ROBERT MORLEY
Sydney
1/2/78

PS

NOW that we hear of some new tax reforms to come, may I add my own point view? No man of my age (I am 74) should have to worry any more about income tax. Surely a man has paid enough to the country by the time he retires.
SALI HERMAN
Avalon Beach, NSW
25/6/72

Celebrity

The ballet's path to impotence

MR Harry M. Miller is to be congratulated on having helped the Australian Ballet to enlarge its audience. Surely this is one of the aims of all bodies seriously caring for the health of the arts in Australia.

This being the case, the company, now having reached maturity, should progress from the commercial venture it has been to a point where it will acknowledge its responsibilities as a national ballet and a federally funded organisation. Certainly, only in Australia could the tax-paying public be expected to subsidise so successful a business on top of paying for tickets.

My own contributions to the Australian Ballet repertoire — Romeo And Juliet, Onegin and Swan Lake — have been popular with the public and, presumably, good for box-office, yet the profits have not been recycled to improve artistic standards, provide the Australian public with a "creative" national company or take steps to ensure that the best Australian dancers are promoted at home and overseas.

The company, advertised as "internationally acclaimed," made no foreign tour in 1977 and is scheduled to play for three days in Jakarta only during 1978. Is this really international? The dancers have been told an overseas tour cannot take place because their claim to the normal equity overseas allowance is prohibitive!

I agree with Mr Miller's colorful language, but would suggest it is the national company which is taking the path to impotence and not the several small, struggling and creative companies, busily copulating on their meagre subsidies which are, in no way, comparable to those of the Australian Ballet.

ANNE WOOLIAMS
Carlton, Vic
1/5/78

A blow to the theatre

I FEEL I must reply to Dale Turnbull's repeated assertion (17/1) that the Old Tote encouraged me to start writing again for the theatre.

The facts are these: Jim Sharman asked the Tote if he could direct my Season at Sarsaparilla. If he hadn't asked, I'm pretty sure that play would still be lying on the shelf. It was Sharman's understanding of what I am writing about and his direction of The Season which persuaded me to write Big Toys. He had already encouraged me to adapt my story The Night The Prowler as a screenplay, the film of which he finished shooting just before Christmas. He had also asked to direct A Cheery Soul in the season of more adventurous plays scheduled for the Seymour Centre.

All those playwrights, actors and designers who have worked with Sharman and Cramphorn would agree that they are our most creative directors. Cancellation of the season at the Seymour Centre and the resignation of Sharman and Cramphorn out of disillusionment is an immense blow to theatre in Sydney.

As I feel that these two are most likely to give us the living theatre for which a new audience is waiting, they will have my full support in any venture they may attempt to launch.

PATRICK WHITE
Centennial Park, NSW
20/1/78

Deprived

I MOST wholeheartedly support Dr David Cooke's letter (6/4) in support of medical benefits for hair transplants to those who "suffer this deformity," i.e. baldness.

As a deformed member of society, I feel we should take this a step further.

I am in the process of suing my father for compensation for the strain congenital baldness has brought to my marriage.

My sex life is still good, but I have been deprived of the pleasure of combing hair (a pastime my wife and I pursued every free weekend).

Also I am considering sterilisation so that this deformity will not be passed on to future generations.

Actually, Dr Cooke, shouldn't we be more humane and encourage euthanasia for any child born bald.

GARRY McDONALD
Bellevue Hill, NSW
9/4/79

The cost of living

Inflation

Disturbed by £1 rise

WE are greatly disturbed at all this talk of rising cost of foodstuffs and essentials. The Arbitration Court, after a long and thorough inquiry, concluded that the economy of the country could stand and absorb the 20/— rise in the basic wage.

Yet immediately we hear of a rise in milk, butter, cheese and bread, and other commodities. It seems to us that those associations who control our day-to-day living need simply decide among themselves to charge extra. We ask: is this right and just?

With this developing situation, it is becoming absolutely necessary to bring the pension rate to a level of half the basic wage if pensioners are to buy the nourishing food they need.

(Mrs) I. ELLIS
Brighton, Vic
4/8/64

PS

THERE is one absolutely certain cure for inflation: that is to increase the working hours per week from 40 to 44 hours. Result — increased productivity, less overtime, lower costs of production and immediate reduction in retail prices.

DINAH CARTWRIGHT
Avalon Beach, NSW
24/10/73

Inflation

High cost of children

MAY I issue a plea on behalf of the young married couples throughout Australia who want children but can't afford them?

Australia cannot rely on its future survival by immigration alone.

Most young women start their married lives working to assist their husbands subsidise their meagre income.

A husband can earn $50-$56 a week if he is prepared to work three extra nights a week, or work all day Saturday.

Where is our 40-hour week? Most of us must work at least 56 hours a week to survive. Mr Holt, when Treasurer, was alleged to have said that the average man earned (at that time) £27 ($54) a week.

Did he take into consideration that such money was earned only because of the excessive hours worked?

Many of us are still lucky to clear $39 a week.

Every second week, I work 67¼ hours to yield a fair pay.

Come on, Mr Holt, help us. Give us some incentive to have a family. My wife and I are still childless after two years married; I know of childless marriages after four years.

I offer the following two suggestions that I know would encourage young married couples to have a reasonably-sized family.

THAT the Commonwealth Government pays all prenatal, operative, post-operative and post-natal expenses from the first through to the fourth confinement for seven years as from July 1, 1966.

THAT the Commonwealth Government pay a grant of $300 for each child born, from the first through to the fourth.

ROBERT E. BEST
Cronulla, NSW
1/3/66

Horrifying rise in fares

I WOULD like to ask the Department of Railways just what we, the public, may expect to receive in the way of benefits following the horrifying rise in the rail fares.

I have just returned from two weeks' vacation to find that it now costs me $1.81 a week to travel from Strathfield to the city compared with $1.53 previously. This seems out of all proportion.

Most people I have spoken to feel the same way — and there must be vast numbers of office workers who have not benefited from the recent rise in the basic wage. I know that I certainly did not.

The state of trains does not seem to have improved very much, either. There are still doors that do not close; windows that do not shut; lights that do not function; seats are still broken down, slashed and marked; walls are still scratched, filthy and in a general state of disrepair.

If I could be sure that the public were going to reap some benefit, then fair enough.

Meanwhile — what are the railways going to do with all that money?

(Mrs) J. B. TAYLOR
Strathfield, NSW
11/10/66

Big leap in inflation

IT is time Mr Whitlam stopped blaming Australia's present economic situation on the "worldwide" recession and faced up to the fact that the blame rests squarely on his own Government's mismanagement of the economy.

You have only to look at the figures contained in the July issue of Economic Outlook, the journal of the Organisation for Economic and Co-operative Development, of which all major Western industrialised nations are members.

Between 1960 and 1972, Australia's average rate of inflation was 3 per cent, the third lowest of the 20 member countries and below the average of 3.5 per cent.

At June this year, under Whitlam's mismanagement, we had the third highest rate of inflation — 8 per cent above the average!

The same journal points out some enlightening facts concerning the rate of unemployment in Australia compared to other countries.

Since 1972, the rate of unemployment in the U.S. has risen by 81 per cent, in Great Britain by 83 per cent, in Canada by 47 per cent, in Japan by 67 per cent and in Australia (under Whitlam) by a staggering 233 per cent.

Add to this the fact that while most other countries suffered a worldwide energy shortage, Australia escaped unscathed, then you have cause to worry about how Whitlam and his boys are running the country.

(Mrs) J. K. KING
Dulwich Hill, NSW
5/11/75

Inflation

Savage blow to home loans

HOME loan repayers have been dealt the most savage financial blow in their lifetime without a bleat from a politician, a church leader, or members of the community who are vocal on a wide variety of controversial issues ranging from Vietnam to the pill.

I refer, of course, to the latest iniquitous increase in interest rates from 5¾ per cent to 6¼ per cent in private sav-

ings banks' home loan charges and from 5½ to 6 per cent in the Commonwealth Savings Bank as from August 1.

This increase follows charge rises from 5¼ to 5¾ per cent on April 1, 1965.

These two increases have added hundreds of dollars to loan repayments.

No private financier is permitted to increase his lending rate on an existing loan but banks, with the blessing

of the Government, are able to do so at a time when they are making record profits.

The rise in home loan interest borders on a national calamity for the newly-weds struggling to establish a home, despite land exploitation by government, local government and developers.

C. J. FITZGERALD
Jannali, NSW
22/8/68

Unjust costs for house buyers

I WOULD draw attention to some extraordinary expenses involved in the purchase of a reasonably modest home where a building society provides 90 per cent of its valuation towards the purchase price.

A young couple with four children have just purchased a home, comprising three bedrooms, lounge room, dining room, kitchen, bathroom and laundry and a detached brick garage. The purchase price was $14,550. The purchasers were involved in the following expenses:

APPLICATION fee and valuation fee paid to building society, $50.

STAMP duty on contract and transfer, $185.10.

SEARCH fees and inquiries re rates, etc, $15.85.

SURVEY, $25.

PEST inspection, $6.

FIRE insurance, $26.60.

MORTGAGE insurance premium, $140.

COSTS paid to building society's solicitors, including registration fees, $114.50.

PURCHASERS' legal costs, $200.

A total of $763.05.

It would appear from this that a reasonable case could be made out for a legal benefits scheme to aid genuine home buyers.

It is clearly unjust that a home purchaser should be saddled with these extra costs, all of which he would have to pay — with the exception of the last $200 — even if he acted for himself in the transaction.

SOLICITOR
Sydney
(Name and address supplied.)
21/2/69

Disenchanted over mortgage repayments

AS a young Australian family man, just how does this present Government expect me to swallow the new interest rate levels on housing loans?

It has become necessary, it says, to restrict liquidity in the finance sector as a check against inflation.

After much negotiation, I have arranged a housing loan of $17,500 with a major savings bank. I am now expected to pay 9 per cent in-

terest to this institution and the monthly mortgage repayment will be $155 a month for 20 years.

Sure, the bank calculates interest levels on this loan daily (which I am told is the most advantageous method), but when you calculate $155 a month for 20 years I find I have to repay $37,200 on a loan of $17,500. I ask you, where is the justice in this?

I'm trying to raise and edu-

cate three children and feed a family, I must work like a black to keep pace with costs.

And then our Government says I must pay more for the privilege of putting a roof over our heads. To add salt to this wound, the Government now says it will not allow mortgage interest to be tax deductible.

P. J. SMITH
Campbelltown, NSW
29/10/73

Inflation

Lucky country indeed

HAVING just returned from an overseas study tour, one realises that indeed we are in the lucky country. I have compiled a record of fuel costs in the countries I visited.

They are:

Country	$ per gal	$ av. wage p.w.
Australia	1.44	270.00
Greece	3.44	32.00
Yugoslavia	2.50	27.00
Italy	3.44	100.00
Switzerland	3.05	214.00
Germany	2.73	250.00
France	3.43	271.00
Norway	3.18	245.00
Denmark	3.60	240.00

Something to think about?

ELLISON BENNETT
Maitland, NSW
16/10/80

We are being robbed

IN newspapers we see articles about bank robberies and company frauds, but no reference to the robbery through the medium of inflation.

This robbery is as real as any other, but difficult to demonstrate clearly as not one dollar is taken from the people robbed.

In the financial year 1973-74, a year with inflation at a rate of 14.6 per cent, an average of $10,700 million was held as deposits by savings banks throughout Australia and in that year the depositors were robbed of value equivalent to $1562 million. Certainly a major robbery. In this year, the amount of the robbery from depositors will be even greater.

Some people may condone this type of robbery, justifying it as a redistribution of wealth. In the case of savings bank depositors, the people robbed are unlikely to be wealthy, but almost certainly average people saving for a holiday, a new carpet, or some similar purpose. This robbery can in no way be justified and it can be stopped.

If a stable unit of value is created and deposits and loans recorded in these units with deposits and payments converted from and to dollars at the time of lodgment or payment, the real value would be maintained.

Interest rates and deposits and loans expressed in units of value would be low and constant and would overcome the hardship to borrowers caused by the rapid increase in interest rates which accompanies a rapid increase in the rate of inflation.

Payments on loans would increase at a general rate in keeping with wage increases.

A. M. McKENZIE
Booragoon, WA
28/11/74

Great wail on prices

AS an invalid pensioner, I strongly protest against the outrageous steeple pricing which is going on in the supermarkets. To me it is completely Chinese that one pays one price one week and an extra rise on the same item the following week.

Two weeks ago, I purchased a 4oz tin of continental roast coffee for 66c and last Friday went back to buy a further tin and found that it had been marked up to 79c, a rise of 13c!

While I can appreciate the international complexities of inflation, I cannot understand how Australians can be so complacent about this. On a radio talk-back session in Melbourne, one can hear almost daily the great wail going out from many housewives — voicing their protests and telling how their weekly budgets are being repeatedly raped to the obvious advantage of the manufacturer.

But I have yet to hear any of the same women resolving to take concerted action to bring this anomaly before the attention of the prices tribunal.

MARCUS FINNANE
St Kilda, Vic
1/6/74

PS

I GOT up this morning, went to the supermarket and had a great realisation — I can no longer afford to eat. What do you intend to do about it?
IAN MORGANS
North Caulfield, Vic
27/11/74

The Cost of living

Pensions

─Australians in poverty─

MR Philpott's recent statements in *The Australian* concernng the achievements of the Menzies Government, particularly in the field of social services, should not go unchallenged.

Many people in Australia live in poverty and in fear of unexpected catastrophes.

With the exception of the lucky few who received increases in the 1965 Budget, the majority of pensioners have received no increase since the 1964 Budget. The cose of living has risen steeply since that time and all workers have received wage increases.

Consider the plight of a widow with three children, struggling to keep her family on $20.50 a week. When one realises that the latest Department of Health basic food charts puts the minimum cost of feeding a family of four at $15.45, one must see how impossible it is to cover rent, fuel and clothing, and other necessities.

However, the unfortunate family living on sickness or unemployment benefit has only $17.25. This barely covers the cost of food for four. But the unskilled worker on the basic wage who gets no concessions by way of rent, rates, fares or medical costs, is also poor. On $31.50 he cannot hope to pay high rent, feed and generally keep his family. Much of the greatly publicised rise in prosperity is based on the fact that income is swelled by a working wife.

CORALIE MALLITT
Beverly Hills, NSW
25/2/66

Our pension benefits 26th on world list

YOUR valuable paper is the only one that seems interested in the ordinary person who is not getting a fair deal.

I refer specifically to those who are receiving old-age pensions — paupers' pensions, as they are often called.

They are forgotten people as far as our Government is concerned.

According to latest figures, Australian pension benefits for old and infirm people rate only 26th on the world list.

The most favorable benefits are paid by the governments of Norway, Sweden, Denmark, Canada and England; nearer home, New Zealand has very good benefits.

Pensioners should receive at least half the basic wage and they should be allowed to earn more than a paltry $7 extra with our cost of living increasing every day.

The Minister for Social Services is not interested in the plight of pensioners.

He will not make any effort to make this country's benefits the best in the world and prevent Australia from becoming stagnant politically.

H. CAREY
Parramatta, NSW
15/6/66

Humanitarian principles

THE sooner Australians are aware of the facts on pensioners, the sooner will the humanitarian principles of the UN Charter be put into effect: "Everyone has the right to a standard of living adequate for the health and wellbeing of himself and of his family."

It is true that a married couple can receive £18 a week (when the 5/— increase is received), but I have never met a pensioner couple on the possible maximum.

(Mrs) I. ELLIS
Secretary
Commonwealth Pensioners Association
Brighton, Vic
27/8/64

Pensions

Why tolerate such inhuman treatment?

MAY I draw readers' attention to the latest figures released in Canberra by the Commonwealth Statistician, revealing that the average weekly earnings of a male employee engaged in industry in both NSW and Victoria have reached an all-time record figure of $80.50, compared with $74-odd for the same period last year.

May I also suggest this was the underlying reason for the unanimous decision of 133 accredited delegates from 140-odd branches of The Original Old Age and Invalid Pensioners Association at the annual conference of that body in Sydney in February last.

That body declared the present pension rate of $15 a week for unmarried pensioners and $11.75 a week for each of married couples were totally inadequate and called on the Prime Minister and the Leader of the Opposition in Canberra to request the Parliament to grant an immediate emergency increase of $3 a week to enable ALL pensioners to cope reasonably with living costs.

We hear much talk from Mr Gorton about abolishing poverty in our affluent society and our rich and wonderful nation; but evidently the talk is not supported by parliamentary action.

One may be pardoned, surely, for asking why an enlightened society tolerates such inhuman treatment towards our elderly folk!

CHARLES JOHNSTON
Corrimal, NSW
20/3/70

Iniquitous means test

CONGRATULATIONS on your sub-leader headed An Inquiry Into Poverty (11/5) and congratulations also to the Opposition Leader, Mr Calwell, for demanding that the Commonwealth Government should fully investigate poverty.

On behalf of the South Coast Council of the Original Old Age Pensioners Association of NSW, we wish to point out that approximately 50 per cent of the 600,000 people and the 150,000 families trying to meet living commitments on less than £17/10/− a week are aged, invalid and widow pensioners, and many incapacitated and totally disabled war pensioners, too, not to mention thousands of superannuees debarred by the iniquitous means test.

Social service pensioners are − and have been for years − relegated into a "resting paddock" to eke out the remaining years of life on a miserly £5/15/− a week!

We thank *The Australian* and Mr Calwell for the timely jolt to the public conscience on the question of mass poverty in a country bursting with untapped wealth and undeveloped resources.

C. E. KOHLER
Chairman

C. L. JOHNSTON
Honorary Secretary
27/5/65

On being obsolete

AT the end of last year, I became an obsolete, non-productive unit; I reached the age when I was banned from work.

I cannot pass a car wrecker's yard without a feeling of sympathy with the inmates. Having had all the assets and income of myself and my wife examined, I may draw about $5 a week provided that I vegetate quietly and don't try to earn any money.

Although my income has been reduced by 75 per cent, everything still costs the same. Had we used our savings to take a luxury cruise round the world, the taxpayers would have had to pay us more because we had managed to reduce our assets. If my pension were not means-tested, about half of the extra $45 would be returned to the Treasury in income tax.

There are two ways of looking at an age pension. It can be seen as money returned in reward for 40 or 50 years' service to the community and a refund of some taxes paid during those years. This is the non-means-tested pension.

The other way is to see it as a charity hand-out to those who have been stupid enough not to accumulate vast assets in order to pay the inflated prices in their old age. This is the means-tested pension.

At election times, political parties promise the former; when they are in government they quickly revert to the latter view.

S. A. ARMSTRONG
Darlington, SA
20/3/75

Pensions

The geriatric elite

I HOPE C. J. Connelly's letter will stir up a veritable hornet's nest.

After a lifetime of hard work as a self-employed practitioner grappling with the perennial problems of high provisional taxation, I managed to accumulate sufficient of this world's goods to enable my wife and I to live our last few years in modest comfort, provided we practise austere personal economies.

We now live in a beautiful Queensland coastal town which population is rather heavily sprinkled with retired fat cats of Australia's only growth industry, the various bureaucracies.

Mostly these people have taken the lump sum pot of gold to establish a luxury home and their BMWs or Volvos and their fishing cruisers, because they know that come their "coronary" — the killer disease of the idle self-indulgent — their widows will receive a further hand-out from a grateful community of $400, $500, or $600 or more a week.

The rest of the fruit of the embezzlement has gone to income avoidance schemes, or has been secreted away with their family so that they can add "petty theft" to their sins. Of course, they do not regard this rape of the public purse as a crime. They believe their arduous service in the maladministration of the nation entitles them to the same "perks" as ordinary mendicant pensions.

The fortnightly pension cheque is essential to their lifestyle. How else could they keep capital intact while maintaining membership of clubs, the essential car and boat, to say nothing of the costs of overseas trips and keeping a well-stocked cocktail cabinet and vintage wine cellar?

I would normally proudly sign my name for publication of a letter like this, but as we have to live among this selfish, strutting, greedy geriatric elite, I fear the consequences of their malicious reprisals on my dear lady wife.

RETIRED & RESENTFUL
19/9/81

A right to live in dignity

WHEN will the Government in Canberra and society look at the plight of pensioners trying to eke out an existence on $96.50 a fortnight?

MPs in Canberra recently received increases of $60 a week and the State members are talking of an increase in the order of $45 a week.

While agreeing that members should be paid according to their duties, we have an obligation to look at the other end of the scale — the pensioners. How would the MPs like to exist on the old age pension?

The poverty level is rated at $154 a week, yet we continue to expect the people who helped to build up this country by their efforts to live on such a meagre income.

I see that all concerned people in Australia must press for an immediate increase in the rate for pensioners, so that they may live in dignity and without undue hardship.

(Bro) LAURIE MURPHY
Christian Brothers College
Gilles Plains, SA
1/4/80

PS

J. McKENZIE (PS, 23/7) should stop whining about the level of the old age pension and start securing her own future. The Australian population is becoming increasingly older following the very high birth rate between 1945 and the early 1960s and our virtual zero population growth rate since then. Consequently, when the people born during the earlier period reach pensionable age, which will coincide with proportionally fewer people earning incomes to be taxed, the Government will be unable to fund an old age pension at its present high level without imposing intolerable high taxes.
RICHARD DALGLEISH
South Perth, WA
4/8/81

ISN'T it about time something was done about the pitiful amount pensioners are allowed to earn before their pensions are affected? Surely those who could work a couple of days a week should be allowed to do so without being penalised. On today's standards the $20 they are allowed to earn is not even a day's pay!
(Mrs) A. DANIELS
Brighton, SA
2/3/76

IS there to be no peace for pensioners? Your editorial and Opinion (14/9) continue to harass us and will probably help to reduce the ranks with sharp distress. Resource-poor countries like Holland and Austria can pay 80 per cent of the standard wage in pensions. What is wrong with this per capita resource-rich land of Australia that our Government can't do the same?
P. MAHONY
Byron Bay, NSW
22/9/81

Dear Joh

Be thankful we've got Joh

I REFER to J. I. Eberhardt's repudiation (Letters, 15/5) of Mr Bjelke-Petersen's leadership. I, contrarywise, wish to inform the Premier that I am glad he represents Queenslanders, whether he is at home or abroad. I hope he leads Queensland out of a Commonwealth that has become anathema since Labor took over last December.

R. PEPPERS
Isle of Capri, Qld
22/5/73

Choosing Joh was a disgrace

YOUR choice of Mr Bjelke-Petersen as Australian of the Year is a disgrace. If "striking impact" is a criterion and the fact that his exploits "lead inexorably to political victory" is cited as justification, then such noted friends of humanity as Attila the Hun, Joe Stalin and Adolf Hitler would be lining up for the "Human Being of All Time" award, should your paper choose to award one.

MICHAEL SPROD
South Hobart, Tas
2/1/75

What else can one say?

THE Bjelke-Petersen Government knocked down Brisbane's most beautiful building without warning after midnight last weekend because it feared the strength of feeling among the people of this city for their Belle Vue. What else can one say?

HUGH LUNN
Your shocked Queensland correspondent
26/4/79

The fastest growing State

MALCOLM Andrews (Perspective, *The Weekend Australian*, 1-2/11) asked where but in Queensland would you find a Joh Bjelke-Petersen supporter. The obvious answer is wherever in Australia people still admire conservative government which encourages free enterprise. If Joh's supporters are not standing up to be counted, the probable reason is that they are too busy planning to migrate to Queensland or, like us, have done so already. It's not just the climate which makes Queensland the country's fastest-growing State.

MARGARET TROST
Cairns, Qld
8/11/80

PS

THE efforts of Northern Territory Aborigines to make the Premier of Queensland, Mr Bjelke-Petersen, mentally dead were wasted. They were too late.

P. M. WALSH
Mt Gravatt, Qld
11/1/75

Dear Larry

Extreme insensitivity

I WRITE to express extreme disapproval of the cartoon which appeared in *The Australian* last Wednesday depicting Mr Whitlam carrying a cross.

This showed extreme insensitivity to the feelings of Christian people, particularly as it was published on Ash Wednesday, the beginning of the Lenten season.

Surely your cartoonists should be capable of expressing their points without giving the offence of associating a venerated religious leader with controversial political figures.

(Rev) W. D. O'REILLY
President-General
Methodist Church
of Australia
Sydney
9/3/76

Dear Larry

Cruel to Menzies

PICKERING'S cartoon of Sir Robert Menzies (24/3) depicting him as a fat, senile cripple shoved off his wheelchair into the mud, with a nurse talking to him as if he were a child or an imbecile, was cruel, insensitive and outrageous.

The cartoon was not even relevant to the matter in question. I happen to disagree with Sir Robert's opposition to any retiring age for federal judges: 70 years is perhaps too early to compel all judges to retire, but I think there should be some limit. Contrary to the impression conveyed by Pickering's cartoon, Menzies' mind is clear, powerful and crisp, and he stated his case lucidly and with dignity: Mr Fraser's reply disagreeing with him was also restrained and reasonable.

There are (or used to be) canons of decency and good taste which even cartoonists should not be allowed to transgress and I am at a loss to understand why this grotesque distortion was permitted to appear.

(Sir) HOWARD BEALE
Bellevue Hill, NSW
28/3/77

Editor's Note: Sir Robert has asked if he might have the original of the March 24 cartoon of himself in the wheelchair in the lake and it is being sent to him.

Cop it sweet!

SIR Howard Beale's remarks (28/3) re Pickering's cartoon on Sir Robert Menzies, part quote: "There are (or used to be) canons of decency and good taste which even cartoonists should not be allowed to transgress."

In the light of the above statement, perhaps Sir Howard might like to comment on his feelings and remarks at the time when Jack Lang was hideously depicted with the grotesque head and the body of a bull, during the time he was called the "Ebenezer Bull" in the early 1930s. Or doesn't that count, Sir Howard?

Cop it sweet, Sir Howard. Pickering is the most astute
Continued next page

Dear Larry

Bad taste

MR Berry (5/4) invites me to comment upon the cartoons directed against Jack Lang as compared with Pickering's recent cartoon of Sir Robert Menzies (24/3).

I knew Jack Lang well; I saw a good deal of him in the Federal Parliament between 1946 and 1949 and visited him at his farm at Ebenezer (of bull fame). I certainly did not agree with his politics in 1930 and 1931, but neither did I agree with the tone of all of the cartoons about him.

Even so, there is a great deal of difference between a cartoon about an aggressive political personality like Lang in the prime of his life and at the peak of his powers, and Pickering's first cartoon about Menzies on the referendum, depicting him as crippled, senile and humiliated.

My protest was not a matter of politics (I do not agree with Menzies about the referendum), but about bad taste and insensitiveness.

(Sir) HOWARD BEALE
Sydney
14/4/77

Dear Mr Pickering . . .

DELIGHTED you have caught up with my non-smoking habits.

I hope that pipe will not puff its way back into your cartoons — at least unless I take it up again.

With best wishes,
MALCOLM FRASER

Dear PM .

THANK you for your telegram, I thought you knew smoking is not permitted in the Senate chamber. Have a look at Page 8 today.

Best wishes,
LARRY PICKERING
10/3/77

Cop it sweet!

From previous page

political cartoonist and although many may not agree with his political depiction, a great majority of people enjoy the message and the intended humor.

ERIC BERRY
Calliope, Qld
5/4/77

PS

THREE cheers for Mr Pickering! The mark of a fine cartoonist is an ability to cut through loads of waffle so that the truth is revealed clearly and perhaps brutally.
PETER SONNERS
Townsville, Qld
2/8/80

Dear Larry

Beyond tolerable bounds

IN the course of public life, one must accept barbed personal commentary, if not with good cheer, certainly in good part.

Mr Pickering's cartoon of July 28, however, goes well beyond tolerable bounds. It implies that Neville Wran's ill-health is, at its best, something I do not care about or, more obviously it seems to me, is something I welcome.

That sort of imputation is nasty, offensive and totally unjustified.

The manifest bias of News Limited against the Federal Parliamentary Labor Party in order to satisfy its architects surely does not have to plummet to such extraordinary depths of bad taste and calumny.

BILL HAYDEN, MP
Canberra
31/7/80

Disturbing

THE more I see of Mr Pickering's cartoons of unionists, the more disturbing I find them, for he appears to hold a deep dislike for most of the people in this country. Another figure he gives no dignity to is "Mr Average."

Am I not right in believing that (a) several million Australians are members of trade unions and that (b) most of us are "average" by definition?

Mr Pickering chooses to depict this large section with contempt and ridicule. His unionist, militant or otherwise, is always a brute: gross, piggy-eyed, a sloth, incapable of any fine feelings. "Mr Average" fares little better. He is dull, has no drive, little self-esteem and no dignity.

I believe there is something unpleasant — even fascist — in Pickering's cartoons: they invite the viewer to despise the ordinary person.

Isn't there enough bitter division in our community already Mr Pickering? You don't, as a cartoonist might claim, merely reflect this, you stoke it daily.

B. PAUL
St Ives, NSW
31/10/77

Sickening

PICKERING'S cartoon *(The Weekend Australian, 23-24/6)* where he advocates shooting communist trade union officials involved in strikes, is most disturbing — if not sickening.

Industrial conflict and strikes are inevitable in a modern industrial society and are not caused by communist leaders who create them out of thin air.

In the NSW petrol strike none of the leading actors is communist; and in the WA dispute, while left-wing leaders are involved, the resulting strike action was endorsed by conservative trades and labor councils and the ACTU.

Communist trade union officials act in the open and, while espousing change to the existing social system (and winning concessions for their members here and now), confine their acitivities to traditional democratic methods — contesting parliamentary seats and disseminating literature/propaganda. They do not advocate killing political opponents.

One of the strengths of a democracy is the tolerance of competing value systems. Pickering, with his advocacy of killing those involved in strikes, may be more at home in nazi Germany than Australia.

BRAHAM DABSCHECK
Lecturer
Department of Industrial Relations
University of NSW
Kensington, NSW
27/6/79

Fair comment

TO misinterpret a cartoon to such an extent that Mr Dabscheck has (Letters, 27/6) prompts me, for the first time in 10 years, to reply to a letter to the editor.

To suggest that my cartoon advocated shooting communist unionists is akin to suggesting black resembles white.

The cartoon said simply that if communists were suc-

Continued next page

Dear Larry

From previous page

cessful in their attempts to create a new communist State in Australia, they then would not be afforded their present democratic right to hold a country to ransom.

If they acted in a communist State in the same way as they do in Australia, they would be convicted as enemies of the State and shot or sentenced to an asylum by the very system they advocated!

That, my university lecturer friend, is fair comment.

LARRY PICKERING
Surry Hills, NSW
28/6/79

With sincere regret . .

IT was with sincere regret that I watched Larry Pickering speak of his resignation from the media scene during a recent television interview.

I have always respected and admired his skill with his cartoonist's brush, although my teeth have been set on edge by the latent cruelty sometimes displayed in his work.

But my respect for him as a human being sharply increased as I listened to his own obviously sincere regret that he had perhaps been a part-cause of the hatred that is physically affecting this country at the present time.

Some solace can be sought by Mr Pickering in the fact that he alone is by no means to blame and that all humor, political or otherwise, is based on cruelty.

I trust, for his sake, that his torment may be eased in the atmosphere of his farming property.

ROBERT WEBB
Woodridge, Qld
31/10/80

Dear Max

That love/hate feeling

I HAVE just returned from abroad and read Max Harris' witty and generous review of my forthcoming book, Boomerang.

I enjoy his praise; and accept his critical remarks with a bow. May I be permitted, however, to make three brief comments?

1. Lavatory doors have no locks in Australia (I wrote) and this is a heritage from convict days.

The comment was mine and meant to be facetious; the fact, however, is true as far as my experience goes.

I admit it is not a special observation of great significance, but I declare: nowhere in the world are there so many lock-less lavatory doors as on your happy and prosperous island.

2. I wrote that passengers are expected to ride next to the taxi driver and Mr Harris called this the "most stupid of canards."

He admits, however, that "the driver will open the front door for you." If you were not expected to sit next to him, he would, of course, open the back door.

3. I complained that bathtubs in Australia lack an overflow. Mr Harris says that "no one told our ill-educated visitant that we reserve baths only for the old, the sick or the occasional migrant."

In fact, your ill-educated visitant has been so informed, but he still maintains

WHY do you print Max Harris?

M. J. BROWN
Subiaco, WA
Why not? — Editor
11/1/68

THANK God for Max Harris!

J. MOXON
Chelmer, Qld
14/7/79

that the old, the sick and the occasional migrant would find an overflow useful.

GEORGE MIKES
The Garrick Club
London
22/7/68

"THE age of the cultural bludge" — for God's sake! Will Max Harris come off it and think for a whole minute about what he's saying when he lambasts the grants to writers (17/8).

Does he think the Australian Society of Authors rigged the survey of authors' earnings that showed them averaging so much less than the basic wage?

How can he think that the people on the Literature Board, the ones he calls a "hard-headed mob," don't know what they are doing?

Does he really believe that old mularkey about writers writing better in garrets? Is he naive enough to think Shaw Neilson wouldn't have written any poetry worth a damn if he hadn't had to

work as a navvy?

I've always wondered why Max fell so hard for Ern Malley. Maybe he thought Ern's being a garage mechanic on Taverner's Hill meant that his verse had to be great.

I didn't get a grant, nor did I apply for one. Had I been a recipient, I suppose I would have qualified as one of the "rich bastards" Max talks about — which would have been news to my bank manager.

Who are those "notoriously affluent" authors the list is studded with the names of, anyway? But suppose I could think of just one who was netting $10,000 a year and he'd got a grant of $5000. The tax man would take $5491 instead of $2889 (an accountant assures me), meaning that the grantee would lose half of his grant in extra tax.

I honestly believe that the grants will produce some better books for booksellers to sell.

Incidentally, Sweden has been spending for years on its authors the kind of money the Australian Government is spending for the first time. Has Max thought of tipping off the Swedes that they are just being a bunch of over-civilised Nordic softies and wasting their kroner?

COLIN SIMPSON
Gordon, NSW
23/8/73

Dear Max

Spare me Mr Harris

DURING several months in Australia, my directors, researcher and I meet hundreds of people; some of these conversations we film, some not.

Mr Max Harris was, I fear, judged to be of insufficient interest. Because of this, he bursts into affronted print (30/5), laying about him with his tiny bludgeon and attacking programs not yet written, let alone transmitted.

There is, I know, a stunning inevitability that any television film on Australia will eventually be castigated by the Harrises, longing for Bloomsbury, as obvious — or unrepresentative; but one notes the subjects he selected for an accurate (at last, at last) picture of Australia: The Geelong Grammar rebels, Manifold, Dutton — Harris even. Such a scene is, I read, not "the old, old bit."

Well, yes. Though we have not, as he insists, filmed Abos, winemaking or British migrants . . . faced with his new, new bit, they begin to look good.

I don't object to his cloudy crystal ball; I can appreciate his feelings of inadequacy, now unhappily reinforced; but when Australia is so full of interesting people, must I be rubbished in such an intelligent newspaper because a director is experienced and perceptive enough to spare me Mr Harris?

And not only me; some 30-40 million people around the world will see these seven programs and, let's face up to it, as a figure of international interest, Mr Harris remains a great little Adelaide bookseller.

ALAN WHICKER
(Of Yorkshire Television)
Broken Hill, NSW
4/6/70

┌─There are no fairies─┐

I DON'T want to join in the "Knock Maxie" game, but this time I must object.

Mr Harris has been cheap and glib at the expense of literature and somebody has to object.

I know the informality, chirpiness and so on are part of his "charm" — he is the Sid Barnes of literature and so on — but the note on Tolkien's The Lord of the Rings *(The Australian*, April 23) is appalling.

First, it shows ignorance to call the trilogy by the title of the first volume, The Fellowship of the Ring.

Second, Mr Harris has some notion the books are about fairies (he may not have been responsible for the heading, Paperback Battle Of The Fairies, but he was certainly responsible for calling the books a "fairytale saga").

There are no fairies, in any sense of the term, in Tolkien.

To correct some of the misleading impressions of the books, I'll simply say that the "oddies" (Mr Harris' charming twit-in-the-street term) are different.

The Hobbit is for children from 8 (7 maybe) to 13 or so, though a willing ingenuousness can enable adults to enjoy it.

It is amusing and exciting enough, with a fine grasp of narrative techniques and evocative (even archetypal) situations.

The Lord of the Rings is not a book for children at all, though I've met two 12-year-olds who enjoyed parts of it (they were both very smart and sophisticated 12-year-olds).

It is an adult work as Orlando Furioso is adult and the unsophisticated thrills come through a greatness of vision, which is difficult for children to begin to appreciate.

Parts of the book, especially the appearances of the Nazgul and the journey into Mordor, can be badly frightening even to adolescents.

If The Idylls of the King or the Morte D'Arthur, The Odyssey, The Faerie Queene are children's fairytales, so perhaps is the trilogy.

These comparisons are not absurd and the merciless folktales haunt the reader here as they do in Shakespeare's last romances . . .

But never mind the lecture on Tolkien — just make Max Harris read books before being charming about them, please.

NORMAN TALBOT
Department of English
University of Newcastle
Newcastle, NSW
16/5/66

The highest regard for Max

I READ with interest Mr Max Harris' spirited attack (17/7) on the mediocrity of the average Australian, as personified by the popular serial, Bellbird.

Ever since Mr Harris discovered my own latent genius by publishing my poems in Angry Penguins in 1944, I have held his opinions in highest regard.

ERN MALLEY
West Heidelberg, Vic
26/7/71

Dear Max

You were so right, Max

AS a long time admirer of Max Harris and his razor-like ability to get to the very heart of his subject, I must take issue with W. H. Perkins (7/9) of Tasmania.

I thought Mr Harris' description of the inept and dull Gunston as being appropriate for "mental cripples" to be accurate beyond any argument. Anything more inane and puerile would be impossible to imagine.

Personality is an essential requisite and it staggers the imagination that anyone with nothing to offer can continue to be the object of payment from the already overtaxed citizens.

If we must pay, surely we should have entertainment and not be subjected to the meanderings of untalented and persistent amateurs. Max Harris expresses the opinion of those accustomed to professional entertainment.

(Lady) VIOLET BRADDON
Woollahra, NSW
14/9/76

Just dripping with scorn

IT'S good to see Max Harris back in form again.

For too many months — beginning I should say with his extravagant puff for an obscure volume on Australian privies — he seemed to see his role as little more than that of a book tipster.

You read Harris to be told what book to put your money on, just as you might read *The Australian's* Racing Lift-Out for a likely horse.

Last Saturday's contribution, two full columns long and dripping with scorn, was more like the old Harris.

And was it welcome? My word!

ARTHUR CLIFFORD
Fairlight, NSW
13/6/66

Lofty parsonical tone

IT seems to me that anyone who can write: "Tendentiousness, if expressed this side of absurdity, is acceptable even if it should be defined as something other than the pure historical genre" is hardly in the position to suggest that Manning Clark writes "ghastly prose." Perhaps Max Harris should save his own "lofty parsonical tone" for something he knows more about.

JOHN COLLINS
Ferntree Gully, Vic
1/6/78

Prognostication off beam

MAX Harris seems to have been completely off the beam recently with his opinions on the Airbus, his resolution to "scrub" public charities which publish lists of donors and his inept prognostication that 99 per cent of the population would weary of the recently televised royal wedding in the first half hour. He should gracefully retire, or refrain from public utterances on subjects other than literary.

D. R. A. MURRAY
Northbridge, NSW
18/8/81

Evasive? Too bloody true . . .

MAX Harris generally concerns himself with the well-being of the earnest reader's cerebrum. In the dramatic volte-face (23/5), however, he has re-focused his attentions (through a 90-degree physiological arc) to the pudenda and its adornments.

During his discourse he chose to say some nice things about my new book, Of Woman, Love and Beauty.

But he also said one very naughty thing, which I hasten to rebut, lest the creaking beams of my mortgage-laden home be supported by nothing but stacks of unsold books and my children go shoeless.

Max Harris says of my book of nudes that "everywhere, that disgusting touch-up brush had had to do its compulsory work." I proudly report that all the models who appear in my book are totally intact, speaking photographically; nothing whatever is deleted.

Max has one particularly perceptive observation, however, that makes me very sad.

I had always felt that in terms of my talent I had been un-got-at, but Harris had to go and say, "Instead of a joyous, unconfined response to his subjects, De' Lisle has had to apply the usual unnatural and evasive poses."

Too bloody true.

But will Max show me some compassion for 47 years of Victorian fear?

GORDON DE' LISLE
Brighton, Vic
28/5/70

Max Harris

MY old sparring partner, Max Harris, has forced me to enter the ring for another bout. He drags the Power Without Glory series into a column devoted to proving that television programming "attempts to equate precisely with the cultural receptivity of the greatest number of people" (May 7).

To achieve this worthy aim, he tries to link Power Without Glory with John Singleton's ads, Bellbird and Don Lane.

He argues that the Power Without Glory series is a further example that audiences are "dragged down to an unworthy level of nitwittedness."

The very opposite of what Max says is true of Power Without Glory: it was planned during the Whitlam era and was aimed at raising public taste to seriously study Australia's history in dramatic form. The dishonesty of Max's column is further compounded by his statement that British audiences are "that fraction more sophisticated than here," then adds that the program was shown beyond midnight. Come off it, Max! To argue that the Power

Round 1

Without Glory series dragged audiences down to an unworthy level of nitwittedness because British television audiences are not seeing it, is worse than tautology, it is a load of old rusty rabbit traps.

The reaction of the sophisticated London audience to Power Without Glory being shown so late was a great number of letters from viewers praising the series and requesting that it be shown earlier. Thames Television responded by taking a decision to repeat the series in a much earlier time slot.

Max quotes the only unfavorable review which the Power Without Glory series received in the London press (Evening News). Martin Jackson, for example in the Daily Mail took a different view. Jackson wrote: "By BBC and ITV drama standards, it is a very adequate production indeed . . . it does for the Aussie in part what Roots has done for the American Negro. It has given him a history and one that is not of Ned Kelly, billycans and tie-my-kangaroo-

down-sport . . . Certainly it deserves a wider audience and a better time than the hidden-away late night slot allocated by Thames."

Perhaps my opinion of the series should be briefly stated: I thought the writing, especially in its handling of the social and political background, was of a high standard. The acting was fine (we have a grand body of actors in this country). And the costuming and period designing was first rate. The main fault was that some scenes in some episodes were not effectively directed and should not have been permitted to go to air. I understand that Oscar Whitbread, the executive producer, wanted to reshoot these scenes but the ABC brass said there was no money for such an exercise.

I agree with Martin Jackson that, in every other respect, the series was very adequate, even by British standards.

I've told you before, Max: if you are going to throw wild punches — keep your guard up.

FRANK HARDY
Manly, NSW
16/5/77

FRANK Hardy has written and taken me to task for my assessment of the TV Power Without Glory production.

Frank may be physically Hardy, but he'll never learn. So I'll say it again.

His novel, Power Without Glory, was an immature, badly written sociological soapie. There is no need for the man who came to write But the Dead Are Many to be bovinely obsessed with his own dried-out cow-cake. This judgment is not much debated among his peers, but Women's Weekly readers and less-literate boilermakers would disagree. Frank Hardy has had 20

Round 2

years to choose which critics he prefers to believe.

The television series based on Power Without Glory was inferior to Bellbird in sociological content. Its acting was only up-market of Number 96 in terms of its pompousness. Its production and direction compared feebly with such a modest endeavor as The Sullivans. It was in short, bloody terrible except to the inveterate consumer of standard soapies. And they'll enthuse about anything so long as it has a sort of laxette regularity.

Let Frank make a fat media dollar. There's no harm in that. But he shouldn't try to play with us rough Grub Street boys. We have no desire to poke him one with a bunch of critical fives, especially when he could now be writing like a major writer. He has only so much time before the old literary menopause sets in.

So to use a Larry Pickering vulgarism, pee off, boofhead. You do the professional writing and we professional critics will do the evaluations. Fair enough?

MAX HARRIS
Adelaide
20/5/77

Dear Bruce

"ITS OUR STABILITY THAT ATTRACTS THEM."

Dear Bruce

Not bad going

CORRESPONDENTS "Dreadful" and Patricia Ewens agree that Bruce Petty's graphic work is childish and incompetent. Do they make their judgment from lofty critical standards — or dead ignorance?

Petty's work has been published by a host of overseas magazines. I've come across it in Punch, New Yorker, Esquire and Economist.

His splendid book, An Artist in South-East Asia, won wide critical praise — and an important publishing award.

And he was rated among the world's leading artists and designers in a definitive survey by the Swiss magazine Graphis.

Not bad going for someone who allegedly "can't draw."

For me, Petty remains the main attraction of *The Australian*, but then, I haven't seen the work of Miss Ewens' children.

PHILLIP ADAMS
Toorak, Vic
30/7/64

Tickled pink

IN reply to Patricia Ewen's letter criticising Bruce Petty's cartoons, I would like to mention that I find his daily comment one of the most pleasing features of your newspaper.

I enjoy his drawings immensely and have been tickled pink on numerous occasions by his contributions to overseas magazines such as Punch.

Legend has it that the late Fats Waller, the Negro jazz pianist, was once approached by a woman who posed the question: "Mr Waller, what exactly is rhythm?" Mr Waller replied: "Ma'am, if you don't know, you 'aint got it." Patricia Ewen resembles that woman.

CAMPBELL BURNAP
Edgecliff, NSW
5/8/64

Tony Hancock

So moving

YOUR cartoonist, Bruce Petty, has a rare ability to express feelings that have appeared inexpressible. I have felt this since first seeing his work in your pages — but until now I had seen nothing so expressive as his cold anger at the death of Robert Kennedy.

But nothing of Petty's has ever moved me as much as his reaction to Tony Hancock's death. To many of us, Hancock at his best did not fall short of greatness in his ability to articulate the pomposities, absurdities and cruel obliviousness of much of our civilisation.

Petty has somehow expressed completely the grief of many at the tragedy of Hancock's life and death.

He has summed up as far as is possible the bitterness that this human being should fall victim to the very failings in all of us of which he was so conscious and about which he could be so articulate.

On Hancock's death, this insensitive, rat race-infested world seems even more than usually nauseous.

KEVIN H. J. BRYANT
Aranda, A.C.T.
5/7/68

The squiggler

NOW that the election is over, would it be possible to instruct your "squiggle" cartoonist to vary the diet of depicting the Prime Minister, Mr Holt, as a diseased gnome?

It is funny the first time, amusing the second time, but it palls after numerous doses.

Ask whether he can think up something else.

Also would it be possible to add a little printed explanation of the meaning of Petty's cartoons?

He also is much given to squiggles and the only item one can understand about his efforts on most occasions is his name.

One can understand that.

N. V. WALLACE
Naracoorte, SA
6/12/66

Picturesque

MAY I suggest to your correspondent who requires an explanation of Petty's cartoons (Letters, 6/12) that he read *The Australian* as well as just looking at the pictures, cartoons and comic strips?

However, a word of thanks to him for his wonderfully-picturesque description of Mr Holt (and Mr McMahon for that matter) as a "diseased gnome."

This even excels the ability of Petty to interpret a complex individual or situation with a few strokes of the pen.

G. M. RICHARDSON
Kiama, NSW
14/12/66

Dear Bruce

NEW BROOM

That nose

YOUR correspondent, Jack Burns, is hypersensitive, too, in condemning cartoonist Petty for depicting the Israeli Prime Minister, Mrs Meir, as having a large nose.

The plain physiological fact of life is that Negroes have black skin, Chinese have slant eyes, while frequently Jews (and Arabs) have large, Semitic noses. So what!

President Nasser's nose has for many years been a cartoonist's delight (along with de Gaulle's), and to claim special treatment for Mrs Meir is to do her no favor. Rather would it be a form of unwelcome discrimination.

Finally, it would seem that Mr Burns is a new reader of *The Australian* otherwise by now he would have appreciated that Petty preserves an admirable impartiality to Middle East affairs, erring only slightly to the pro-Israeli viewpoint.

DEREK BARSON
Smithfield, NSW
25/10/69

How unfair

PETTY'S cartoon, "Gorilla war" (15/6) is unfair to gorillas.

George Schaller, in his book, The Year of the Gorilla, shows these amiable creatures to be kind spouses and loving parents.

Living peaceful lives in remote areas, they are careful not to trespass on the territories of other gorilla tribes and are tolerant of well-intentioned human observers.

When alarmed they show a pantomime of menace and resort to violence only when attacked.

HOPE BURGOYNE
Reid, A.C.T.
28/6/68

PS

THE Governor-General, Sir Paul Hasluck, in his Australia Day message, appealed to people in Australia to ponder the question of what sort of people Australians have become, or are becoming. Petty's facetious and childish cartoon, ridiculing Sir Paul and his message, gives one answer. It is to be hoped that it is merely the answer of the loud and vulgar minority to whom even the word dignity, as applied to the Head of State, is a dirty word.

CRASTER USHER
Hornsby, NSW
21/2/70

The Poms

Give me decadence

WHAT'S so wrong with being decadent, anyway?

The word is cast about pejoratively and yet I know a lot of people who would give their eye teeth to be called decadent.

France has always been held synonymous with that word and, apart from being way ahead of Britain in the cultural stakes, she's a damn sight more pleasant place to live.

Phyllis Bentley recently summarised neatly the change that has come over Britain by saying that where the British used to live like Romans (empire-building, puritanical etc), they have now become Italians (pleasure-seeking, easy-going etc).

If this is true, then I think it an excellent thing, both for Britain and the world.

Anything to terminate those eternal schooldays in which they spread all those middle-class shibboleths which make life so dull in Australia and Canada!

The last time I was in London — the rest of the country is and always will be a wilderness to me — I found the scene to be stagnant, full of xenophobia and of a particularly deadly form of boredom.

That was three years ago — but NOW?

If half of what I read is true, then I can't wait to get out of vital, progressive, liberal Melbourne and hurry back over there while I can still get me some of that decadence.

RAY TAYLOR
c/o the nearest shipping office
Melbourne
30/6/66

Seeing the light

GLORY be! So 50,000 Australians have gone underground in Britain rather than face the risk of being returned to Australia!

Can it be that the intellectual, political and social climate of Britain is more attractive to adventurous and discerning Aussies than the much vaunted sunshine of their own over-governed, over-censored and over-indulged country?

Can it be that 50,000 expatriots are disinclined to exchange the civilised amenities of a comprehensive national health scheme and humanitarian social services, for the devil-take-the-hindmost, sick-at-the-thought-of-being-sick atmosphere of Australia?

Have the 50,000 explorers discovered the real freedoms . . . of being able to read what the big outside world is reading, without the vice squad looking over their shoulder; being able to think and express themselves publicly and to oppose government policy without being subjected to the sneer and smear of fanatical anti-communists?

Is it that 50,000 enthusiastic Australians have discovered a place where education, the arts, science, politics and industry, are still very much alive and going places?

A place that was not afraid to stand perilously alone, on a matter of national and international principle!

Could it be that 50,000 Australians have seen the light? It seems highly possible; and, I can only repeat, glory be!

EDWARD KNOX
Ashburton, Vic
23/11/66

She'll be right, mate!

THE disintegration of England has been foretold many times by much better qualified judges than Peter (Morbid) Smark (Where It's All Happening And Most Of It Bad).

"There is scarcely anything round us but ruin and despair": William Pitt.

"I thank God I shall be spared from seeing the consummation of ruin that is gathering around": Duke of Wellington, 1851.

"Nothing can save the British Empire from shipwreck": Lord Shaftesbury, 1848.

"Unless our Budget is reduced, we shall languish and decay; we have upon us all the visible marks of a declining people": Davenport, 1699.

"Our revenues mortgaged, our credit sunk, our people exhausted and dispirited": Lyttleton, 1739.

"The endless increase of national debts is the direct road to national ruin": Hume, 1776.

"When America gains independence, the star of England will set and her glories will be eclipsed forever": Shelbourne.

"It would be as easy to bring down a bit of the moon as to light London with gas": Humphry Davy.

But — "The most hopeless hour in England's history has always been the most hopeful:" G. K. Chesterton.

So, not to worry, Peter; she'll be right, mate!

A. C. HADLOW
Toorak Gardens, SA
20/2/68

The Poms

Gauche lout

AS a proud citizen of "that bloody little island off the coast of Europe" that Mr Hawke makes the target of his foul-mouthed abuse, may I say that if his "bloody big island" should ever manage to achieve just 1 per cent of Britain's glory and contribute just 1 per cent of Britain's gifts and example to world justice and civilisation, it will be doing more than well.

However, as your major export to date has been the gauche, uncivilised lout whose language almost matches that of Mr Hawke himself, one doubts very much if the world at large would welcome any Australian contribution to its culture.

RALPH SCOTT-MAINWARING
Windsor, Vic
7/7/76

A big snag

I WAS told before I migrated from England that one of the things I must never do was criticise Australia to an Australian. So I never have done. After all, I can think what I like and say what I please in the privacy of my own home.

But I am not writing on any major issue; oh no, you have plenty of well informed readers doing that, I am just daring to sound off on what I have come to the conclusion is a very minor issue where your sausage makers are concerned: your sausages — they are damned awful. Believe me I have tried plenty and never a decent one among them.

In a country where good food abounds I cannot help but feel that some enterprising sausage maker would benefit greatly from a course on sausage-making in England.

A plate of really first-class sausages would convince me that there is, after all, more smooth than rough in Australia.

(Mrs) E. BRENNAN
Cronulla, NSW
22/8/69

Ashamed

ON behalf of many thousands of us in Britain, I wish all Australians to know that we bow our heads in shame at the disgraceful way you and our other Commonwealth countries are being treated under Edward Heath's immigration bill.

Though a debate in Parliament may alter things somewhat, nothing can hide the fact that continentals are given preference.

We in the anti-Common Market organisations, of which there are over 120, have worked extremely hard to prevent Britain's joining Europe.

We do not forget 1939-45.

(Miss) JOYCE DEAN
Bristol, UK
12/12/72

(The writer is a member of the Bristol Anti-Common Market League.)

The Poms

Sick joke

SOME months ago I returned to live in Australia after an absence of more than 15 years on transfer to my company's London office. I feel I must express my utter disappointment, disillusionment and even disgust at the complete national neglect of any sort of real progress here at home in those years.

The fact that I spent them in Britain — a country which has been constantly and roundly condemned in the Australian media as lazy, bankrupt and generally hopeless, as against my own homeland here with all its self-styled enterprise, energy and national prosperity — led me to believe that I was leaving Inertialand and returning to Utopia.

What a sick joke it all turned out to be. In those 15 years, the mocked-at and written-off British have, for all their very real economic crises, built magnificent new motorways, invented and introduced super-speed luxury rail travel, improved their huge range of social services and tackled 101 socio and economic problems we here have never known.

While here in Australia it is still the same old story of mess, muddle and waste as ever. No matter where one looks, there is virtually nothing to show for that mythical energy and enterprise or for all those very real billions of tax-dollars handed over to our legion of federal and State governments and "empires."

Good God, Australia, we haven't even got one decent national highway worth the name — Melbourne and Sydney are still linked by that medieval monstrosity called the Hume Highway. Here in Melbourne, I even feel and recognise the same old potholes in the same old roads that used to shake my

┌You cad, Sir/Madam!┐

IF I may use a restrained diplomatic term, I thought your editorial of May 2, entitled Male Chauvinism At The British Polls, took the biscuit.

You said that Britain was "giving the world a flawless performance of mass male chauvinism" because the 20 per cent Tory lead in the public opinion polls just over a month ago had been transformed into a neck and neck Labor-Tory struggle.

For lack of logic, this argument would be hard to beat.

Mrs Thatcher was already the nationally-known leader of the Conservative Party when the original polls were taken. So the leadership of a woman was as much responsible for the original 20 per cent lead in the polls as it was for the subsequent supposed decline.

To ascribe the latter to male chauvinism without ascribing the former to an absence of it, is ridiculous.

But, of course, events are an even stronger proof than logic. Now that the British electorate have returned the Conservative Party to power with a woman at the head of it, your allegation of mass male chauvinism has been blown sky high.

I look forward to an honorable admission that you have demonstrably slandered the British electorate and in particular the British male!

If you do not retract gracefully and in a gentlemanly manner, I shall not actually challenge you to a duel; but in that case I think your readers will recognise that male chauvinism resides, not among the British electorate, but in the editorial rooms of *The Australian.*

DONALD TEBBIT
British High Commission
Canberra
8/5/79

EDITOR'S NOTE: As you say, Sir Donald, Mrs Thatcher was a nationally-known leader when the opinion polls showed her with a 20 per cent lead. Then, as the real polling day drew near, people who said they would vote Thatcher fell away in droves, although her performance on the hustings did nothing to warrant this desertion. Strange, that. But we take your point that Mrs Thatcher was eventually elected by a comfortable margin and for this much credit must go to British manhood. So congratulations to the British male. And congratulations to Mrs Thatcher.

car and my frame 15 years ago. What with bridges that either fall down or never get completed, railway rolling stock out of a museum and timetables like Tattslotto in one's chances of satisfaction, septic-tank suburbia,

the same old wooden-box schools, hopelessly inadequate police protection, etc, etc, etc, I am beginning to wonder if I ever went away.

J. R. BISHOP
South Yarra, Vic
4/8/76

The royal Poms

A send-up

THE letter from Mr Ferrers-Guy appears to me to be in itself almost a self-contained script for the Bramston people to utilise.

These verbose old-world ramblings invariably end up in their final thrust with a quotation, which just as invariably as always is a misquotation.

Your correspondent, true to form, quoted Voltaire as saying, "The secret of being a bore is to tell everything."

What the French gentleman actually said was, "The way to be a bore (for an author) is to say everything."

Dear me, how aptly the true quotation turns back and gives Mr Ferrers-Guy a little jab.

If we stay with Voltaire then for the purpose of the exercise, I commend to readers who have been following this send-up of the Queen Mother a quotation contained in the preface of Voltaire's L'Enfant Prodigue — which says, "All styles are good save the tiresome kind."

There was certainly nothing tiresome about the style of the Bramston send-up of the Queen Mother; but, in my opinion, a great deal was tiresome in the style of your correspondent's letter.

Mr Ferrers-Guy finally asks what Voltaire's reaction would have been to the television send-up.

I suggest his statement could possibly have been, "Please do not misquote me and as soon as the Cooma snows start to fall, take a fast dip in the nearest icy river; for it may bring upon you the realisation that we live in 1966 and styles do change."

HARRY M. MILLER
Sydney
25/4/66

Pro the Queen

DONALD Horne in his book, The Lucky Country, states that "to people who are under 35, there is no basis of power, or performance, or reason in the monarchy."

As a member of the age group whose view he so flagrantly misrepresents, I feel compelled to register a strong protest.

Mr Horne has completely ignored the value of the monarchy both as an actual power and as a symbol.

As an institution it serves to protect the rights of the people from the avarice of power-hungry politicians. The symbol of the monarchy is one of the greatest unifying forces of the Commonwealth which, far from being a mere sentimental relic, is of vital importance in the struggle against world communism.

It would serve a far better purpose if people of literary talent would turn their attention to educating youth in the true history and function of the monarchy, rather than subjecting this noble institution to unwarranted derision.

MERLE HORTON
Parkville, Vic
21/12/64

Anti the Queen

MY forebears came from Ireland and a lot of my mates' parents came from Italy. We would lay down our lives for this country, but never in the name of the Queen of England.

Are we traitors? I don't think so. We are more inclined to think that any Australian who swears allegiance to the Queen of England is a traitor to his own Australia.

Those Australians who would still like to be British colonials should start deporting us immediately so that they can have a country which is totally true to its foreign monarch.

JOHN E. O'LEARY
Concord, NSW
14/9/64

Disgusted

AS one who has read your paper since its inception and have always regarded it as a notable and valuable addition to those available in Australia, I am surprised, concerned and disgusted that you should find it proper and necessary to publish, in your issue of October 25, a letter signed by Robert E. Best, which contains such references as it does to the Queen.

To say the least, these display a vulgarity which, to my knowledge as a third-generation Australian, is not a characteristic of the race.

Additionally, to write that "the Queen, after all is said and done, is just a (royal) Pommie" is not only entirely lacking in the chivalry due to a lady (whoever she may be), but overlooks the fact that she is, by law, the Queen of Australia.

A. A. SALTER
Lindisfarne, Tas
9/11/66

The royal Poms

The British Raj and modern Australia

ON the arrival of Queen Elizabeth II, it is reasonable to speculate on the impact the visit will have on Australia.

The visit by our absentee head of State may serve to kindle the issue of whether the British Raj is relevant to modern Australia and whether its un-Australian imprint on our society hinders our search for a national identity and sense of national responsibility.

The popularity of the tour will no doubt influence the policies of our office-bearers for the next few years.

I believe that Elizabeth II should be welcomed as the head of State of a country with which we Australians have had many fine associations — she should be rejected by patriotic Australi-

ans when she comes in the guise of the colonial empress, addressed as Australian head of State, but flying English colors.

Her presence in this role will be an affront to the dignity and worth of our people. That we should view ourselves as people too inferior to provide our own national

Continued next page

The royal Poms

From previous page
leader is a bitter humiliation: that we should look to a foreign aristocracy for inspiration is directly contradictory to our egalitarian principles.

It is true that we owe much to the British people — we owe to those Britishers who had the courage and tenacity to come here and forge this nation.

We owe our allegiance to those Britishers who became Australians and we owe nothing — especially not sycophancy — to those who saw Australia's growth from prison camp to nationhood as an incident they could not prevent.

Observation shows that the British royal family does not consider its responsibilities to Australia important enough to warrant the settling of a member of the family permanently in Australia.

They retain their positions relative to Australia for the benefits and prestige it accrues to Britain — they are British to the bootheels and rightly so.

Let this year be one for discussion of the issue and for positive movement in the direction of our coming-of-age.

We could make a good start by ignoring the royal visit, by supporting the quest for an Australian national anthem and by agitating for the removal of the Union Jack from our flag.

W. SCHIEMER
Mudgee, NSW
1/4/70

The cultural cringe

I WISH to protest, politely, against the opening of the Sydney Opera House by the Queen of England.

I make this protest as an Australian artist and I diffidently but warmly invite other artists, and other Australians, to join me in it.

Lest it be thought that I am some kind of fanatic, I must say that I have nothing against the Queen as the head of State of a friendly foreign power, I merely think that, at this stage of our history, she is wholly irrelevant to Australian art and the life of the country, except to the extent that she symbolises a tie of colonial dependence which continues to harm them.

This is not her fault; the fault is ours that we have persisted in habits of colonial inferiority. The famous cultural cringe has been a baleful fruit of this. Doglike dependence in the past on certain great and powerful friends has been another.

My contention is that sovereignty is indivisible and cannot be effective unless it is complete. You cannot be three-quarters self-confident, or three-quarters free.

Against the contention that the Crown symbolises our origins and tradition, I would say that it has been against this origin and these British traditions that all that is distinctive in Australian life and art have developed. And it will surely be granted that by no means all Australians are of British origin now.

Many people think that symbolic matters are somehow unimportant and that to bother too much about them is un-Australian. Maybe they're right; my own feeling is that while ever we allow our symbolic life to remain ultimately colonial, our national life will remain tinged by dependence, by deference — and by rancorous resentment of those to whom we defer.

For the above reasons, I suggest that, in the absence of an independent head of State in either Australia or NSW, the Opera House be opened officially by either an elected head of government or, better, by an Australian musical artist of distinction.

An even happier idea, of course, would be to regard it as already opened — by music!

LES A. MURRAY
Sydney
12/10/73

Annoyed at frumpish image

I TAKE exception to Pickering's cartoon of March 8, in which he portrays the Queen as frumpy, dumpy and with a double chin.

To my conservative eye, her trim figure is always elegantly and appropriately clad. Imagine the public outcry were she to appear in slit skirts and plunging necklines.

Vive la reine, just as she is.
KATHLEEN HOWE
Yeppoon, Qld
17/3/77

From the heart

I AM writing this from a cell in the guardhouse at Bardia Barracks, Ingleburn, NSW.

The cell is eight shoes long by five shoes wide (about 7ft by 4½ft). It is steel-lined and a draught blows through, and it is cold.

The thick grey paint on the steel hasn't quite obliterated the etchings of some past prisoners: "Pte Anderson goes on strike 21-2-63," "I love Christine" and "The Rebels, '56."

More recently, in the grey paint, a Private Hartwick has declared, "I hate the army" and "Dusty" has made 20 small strokes and the proclamation "one day to go." Wishing to leave my mark also, I've used the inclined edge of a one-cent piece to carve: "Wars will cease when men refuse to fight."

All that scratching filled in a few hours in this lonely, boring hole, but as I survey my handiwork again I wonder vaguely if a soldier was locked up with these eight words for a few days, whether they'd make an impression.

If I didn't believe those words and insist on acting them out, I wouldn't be here now.

Nearly three years ago, I decided I was a pacifist — that I believed war was a crime against humanity, that I could not take part in any war, or preparation for war and that I should help to remove the causes of war.

A few months later I helped establish the Sydney Conscientious Objectors' Group, which helps intending objectors sort out and clarify their thoughts through weekly discussions.

Wars will cease when men refuse to fight

Simon Townsend

During 1966, a magistrate and a judge refused to exempt me from compulsory military service because I was "not sincere." I'd managed to "fool" hundreds of other people, but not those learned men of the Bench.

My family (none of whom are pacifists), friends (a tiny minority who are pacifists), many journalist colleagues and lots of acquaintances, including psychologists, academics, politicians and a few soldiers had all been "fooled."

Driven by this "insincerity," I openly refused to take a medical examination ordered by the Department of Labor and National Service and consequently, in early 1967, I spent a month in Long Bay Jail, Sydney.

I applied again to a magistrate for exemption. He made no judgment on my sincerity, but refused the application on a technicality. I appealed to a judge — who started the case by relating his own war service and telling of his present work for a semi-military organisation — and he declared me, in effect, some kind of giant hoaxer with a martyr complex and a desire to stir up trouble.

During these years, the hoax had included chairing weekly meetings of the objectors' group, extensive reading both for and against pacifism, speaking publicly and writing about my beliefs, and acting as legal representative in court for six other objectors; but what took most time, energy and patience (and probably the most important in the pacifism cause) was the dialogue — when you're a "conshie," everyone wants to know why and most people want to talk it over.

Continuing the "hoax," in February I again refused to take a medical and in March I defied an order to report for military duty. I was charged with these two offences in the Special Federal Court, Sydney, on May 15 and was committed into the custody of an army officer waiting in the court.

I disobeyed his order to accompany him and he called on two Commonwealth police who escorted me, an arm each, to a car outside. On our way to Eastern Command Personnel Depot, Watson's Bay, the officer

Continued next page

From the heart

I am going to see this out . . .

From previous page

told me I was under close arrest.

That night, I slept in a room guarded by eight soldiers, two of whom, in rotation, had to stay awake.

On Thursday, I had a long chat to the army psychologist and did one of those circle- the- yes- or- no- question-mark tests with questions like "Can you stand as much pain as others?" (I circled the question mark. How the hell would I know how much pain others can stand? From movies? And does standing pain mean without wincing, without crying, before fainting.

The psychologist thought I was pretty stable. My consciencious objection was an administrative matter, he said.

A little later, the regimental sergeant major ordered me to draw and sign for army clothes. I refused. He told me the possible consequences of disobeying could be imprisonment and ordered me again to draw the clothes, and again I refused.

A summary of evidence was taken by the officer-in-command and I was remanded for court martial.

On Thursday evening, I was brought, in a cage on the back of a utility truck, to Ingleburn and locked in this cell.

My continual requests that my family be told of my whereabouts were politely noted, to be referred to someone higher up who was always "away" or "busy" or "trying."

I realised I was being kept incommunicado to avoid any publicity or demonstrations.

I was getting pretty miserable. No one was allowed to converse with me, I had nothing to read but a book of psalms, no pen or paper and I was kept locked up except for shower time, and three short exercise periods a day.

Then late Saturday, my younger brother and the girl I'm to marry turned up. My brother had sought help from Gough Whitlam and the member for East Sydney, Len Devine, and eventually the Army Minister, Mr Lynch, had ordered they be allowed to see me.

Suddenly I was allowed book and writing equipment. I'd refused to wear a uniform or army pyjamas and so had been living day and night in one suit and one set of underwear; this morning, Sunday, my girl friend returned with fresh clothes.

Except for a flustered officer who took a stick from under his arm to shake it in my face, and say loudly, "You're in the army now, son, and it's 'Yes SIR'," I can't complain about the soldiers I've come in contact with, who have treated me as fairly as possible.

I wish not to dwell on the absence of principles of British justice in the Australian Army, but this taking away a man's privileges before he's convicted seems an incredible infringement.

Personally, I'm resentful that I've been placed in close arrest instead of open arrest (which means I am trusted to stay in the barracks) when I have given every indication that I have no intention of escaping.

I am going to see this out. I have never intended to and I never will obey military orders. The army doesn't want me, of course, but it can't "lose face" by dishonorably discharging me now.

I expect a sentence in Holsworthy Prison and maybe even further court martials and sentences.

The "hoax" goes on . . .

SIMON TOWNSEND
Potts Point, NSW
22/5/68

PS

IF aliens are to be given the choice of being conscripted for military service or leaving the country, then surely it is only fair to offer the same choice to our own boys.

KEN NOLAN
Chadstone, Vic
25/8/66

IWASMO stint erested in y our news pap erre port of Aug819 77 onthe Quee n's vis itto Northern Ire land. I pre sume fromyour referenceto "soldiersan dpo licewill" tha tit wascom posed byajap anese mig rantty pe setter ofiri shori gin. An yway itwaso ne ofthe mostinter esting of fart icles Iha veread recently.

P. BAYLY-JONES
Hawthorn, SA
17/8/77

WE do TRY to correct all the literals before we go to press, but gremlins will be gremlins. It was corrected in the second edition and thanks for the laugh -EDITOR.

From the heart

Are we celebrating mass hypocrisy?

OBSERVATION and meditation of the events occurring during the recent Christmas period confirms the opinion that the origin of this celebration is entirely lost to Christianity.

Perusal of the daily press leads one deeper and deeper into gloom and cynicism, as the realisation grows of the absolute lack of sincerity of humanity in general.

During this time we have been informed that:

(1) Prison breaks, murders, rapes and brawls are prevalent.

(2) Concern is expressed over the ease with which under-age persons of both sexes are served with intoxicating liquors in bars and bottle departments, and the orgies indulged in consequent to the titillation obtained from these beverages.

(3) A gentleman, 16 years of age, has expressed an opinion that "drink and sex are now **in**; otherwise one is not **with it.**"

(4) Cripplings and fatalities on roads are increasing steadily due to the lack of co-operation by everybody.

(5) Derelictions of duty among officers of law enforcement are continually being uncovered.

(6) Alarm is expressed at the rate at which Australia's minerals and industries (light, heavy and primary) are being "sold out."

(7) America is preparing to escalate the war in Vietnam, under cover of unacceptable peace proposals, in order to spread further the terror (depicted in photographs) of women and children caught in barrages of artillery shells, high-explosive and napalm bombs.

(8) Americans of doubtful qualification are welcomed, with open arms, as migrants; while colored persons of high qualifications are denied admission to the country.

(9) Dr Subandrio is quoted as having expressed interest in the discussion between President Johnson and Mr Wilson concerning the role to be played by Australia in the defence of South-East Asia.

He asks, with understandable amazement: "Where was Australia?"

Complaints are registered that toys in the shape of death-dealing weapons are being conspicuously offered for sale and that pre-Christmas spending was most satisfactory.

In culmination, one sees published in the daily press a photograph of a Christian South Vietnamese kicking at a prone Viet Cong prisoner under the casual observation of some Christian Americans — who, by their facial expressions, could not care less.

Adjacent to this is the information that the Pope is appealing for peace in Vietnam and enlisting the aid of Russia (with trust) and China (without trust).

Headlines, above all this, proclaim the recipients of New Year honors, among them some, who in my opinion, could have a measure of responsibility in the foregoing.

By now, thoroughly nauseated, one is convinced that Christmas has become the celebration of a mass hypocrisy.

W. H. BROND
Yarrawonga, Vic
12/1/66

Why I left the Church

AS one of those "runaway priests" attacked by the Pope recently (reported in *The Australian,* 10/4), I feel an obligation to speak up briefly.

I speak out not only to explain my own position, but also for many other priests who in recent years have slipped away quietly from the priesthood or from the Church with grievances unaired and their situation unclarified in the eyes of the average Catholic.

Why did I, as a priest, leave the Church? Basically for the same reasons that laymen leave the Church — because I found the Church to be no longer a helpful or credible framework in which to live my life.

The question is an even more urgent one for the priest than for the layman.

For some time, I was content to explain that I did not agree with this or that decision of my bishop or Church. Then the day came when I realised that by wearing a collar and calling myself a priest, I was identifying myself so much with injustice and narrow-minded conformity that no amount of explaining could excuse the compromise.

I received my first indications of these gross defects in the Church's practice in the seminary.

The bitterness and heartbreak of seven years in such a loveless community as the seminary has to be suffered to be believed: all the machinery of friend informing against friend, the subtle spiritual weapons of making minor breaches of rule **Continued next page**

From the heart

A 'runaway priest's' view

From previous page
"sins," conformity being equated with virtue and those who left the seminary being branded as spiritual inferiors.

I struggled on to ordination in the hope that the seminary was an anachronism, that outside the Christian virtues of love and justice would still be flowering in the Church in which I was to work.

Great was my disillusionment: when I started in parish work, I found the same authoritarianism, but this time structuring the whole Church from the bishop down.

My first open conflict with my bishop came over my opposition to the war in Vietnam. Now accepted as a commonplace, the public opposition of a priest to the war was, in 1967, an event of public interest.

In the interviews with my bishop, when I was called in to explain myself, his arguments could be reduced to the following: that the greatest evil in the world today, apart from mortal sin, was communism and that opposition to the war in Vietnam was wrong because it meant support for communism.

When I tentatively suggested that we could not abandon a good cause simply because communists supported it, he came out with the incredible statement that anything that communists did was evil. I realised then that I was not dealing with a reasonable man.

Another great cause of conflict for me was with the Church's position on sexual morality. Apart from the large families living in squallor and young mothers unable to cope, I think that in my experience of the effects of the Church's teaching on birth control the saddest were several cases of men with five or six children being caused to masturbate rather than have intercourse with their wives and then feeling guilty about masturbating.

As chaplain to a Catholic boys' high school, I also experienced the terrible feeling of guilt that is built up by the Church's attitude that masturbation is a serious sin. Some boys who had this habit, recognised now as quite normal in adolescence, were nervous, extremely unhappy and ridden with guilt because they had been told that they were sinners.

Because of the Church's attitude to divorce, homosexuality and abortion, I also saw needless suffering being caused and I soon came to the conclusion that as the Church had caused so much damage in these areas, it would have been better if she had had nothing to say.

My decision to dissociate myself from the Church has been a completely liberating one — many other priests have experienced this recently and I am glad for them, too. I have not applied and do not intend to apply, for any official release from the priesthood, since I do not believe that the Church has the power to bind a person in any way.

Many of my friends who have left the priesthood and yet wish to remain in the Church have been subjected to various indignities. In order to apply for a dispensation from celibacy and be free to marry, one has to answer in detail questions about all sexual activity since reaching puberty.

The purpose of such information, apart from the titillation of a dirty old monsignor, eludes me.

Looking back at the Church from my vantage point, I see it now as a power structure with very little relationship to Christianity. It is conservative and conformist by its very nature, for its existence depends upon conformity to the status quo.

It is reactionary in its attitudes as it has been throughout history, decrying social and moral reform as evil supporting the most outmoded world-view current.

CHARLES BOWERS
Casula, NSW
3/5/71

PS

THE enclosed letter was signed by 3472 concerned Australians since the Tasmanian Government's decision to hold a referendum on the future of Tasmania's south-west wilderness. As the area is of national importance, like the Great Barrier Reef, we think that ALL Australians should have a say in whether the area is destroyed or not.

MICHAEL FOGARTY
Tasmanian Wilderness Society
Melbourne
5/10/81

From the heart

Racial hatred at the rugby

I AM an Aboriginal Australian employed in a responsible position in the Commonwealth Office of Aboriginal Affairs at Canberra.

Throughout my life, I have been proud of my ancestry and have been a keen participant in sporting activities.

In fact, I have played 20 years of first-grade soccer, often against international and interstate teams.

I wish to comment on an incident which took place in Sydney during the match between South Africa and New South Wales recently.

On this particular occasion, a group of Aborigines, including myself, decided to attend the game merely as spectators.

We are obviously not supporters of apartheid, but felt it necessary that we should get some impression of the atmosphere of these games.

We were absolutely amazed at some of the incidents we witnessed. These were:

1. The vicious and deep-seated racial intolerance and hatred displayed by the overwhelming majority of rugby union supporters in the section of the crowd where we stood.

The demonstrators were merely the catalyst (or the excuse) for this expression of racial hatred, which was horrible to witness.

There seems justification for the claim that rugby union creates animals — and not sportsmen or gentlemen.

To the rugby supporter, the continuation of the game justifies the existence of slavery and deprivation of personal freedoms — in fact, anything goes providing the game goes on uninterrupted.

2. The action of rugby union vigilantes, or self-elected strong-arm groups,
who were intent upon doing physical damage to anyone who dared challenge apartheid or the playing of rugby.

I saw these "sportsmen" of doubtful courage throw cans of beer and other hard objects into crowds of young people — not all of them demonstrators.

It was disgraceful behavior and does not say much for the game of rugby union.

3. And finally, as we Aborigines were leaving the ground before the game concluded, to escape the rush of the crowd, several sections of the crowd saw us and began hurling abuse.

We were called "dirty niggers" and "black bastards" and told to "go to Africa where you belong."

The name-calling was serious and upset us very much. We were challenged on numerous occasions to fight and people continued to use filthy language against us
for no other reason than that we were Aborigines.

We were absolutely disgusted with our fellow Australians.

I really thought white people in this country and Aborigines had come closer together over the past 10 years. In fact, racial intolerance is still rampant, but seems more sophisticated and deep-seated.

If the rest of Australia thinks and behaves similarly to most rugby union supporters, then we have no future but one of unhappy race relations.

My plea is that we should not relive recent terrible American racial experiences.

We have a wonderful opportunity to create the good society and I feel such an opportunity should not be ignored.

CHARLES PERKINS
Hughes, A.C.T.
22/7/71

The death of Lake Pedder

I'M sitting here in Sydney listening to the rain. And I know that it must be raining in south-west Tasmania.

And the water is quietly filling up behind the unfinished Serpentine River Dam. Already the swollen Serpentine is breaking its banks and confused possums, wildcats and wallabies are moving off to battle for new niches in a habitat where there are no niches to spare.

Another month's rain and the swamps around Crumbledown will be a vast sheet of water. Another month again and Lake Pedder — Australia's most beautiful lake — will have disappeared. With it will have gone sweet
Lake Maria and a host of little reed-fringed pools and bushy thickets.

In 40 years' bushwalking, I have never seen native wildcats except at Lake Pedder. They were fed by hand by our party and they clambered over us in our sleeping bags like domestic cats.

In the morning their tracks sprinkled the marvellous Pedder beach. In two, three months, they will be dead.

Destruction of Lake Pedder, Lake Maria and their wildlife is nothing more than a plain bloody outrage. It is being perpetrated by the most philosophically backward and arrogant bu-
Continued next page

From the heart

Lake Pedder

From previous page

reaucratic machine in Australia — the Hydro-Electric Commission. The commission still talks of conquering the wilderness while the rest of the world talks of preserving the little left of it.

The HEC obviously aims to put dams on all the major rivers of Tasmania, irrespective of their effect on the natural river systems, on scenery, fisheries, wildlife or forestry. It will submerge $50 million worth of timber with the Gordon Scheme.

Its assessment of the costs of various alternatives are false. The Gordon Scheme is simply uneconomic. If indeed any more power is needed in Tasmania, it can be provided more quickly, with smaller capital outlay and at cheaper rates from coal or oil-burning stations located near the sources of demand.

The Gordon River Road, which gives access to the Gordon Scheme dams, was built largely with Commonwealth funds. It is an environmental disgrace — a vast series of untidy and eroding gashes.

But Lake Pedder can be saved. The 100,000 fee-paying members of conservation societies must surely feel that preservation of Australia's best wilderness area is worth a visit to their federal parliamentary representative.

They should be persuaded that we will not only **vote against,** but actively **campaign against,** politicians who support the use of federal funds for environmental savagery of this order.

Why should Australians listen to the rain in growing anger and shame?

MILO DUNPHY
Sydney, NSW

(The writer is honorary secretary of the Colong Committee.)

19/1/72

The right to be allowed to die

I WRITE to express the feelings of a grandmother with a grandson born prematurely with severe spina bifida and hydrocephalus.

Without any treatment (that is humidicrib, oxygen, tube feeding and operations), he would probably have died, but once such a child is put on the conveyor belt of the preservation process it cannot be stopped.

He is now three years old. He will never walk, never have control of his bowels or urine, never have any sexual powers. He has a squint and needs glasses.

With splints on his legs, he is able to sit up and shuffle very slowly a short distance. He can talk, but movements of his hands are jerky.

He is as yet unaware of his plight, but in a few years he will probably wonder bitterly why he was born thus and was allowed to live.

His mother is required to take him to six different clinics — spina bifida, neurological, orthopedic, urological, psychiatric and physiotherapy.

Two full fares on public transport must be paid as the child, heavier as he grows older and already very heavy in his splints, can only be conveyed in a pusher.

Help must be obtained to care for his younger brother and baby sister during frequent lengthy absences, or all three taken to hospital (a formidable task) and the toddler and baby left in the hospital creche.

A charge of $1.80 is made for each attendance and none of this is recoverable from benefit funds. The child requires callipers, special boots, standing frame, urine bags and adhesive for them, and even at subsidised rates the cost is heavy.

Getting the child up in the morning and putting him to bed at night with the necessary attention to his various appliances is a lengthy, laborious process. His normal brother and sister are deprived of their fair share of attention.

I sit on the sidelines seeing the physical, emotional and financial problems that his survival puts on his parents and I can say nothing. There is nothing one can say which would help. I must even ask that my name be withheld so as not to distress my daughter and son-in-law still further.

But I can ask here whether all this skill of modern medicine, surgery, nursing and physiotherapy is misplaced in such a case.

Not only does it perpetuate a burden to the child himself and to his whole family, but the cost to the community is enormous. Skill misused in this way is bad medically: bad for the individuals concerned and bad for the whole community.

Children who are born with a severe incurable defect and whose expectation of life would be short without special treatment should be given nothing but the normal care of a normal baby.

They have the right to be allowed to die.

"GRANDMOTHER"
Melbourne

(Full name and address supplied and withheld by request.)

1/8/74

From the heart

Goodbye and God help you!

TEN years ago my wife and I and our two children — then a toddler and a baby — came to this country as migrants from Britain. Next month we are going back home and we shall never return to Australia. There is nothing remarkable nor unusual about that, but having wasted a decade of our lives, I would at least appreciate the chance to get even a few of our disillusionments and frustrations off my chest.

We came to this country believing it to be young, vigorous and promising a much better future for us and for our children in particular. After 10 years here, I leave convinced that Australia is at best a circus run and peopled by clowns and at worst a gigantic lunatic-asylum with half the patients running about in ever-diminishing circles and the other half apathetic zombies.

It didn't take us long to appreciate the truth of the "private affluence, public poverty" tag on Australian society. Behind the facade of prosperity lay the massive neglect of basic community services taken for granted in the other developed countries — roads, education, medical services, care for the aged and so on. I shall never forget seeing the installation of a sewer rating newspaper headlines. And yet there has always been ready money for racetracks, football stands and the like. Good grief — what priorities do you people stand for?

When we arrived and for five years thereafter, we tolerated the plan-nothing, do-nothing, change-nothing euphemistic "Liberals" who had been in power so long they were clearly responsible for the appalling lack of public facilities. Then, in 1972, we, too, decided "It's Time" and helped to hand Australia over to Super-Ego and his motley band of back-stabbing, loan-scrounging, mud-wallowing amateurs who not only emptied the national treasury, but made Australia a bigger laughing stock than ever.

So, in 1975, we, too, swallowed the Fraser "we have the economic answers and policies" bait and voted in this cold, wooden divine-righter and what happens?

After 18 months floundering around, he has Australia in as big a mess as ever, has bled even the few social services we did have, has crucified Medibank in the interests of the AMA, pushed us into devaluation "to help exports" — which it hasn't done one whit, but cost us all millions (in money-value), and now his super-rabbit-out-of-the-hat is this unbelievably naive and stupid three-month price and wage freeze; something which has been tried and failed in a dozen other countries and long since abandoned as useless. What the hell does the wretched man think will happen at the end of the three months — is he blind, or is his Government so policy-bankrupt that they will grasp at anything? Is this the great measure he promised us to cure inflation and unemployment?

So, there we are. We have sat here for 10 years watching an army of utter mediocrities come and go in power and manage to bankrupt what should be one of the most fortunate lands on earth, with a super-abundance of natural riches, no inherent racial conflicts and everything going for it.

I do not have the time, nor you the space, to go into the so-called "education" my children have received here, the suburban wildernesses we have lived in, the glorification of the ocker and the foul-mouthed, and the whole lousy picture that adds up to 10 years' waste and boredom.

This I do promise. If it is ever within my power to help prevent others from selling their native birthright for a mess of Australian pottage, be sure I shall do just that. Goodbye Australia — and God help you!

CHARLES KEMP
Blackburn, Vic
25/4/77

AS an Australian who has been living overseas for the past 14 years, two of which were recently spent in New York, I should like to comment on the noble sentiments expressed by Mr John L. Gilbert. Actually it would seem that the "strident selfish arrogant forces" appear to be emanating from the

A selfish society

"elected representatives of the people."

Could it be the qualities of selfishness, complacency and laziness which have permeated the Australian way of life stem from a superimposed cult of materialistic, unethical values set by the media? Where uncouth ockerism is considered more acceptable in advertising than the "concise Oxford English" used by our forebears.

Continued next page

From the heart

Breakdown in our values

I WOULD like to point out that the germs of the "new British disease" (your editorial, 15/7) have spread to this continent.

We have passed the prodromal stages with all the signs and symptoms, viz, the behavior of mobs at pop concerts, Riverina motor races, Newcastle pub, political meetings and even on the Sydney Cricket Ground.

The unemployment, color and larger population in England may make it worse, but as you said they are not the real causes of it.

Let me suggest to you that the causes are philosophical and when this philosophy was put into practice the "new British disease" was the rational outcome of it.

We, and especially our children, have been subjected to incessant bombardment of philosophies over the past 30 or so years which told us that we have no power over our own fates and that we must be all equal.

We can see these philosophies everywhere around us now. Our and our children's ideas were subverted to such a degree that we accept rubbish in art, irrationality in education, injustice in law, theft in economics and pragmatism in politics.

How else could the thousands of cricket-loving fans accept the degrading searches after the incidents with the drunken louts on the Sydney Cricket Ground — who went free themselves?

How else can you explain the clamor for more strict gun controls on all law-abiding citizens, while most thefts are not even investigated, the courts allow the rapists and robbers to get away with next to nothing and even murderers may be out of jail after some five years?

Can you see how our values were distorted over the past 20 years?

What values can our children have when they know that the politicians are eager to donate them "rights" to anything for nothing except enough votes?

Why should they bother to work when they know that for two thirds of their working life they will be working like slaves for nothing because the Government will rip it off them in one way or another?

The real question is: Why shouldn't your children be part of a looting mob in a society like this? It pays to be a rat.

(Dr) R. I. PLACHY
Millicent, SA
21/7/81

Basic lack of concern for others

From previous page
Where smutty jokes in bad taste are permitted on peak viewing time on TV.

Is it any wonder that our children are unable to spell or express themselves coherently when subjected to this mindless babbling, which quite frankly is an insult to one's intelligence? It is really a question of priorities. Maybe it is just that as a nation we have lost our identity and with that a sense of reality. Australians have allowed themselves to be manipulated.

Our intolerance stems from the immature Australian attitude towards our migrant population, whom we need as a workforce. Peoples whose cultures and heritages date back thousands of years are derogatorily called "Poms," "Wops," "Dagos" and this is indicative of the ocker intolerance, a deplorable characteristic, which does not endear us to people of other nationalities.

I look at the country I knew and loved as a child, which has been raped of its beauty by economic greed, miles of used car lots, junk take away food; semi-illiterate teenagers without job potential, lacking incentive or self-worth; the despised "dole bludgers," maybe victims of an inadequate educational system; the old people who now eke out their meagre pensions in some gloomy room, robbed of dignity in their declining years; people caught up in a mesh of bureaucratic bungling and inefficiency.

It indeed makes me sad to see the basic lack of human concern which has worked its way insidiously into this society. Masses of people being manipulated, imposing a false sense of values, where it is no longer acceptable to do an honest day's work any more.

The rivers and seas are polluted with industrial waste, cancer-forming agents, dogs are allowed to foul the pavements while the very air we breathe is unacceptable due to traffic smog. Crimes of violence are commonplace, muggings, murder and rape an everyday occurrence. Perhaps we should look to our way of life before we become too insensitive to the basic human rights of others.

MARGARET MUIR
Surfers Paradise, Qld
6/7/77

From the heart

Tracey: constant pride to a very grateful father

I RECOGNISE that stirring sewage only makes it smell worse, but I am prepared to pay that price to comment on media reports that Tracey Wickham boasted that she would have beaten Michelle Ford in the 800m freestyle.

I know Tracey reasonably well. To the best of my knowledge, I helped start her off in life. I then had the opportunity to watch her closely for almost all of her nearly 18 years. So I feel as well-qualified as any journalist to comment on any remarks she is reported to have made.

Boasting is not the hallmark of a champion and I have never heard Tracey Wickham make one boast in her short life. She was taught very early in her career that swimming races are won in swimming pools not in the cesspools of newspapers. Her achievements in that regard are a matter of record.

It had also been continually impressed on her from almost day one that the day would certainly arrive when the same press that hailed her would turn against her. Despite that preparation, she was not ready when the day arrived. Alas and alack!

Difficult to believe isn't it, that despite her globe-trotting experiences representing her country at Olympic and Empire Games and world championships, and doing nothing else but bring great glory to her country, she should remain so girlish and naive as not to be able to deal coolly, calmly and professionally with the vultures of Australia's media, and she is almost 18 years of age!

Time and again that poor unsuspecting little girl has been reduced to tears as Australia's journalistic elite have distorted and twisted and edited her answers to their loaded questions, so

Tracey Wickham

that the only thing the truth and the reports had in common was the English language. Imagine at 17 years of age not being able to see through their plausible guile. How could a girl get to be her age and still be so unsophisticated and trusting of human nature? She will probably pass the same qualities on to her children. How sad.

See the pitiful spectacle we present to an unbelieving world, Australia. See how in one foul media swoop, we de-grade one of our finest champions and representatives of this decade and make her look like a sour-grapes loser. How unsightly!

But worse still. Look how by the same deed we diminish the glory of the thoroughly deserved victory of a new champion who won an individual gold medal in Olympic record time. Where else in the world would a media be so pathetic as to divert attention away from Michelle Ford's proudest moment?

She earned the top step on the podium and deserves nothing but our salutes and tributes. Nothing else is relevant — not even the opinion of Tracey Wickham.

I salute you, Michelle, and your family, too, because I have an insight into the price they paid to allow you to express your talent into the ultimate sporting victory.

And I know that Tracey does, too. I also know, because I know Tracey, that any competitiveness she feels toward you outside of the sporting arena is a figment of the imagination of a very sick media.

As for you, Tracey Wickham, you have been a source of constant pride to a very grateful father. For your sporting achievements certainly, but mainly because you are a wonderful, warm human being who has served her country well, been generous to a fault with your time to all sorts of organisations, oblivious to any form of compensation, a wonderful sister and daughter and an example to all those potential champions coming on.

You are a real champion, Tracey, and you do not have to justify yourself to anybody else. So do not bother.

I salute you.

ROGER WICKHAM
Marrickville, NSW
5/8/80

Women

No choice but to work

NAN Wheeler's I'm All For the Home Life (3/3) is typically middle class. She writes solely from the economic viewpoint of a minority of Australian women. To her, there is actually a choice for married women; whether to stay at home or go to work.

The grim fact for the vast majority of working wives is that they have no choice. For heaven's sake, let's be real about this. The never-ending increases in the cost of living are forcing countless thousands of wives and mothers to work outside the home, willy-nilly. Outside the cocoon of the class of women who choose to enter the business world, in an-swer to taunts about contributing their bit to society, is the vast army of women driven desperate by the losing battle to keep their homes going, clothe and educate their children and insure against sickness and accident on only one pay envelope, the husband's.

If they're lucky, they enter the business world, as humble clerks and typists; if they're not, they get varicose veins from endless monotonous hours standing behind shop counters, operating machines in canning factories, working as bus conductresses, railway porteresses, as door-knocking saleswo-men — anything, any kind of a job, that will relieve the crushing load of worry and debt from their overburdened husbands.

And always the constant nagging worry about the wellbeing of the children during mother's enforced absences from home.

For many of them, the only hope of release from this slavery of running both a home and a job and to be able to retire permanently to the haven of being just housewives and mothers, is to win a State lottery.

(Mrs) B. E. JONES
Kings Cross, NSW
9/3/65

Women enjoy many advantages

I REFER to your letter, Australian Women 2nd Class Citizens, (7/10). The three angry misses from Queensland University have not fully grasped the complexity of the problem they have tackled.

When the position of women in Australia needs changing, it will be changed in the same way as all other social changes have come in Australia — democratically and with a minimum of opposition, in this case from the males (myself included).

Changes in the relationship of the sexes must occur, but the problem will not be solved by simply raising the wages of females, having them do the same physical work, or making it legal for them to drink in bars.

Women enjoy numerous advantages over men under the present system. Far more women are able to go overseas than men, who have to think of their careers.

Economically, the average woman finds herself well provided for and with little or no worries about a career or the future.

When women are prepared to swap insults and crudities with men; when they are prepared to pay their way when they are taken out; when they are compelled by society to aim at careers and to support or share in the support of families; when, in fact, the social structure, ideals and norms of our society have considerably changed, then and only then will women drink in public bars and receive equal pay.

ROBIN PERCY
Harbord, NSW
15/10/64

┌─ **PS** ─

THE award of an MBE to the Beatles strikes me as most deplorable. Teenagers should be able to look to their elders for authority, wisdom and dignity; instead we find a shameful pandering which we did not seek and do not want.

EILEEN HALEY
Paddington, Qld
23/6/65

Working wives

A social evil? No!

IN a report in *The Australian* of March 30, Judge Hits At Working Mother," Mr Justice Bridge deemed it necessary to let off a fusillade of deplorable words against the working mother.

We have three young children, aged from eight to 11, and my wife is a working mother, but, to repeat Mr Justice Bridge's words, she does not constitute a grave social evil nor does she contribute to juvenile delinquency.

Why does my wife work? For fun perhaps? No, Mr Justice Bridge, she works not for the fun or thrill of it, but she works to help meeting the ever increasing cost of living, educating and clothing the children. They are, I am proud to say, better behaved, reliable, unspoiled and able to do some household chores, unlike many other children whose mothers are not working.

Recently, the Judiciary had their salary again substantially increased, the amount of this increase alone representing approximately 50 per cent of my annual income. According to newspaper reports, the weekly income of the Judiciary ranges between £120 to £150. My weekly income is something over £20.

WERNER SCHMIDLIN
Edmonton North, Qld
6/4/65

Restore home life

I BELIEVE the Barrier Industrial Council of Broken Hill is on the right track in compelling married women to resign in favor of single girls.

The basic wage is computed on the cost of living of man, wife and three children.

On that basis, there is no need for a married woman to compete against single girls.

I don't want to stick my neck out, but in the main, the extra money earned by the wife does not go into housekeeping, but rather to enjoy the amenities of club life.

As I see it, the replacement of home life by club life is the root cause of our weakened society.

None will deny that home today is just a place to sleep in.

Economics do not enter into it. We are an affluent society.

As an old unionist, allow me to say this: There was always a fear that women competing against men would, through a lower wage, destroy the whole fabric of arbitration — hence, the provision for a basic wage including the wife and three children.

With the restitution of home life, a sick society would automatically return to normal.

C. P. CARSON
Trangie, NSW
25/10/67

Cheap labor

I HAVE been asked by my council to express its views on the proposal made by the Minister for Labor and National Service, Mr McMahon, that female employment be increased to augment the work force.

Mr McMahon is reported as saying that he could see no reason why many jobs, which are traditionally regarded as male preserves, should not be done by women; and he advocated that the attitude to employment of married women should be changed.

My council says that if women are to be employed they should receive equal pay for the job performed. The trade union movement and white collar associations have been to Mr McMahon only to find that he and his Government have stubbornly refused to follow the lead of many enlightened countries.

If his proposition leads to employment of women on the cheap at the expense of family life and general wage and salary standards, it deserves rejection.

(Miss) L. BARBER
Deputy Chairwoman
National Equal Pay
Committee
Australian Council of
Salaried
and Professional
Associations
6/9/65

PS

AS an evacuee of Darwin, I would like to express my family's appreciation of the kindness and courtesy we received in Sydney. The staff and volunteer helpers at the airport, our overnight stop, were just great. We would never have been able to cope without their help and patience. Thanks to you all.

ELIZABETH WYATT
Darwin
6/1/75

Working wives

Idiotic myth on work

IT is a long time since I have read such a socially divisive and dangerous statement as that which occured at the beginning of your feature article on unemployment in *The Weekend Australian* of January 14-15.

It is unfortunate that the authors of the article chose, so early in it, to perpetrate the idiotic myth that working mothers, ipso facto, deprive their children (or anyone else's) of a job. Why not blame working fathers, particularly those holding down two jobs, one of which is lucrative because it is worked at night and over the weekend, or at any other time which enables them to benefit from penalty rates?

Certainly much of the blame for youth unemployment can be laid at the feet of teachers and parents who, for whatever reason, have brought their students and children up ill-equipped to cope with a society which is basically competitive, where responsibilities have to be accepted, standards maintained and goals striven for.

I strongly object, however, to the suggestion that all unemployment problems will be solved if the married woman goes back to what the article seems to suggest is her proper place: namely the kitchen sink. This idea is stupid, discriminatory and as sexist as the heading to the article which reads, If Mum Quit Work, There'd Be Jobs For The Boys (And Girls), as if somehow girls had less right to be employed than boys and are merely an afterthought in the unemployment problem.

The sooner it is acknowledged and accepted that the right to work is not determined by one's age or sex or marital status, but rather by one's ability and willingness to do the job, the better.

JANINE HAINES
Senator for South
Australia
25/1/78

Women cannot go back

B. A. SANTAMARIA (24/9) is fighting a losing battle. We can't turn the clock back. Over one-third of the Australian work force is female and three-quarters of that figure are married women. The family is endemic to all societies. Its fragmentation is not caused by working mums.

There is a mountain of statistics which point out that delinquent children do not come from the families of working mums. On the contrary, working women of the middle class invariably have interests outside their homes and work areas, and their children benefit from a mother who is something other than "servant" to her family.

Mr Santamaria should turn his attention to the thousands of depressed women in our society, particularly ethnic groups, who are factory fodder in the clothing and food industries, and who need his eloquent support far more than do the middle-class working mothers of Australia who are probably the current props of Malcolm Fraser's shaky economic philosophy of "Spend more — with confidence."

MARY WILCOX
Aspley, Qld
6/10/76

Give up your job

PHILIP Cornford's excellent article, Cancer in Australia's Industrial Heart (30/7), is appropriately hard-hitting in its description of the hopelessness of young people desperately trying to get a job.

Perhaps *The Australian* could do a survey of two-income families in the Newcastle area — and in other cities — where the wives of highly paid tradesmen, executives and professional men are working outside the home for a wage. These women, whose worry is more the cost of high living than the high cost of living, should take a long, hard look into their conscience and think how soul-destroying it is for a school-leaver, eager for independence, to be loafing around feeling useless and unwanted.

I would like to suggest to every women whose husband is capable of supporting her and her children that she vacates that job which gives her morale a boost, but that she doesn't really financially need.

In this way, she can rescue the morale of an unemployed boy or girl, man or woman — and contribute to the wellbeing of the whole community.

Could your paper lead the way, which it is doing in so many worthwhile areas these days, in putting out a clarion call to all working women who do not need the money to give up their jobs in favor of the jobless? There are many stimulating, exciting voluntary jobs to do in the community.

(Mrs) S. M. WILLIAMS
Canterbury, Vic
4/8/76

Women

We are being exploited

I AM a woman who earns three-quarters of the equivalent male rates of pay and who pays fees, rent and fares at the same rate as men, so I must disagree with your correspondent (Women's Place, 15/10) who stated that economically the average woman finds herself well provided for.

While these disparities continue, women will be exploited, not only as workers, but as consumers. One-quarter of all adult women in Australia are members of the work force, which suggests that a large proportion of married women either contribute to the support of their families, or support their families entirely.

The adoption of equal pay is urgently needed, not only to establish firmly the status of women in a free and democratic community, but to demonstrate their true value in the work force.

V. McKENZIE
South Yarra, Vic
22/10/64

Women's rights

Women's voices must be heard

WHY do we retain our backward attitudes to Australian women?

Because Australian women are apathetic.

But ask them to organise money-raising activities for charity and they are whipped into a fanatical frenzy, selling home-made cakes and preserves, hand-knitted garments, dolls etc.

In the six State Parliaments, a total of 496 seats (Upper and Lower Houses), there are a mere 10 women members.

Nominations were called recently by a political party

for the Tasmanian House of Assembly, and, as far as I can ascertain, there was not even one woman candidate.

They have no hesitation in forming committees to pool their efforts and make their voices heard in their own area.

When will the Australian Parliament ratify the International Labor Convention on equal pay for men and women for work of equal value?

I answer: "When will Australian women pool their efforts and do some-

thing really constructive towards this end?"

In Federal Parliament, there are only five women senators out of a total of 60 seats; in the Lower House, two members out of a total of 124.

In order to achieve equal pay for men and women for work of equal value, women must make their voices heard in places other than local committee meeting rooms.

(Miss) M. H. McLACHLAN
Hobart, Tas
26/9/67

Feminist, a dirty word?

CAN anyone supply a definition of a feminist? Why has it become such a dirty word with a lot of people?

For nigh on 40 years, our association has been working on the assumption that a feminist (he could be a man) is someone who desires and expects women to take their part in the community on an equal footing with men in regard to both privileges and responsibilities.

Why, then, do so many women state publicly "I am not a feminist but . . . " or "I am opposed to feminism

but . . . ." and immediately go on to enumerate all the points of view that a good feminist really does hold.

Perhaps the word contains some overtones of a hangover from a witch-hunting past which imagined feminists to be some sort of female viragos, stomping the countryside ranting their man-hating doctrines.

M. CHRISTIAN
President
United Associations
of Women
Sydney
15/4/68

Male bastion

THE recent remarks of the Governor-General, Lord De L'Isle, on the backwardness of Australian women in public life deserve some notice.

The majority of Australian women feel they are not backward and the real truth is that in public life, in the spheres that really matter, Australia speaks with a masculine voice.

The absence of women in Parliament is due to a combination of causes, but no one ever hears of a "safe" seat being reserved for a woman candidate.

Appointments to boards are almost entirely male: e.g. the Martin Commission and others of similar nature are always male.

Maybe the Governor-General, before he leaves Australia, could suggest to Sir Robert Menzies that this belittling of women should cease.

L. G. WOODCOCK
President
United Association of
Women
Sydney
12/4/65

The dullest creatures imaginable

AS a recent arrival by way of the United States, it was interesting to read Mr S. Nihal Singh's article (*The Australian*, May 13)

I was especially delighted to note his mention of the segregation of the sexes here, as this is one of the strongest criticisms I have of the way of life in Australia.

Abroad, I find Australian women much more animated and intelligent, whereas in their own coun-

try they are the dullest creatures imaginable.

Socially, I rebel against being relegated to one end of the room to talk "domestic".

God forbid if it should ever come to the matriarchal society of the U.S., but I certainly feel I am in a land where I am forbidden to express myself.

JEANNETTE CHILDS
Queenscliff, NSW
24/5/66

Women's rights

The right to choose

Fair go at home

WHILE sitting in the pub the other night talking to a group of chaps, the subject of the Women's Liberation Movement was raised and my opinion asked, to the accompaniment of sneers and chuckles.

Probably my biggest mistake was that I actually gave an opinion. It was a rude awakening to the fact that women's liberation is a "no-no" unless discussed with a man in sympathy.

A couple of women looked aghast before joining in the general snickering. Of course, there was no point in reminding them that they were involved, either directly or indirectly, in the whole women's liberation bit. They wouldn't have listened.

Later in the evening, I was invited (not dragged) to dance and the chap commented on my feminity and asked how I came to have any sympathy for the obviously aggression-orientated women's cause.

It was pointless saying that I would like to make up my own mind should I ever need

an abortion, that I don't want to lose my identity as a Mrs John Smith (if my parents had wanted to call me John, I'm sure they would have), that I can do more with my life than ugg away in suburbia long before the ripe old age of 25 (which sounds almost menopausal in this country), and that I'd like an equal opportunity to do it.

I don't want to drive a truck, dig up roads, drink stronger liquor or smoke a pipe to prove I have bigger muscles or a stronger stomach than all those lovely men, but I would like a fair deal as a woman if I want to have a child out of wedlock, buy a house, or become an executive.

If women cannot activate, they can infiltrate and we don't have to put up with the greatest male conversation exit of all time: "When we want your opinion, we'll give it to you."

SUE KNIGHT
West Beach, SA
4/9/70

I WOULD like to agree with Mr W. G. Ford, senior lecturer at the University of NSW in industrial relations, who said that gross sex discrimination against women exists in industry *(The Australian*, 15/8).

Even worse, it exists more strongly against women at home, where mothers of very young children are expected to work twice as long per week as a healthy man and be on call the whole time.

While in the past trade union officials have visited the Northern Territory and New Guinea to advise people on how to go about organising themselves, they have done nothing for the woman working at home.

There are, of course, good and bad husbands in the same way that there are good and bad employers.

But it is astounding to realise that even "good" husbands think that it is quite reasonable for their wives to work long hours for years while their children are small, without one day off, even though the average man can play golf, or go to the races on his days off without having to worry about his work or his family.

Legislation regarding working conditions for women at home is the only thing which will give young mothers a fair go.

Trade unions should be ashamed that while they are doing so much for themselves, they are doing nothing to help the helpless to come together to fight for fair working conditions.

B. PHILLIPS
Woodridge, Qld
21/8/72

Women are not idiots

YOUR first-rate Female Mind articles — particularly the excellent and witty piece on marriage by Betty Riddell — have strengthened a long-held conviction that most women, except the semi-literate, are more interested in "hard" news than the useless rubbish purveyed by most other newspapers in their separate section.

The days when most women were completely occupied with running homes, working for charities, attending teas, lunches and bridge parties, went out with button-up boots!

Nowadays, as well as running homes, a big majority of women by necessity go to work — despite UNequal pay — and take just as much interest in world personalities and affairs and what's going on around them as men do.

Women are tired of being regarded as basically mentally different from men; excluded from most of the interesting jobs; and placed in the legal category of "women, children and idiots."

MARJORIE PLUNKETT
Potts Point, NSW
28/2/69

Women's rights

More power to Germaine Greer

BRAVO to Germaine Greer, who refuses to address the (Sydney) Journalists Club while women are excluded from membership and to the ladies who object to such exclusion (Letters, 27/12).

The exclusion of women from clubs and associations representing professions, of which women are members, seems to rest on certain unstated assumptions: that women are poor mixers; that they require to be coddled and flirted with and are therefore a source of danger to married men unaccompanied by their wives; that they are emotionally unstable; that they are over-earnest and therefore spoil sophisticated society; that they will "swamp the place and take it over"; that they are prudish and likely to be shocked by male conversation.

The truth is, of course, that some women have some of these attitudes, just as some men do. But men are not as a rule excluded on such grounds.

Lots of men profess sympathy with women in their stupid exclusion from professional equality of this kind: "I'd let them in if it were my decision, but the others would object, so I won't rock the boat."

There isn't much women can do from outside to reform these organisations; there should be enough enlightened men willing to threaten resignation from organisations which unreasonably exclude women.

T. W. MOHAN
St Ives, NSW
5/1/72

IT is a revelation for an Australian woman to visit a country which is not anti-feminist.

The benighted status of Australian women seems to be a recurring topic, not only among expatriates but also the English — amused but incredulous — who have been getting a deadly accurate picture, perhaps from women migrants.

I'm still marvelling at the range of responsible jobs that would be available if I stayed permanently. There's no question of seconding you to some mediocre badge-wearing male who picks your brains and takes the credit, as in Australia.

I can still hardly believe that a woman can walk into a pub and order a brandy like a milkshake, instead of imbibing sweet sherry in the suburbs by herself. And there are no boorish male drunks lurching home of a Friday.

More power to Germaine Greer. The extraordinary debate about her in the Australian press conjures up a picture of some remote clan of hillbillies whose tribal routines have been disturbed.

CLAIRE WAGNER
London
22/2/72

The battle against sex-ploitation

THERE are a lot of women becoming more aware of the ways that society (including women) discriminates against them.

The obvious examples, like wages and job opportunities, are open, clear-cut issues which can and are being fought and are meeting with some success.

The hardest battle is against the subtle sexist attitudes that bombard women at any age and stage of awareness.

It starts when little girls play with dolls, her children, which is to be her main role and aim in life. She also learns very quickly that if she looks cute, sits on daddy's knee, kisses and cuddles him, she can get whatever she wants.

So she learns to exploit her sex and the stereotype is born.

Advertisers are being attacked over the way they perpetuate the myth — but they didn't invent it. They merely pick up a popular social attitude, make it larger than life and feed it back to the people.

But if they didn't invent sex-ploitation, they do a great job of selling it, which doesn't make the battle easier for women.

A recent example is a TV commercial for a child's toy in which we find mum and the kids (all 20 of them) trooping down to the park to play. Mum is a comic figure (and a large one) in a feather boa carrying a picnic basket.

The commercial goes on to say how childishly simple this toy is followed by shots of kids throwing it and catching it. The last scene is mum catching one by accident — a look of moronic joy spreads across her face as an astonished but still sugary voice assures us that "even mum can do it."

We've got to wake up to these insidious attacks (on women, not on "mumism") — even mum should see that!

CHRISTINA HAMILTON
New Brighton, NSW
12/7/73

Women's rights

Upgrading the Australian woman

YOUR editorial (14/9) and your cartoon (16/9) are examples of male chauvinism par excellence. Both, under the guise of support for women's rights, ridicule the declaration of 1975 as International Women's Year.

International Women's Year, 1975, celebrates the 50th anniversary of International Women's Day which, on March 8 each year, has been used by women's movements throughout the world as a focus for their demands.

Your editorial implies tokenism on the part of the Government in setting up a committee to prepare a national program to celebrate International Women's Year and goes on to accuse the Government of failing to implement action to improve the status of women in this country.

During its time in office, the Labor Government has done more to improve the status of women than any previous government in the history of this country.

Until the election of the Labor Government, the women's movement in Australia battled in vain to gain even token support from governments for any of its demands.

Since the election of the Labor Government, we have seen the introduction of equal pay, the appointment of a woman adviser to the Prime Minister as well as women advisers to a number of senior Cabinet ministers. Women have been appointed to key positions in the Public Service and we have seen the appointment of a woman doctor as governmental adviser on family planning, an appointment which the women's movement feels confident will presage an "intelligent conclusion to the abortion issue."

By far the most outstanding contribution has been the funding of the Leich-hardt Women's Community Health Centre. For the first time, Australian women have had provided for them, through the far-sightedness of the Government and the dedication of the women from the Women's Liberation Movement, a comprehensive health centre where they can get first class gynaecological and general medical treatment combined with in-depth social and psychological counselling, in an atmosphere of warmth and understanding.

The Women's Liberation Movement has before the International Women's Year planning committee four submissions — any one of which if implemented, would be of major significance in "tangibly improving the life and status of women in Australian society," not only in 1975 but for the future.
BETTY PYBUS
McMahons Point, NSW
21/9/74

A mockery of womanhood

AS International Women's Year draws to a close in Australia, I despair that the voice of the majority of home-loving, hardworking, community-concerned women will ever be heard.

The whole project, as put forward by Kurt Waldheim, Secretary-General of the UN, has been frustrated and defeated. Generally, women of the world have not symbolically stretched out their hands sympathetically across the oceans in a global search and response for compassion, justice, love and peace for themselves, their families and their children.

Instead, International Women's Year has become a furore of angry, frustrated, embittered people, railing and wailing over cauldrons of hate; stirring for revolution and the destruction of democratic systems, which in the end means peace for no one; justice for no one; and a horrible future for the little children of the world.

Not the least of the offenders are the Australian women organisers, who are not true representatives of the average woman who loves her country, her home and her family, who extends that love to people beyond her shores and who wants to inspire in all children of this generation the great spiritual values that will destroy the hate and the bitterness and enkindle love, tolerance, forgiveness and above all justice.

These silly, educated, introverted trumpeteers are making a mockery of the rest of Australian womanhood, which has contributed so much to the building up of the Australian lifestyle.

If, for no other reason, I wish the Senate would bring on an election so that even at the 11th hour there would be some chance that the true image of the majority of Australian women would emerge, nationally and internationally.
(Mrs) DOROTHY HAWKES
Devonport, Tas
25/9/75

Women's rights

A question of style

I CAN'T resist having a tilt at Buzz Kennedy re his occasional series on Australian women featured in *The Weekend Australian*. All in a spirit of good fun, of course — after all, a prime requisite of any woman of style is a sense of humor.

Buzz dear, why this fixation with the 30s as the peak of feminine "beauty, style and elegance"? As though having attained this high-water mark, one must remain forever, as it were, in limbo, like a chook in aspic.

These elusive qualities have precious little relation to biological age — either a woman has elan or she hasn't. A photograph published last year in Australian newspapers revealed that Malcolm Muggeridge's wife, now in her 70s, must be one of the most stunning women in Britain today and, offhand, I can think of a certain four-year-old miss who is loaded. Miss Jean Brodie said it all — the prime of life is a state of mind.

Sad to say, in the majority of cases, the outward and visible signs of style, ele-gance and beauty are not reinforced by intellectual and spiritual graces.

After the first favorable impression, the rot of disillusionment sets in. By popular trivial standards, the Jackie Kennedy, Grace Kelly (and one can think of a few closer to home) archetypes are considered to be women who have the lot, but I rather suspect that 75-year-old Margaret Mead has more panache in her little finger than the whole pack of them

And who else but Oscar Wilde to have the last word on a woman's age: "Never trust a woman who will tell you her true age. Any woman who is capable of that is capable of anything!"

(Mrs) PATRICIA CHILDS
Bexley North, NSW

BUZZ KENNEDY SAYS: I do not maintain that women are at their best only in their 30s. My claim, to which I stick, is that they are not worth the worry UNTIL they are 30. I do not place an upper limit. At my age, could I afford to?

29/8/77

She doesn't speak for me

I READ with interest that our Prime Minister has appointed a super-woman as a special adviser on women.

Regrettably, it appears that she is in favor of abortion on demand, pornography and so on. As a woman voter, I am very much against this woman being a spokeswoman for me on such matters.

Advocates of Women's Lib claim that abortion on demand is necessary to liberate women, but I cannot understand their reasoning.

There is a saying, "It's always the woman what pays."

Surely, in the case of abortion, this saying is borne out.

There are other solutions to the problem and perhaps these would be better causes for Women's Lib to adopt.

I would be interested to hear from any person who feels the same way as I do with regard to this matter.

(Mrs) MARGARET BOURKE
Nunawading, Vic
19/4/73

PS

IT does appear that far too many women prop-ounding their rights, lib and such, are unfeminine, untidy, badly dressed, foul of speech, limited in vocab-ulary, badly wanting in the area of attraction and, most striking of all, lacking in humor. They also appear to be unmarried manhaters. Perhaps the obvious and bitter frustration is therefore understandable, alas!
DONALD WYNNE
Woollahra, NSW
5/1/78

JULIE Rigg thinks that no one can entertain the idea of sexual relations without some attendant de-gree of love. I believe that this is true of woman — that is her tragedy. It is not true for man — that is his.
BILL RAMAGE
Bellerive, Tas
30/10/67

I AM glad my comments on tipping spurred the in-terest of Mr Mike Jason (Letters, 30/7) who made the point exactly that I was trying to bring out. He said waitresses and others get wages that are disgrace-fully low and they need tips to live. This is exactly my point: it is degrading to have to exist on handouts instead of a proper wage re-flecting just reward for work performed. My atti-tude is that handouts should not be necessary — everyone is worthy of just payment.
(Mrs) ELLNOR GRASSBY
Canberra
(The writer is wife of the Minister for Immigration.)
10/8/73

Politics

Calwell must go

EITHER Mr Calwell has an extraordinary lack of political nous for one who has been in the centre of politics for so long, or he no longer has the interests of the A.L.P. at heart.

I have yet to meet anyone who believes that the A.L.P. under Mr Calwell has a chance of being elected.

Prominent members of the party, branch secretaries, trade union officials and political commentators have commented in this vein, and with increasing conviction, since the last elections.

If Mr Calwell has inadequate political nous he should be forced to resign.

If he no longer places the interests of the Labor Party foremost, he should be forced to resign.

If the Labor Party keeps Mr Whitlam in the wings much longer, it might have cause to be very sorry — not only when it loses the next elections, but when it looks for a new potential election-winning leader to replace Mr Calwell afterwards.

No one with Mr Whitlam's strength of personality, intellect and convictions can be expected to take this kind of frustrating stupidity indefinitely.

If the Labor Party had taken the plunge a few years ago, its stature in the electorate would be immeasurably greater and it would very probably be in office today.

H. B. LEVIEN
North Bondi, NSW
25/8/65

Like Laurel without his Hardy

I'M in need of reassurance. All the old solids seem to be decaying. The Catholic Church considers contraceptives, the Minister for Customs unbans good books and rumor has it that Sir Robert may soon retire.

Politics without him! Think of it. It'll be like opera without Sutherland, Christmas dinner without plum pud. And poor Arthur Cal-well will be left like Laurel without his Hardy.

Suddenly the "Out Bob" flaking in the railway viaduct is as poignant and nostalgic as one's baby booties. When Sir Robert goes, who will tell us our political fairy stories?

Who will keep us safe from the colored bogey-man?

P. ADAMS
Toorak, Vic
9/8/65

Politics

The arrogance of Menzies

THE persistent rumors about Sir Robert Menzies' imminent retirement recall to my mind the very mild editorial about him printed in *The Australian* on December 22.

To me and to many others, he will always be the man who, just returned from Germany in 1939, was full of enthusiasm for Hitler and his methods. He remains the man who, in 1960, pompously declared that he was taking full responsibility for his Government's financial policy which later resulted in unemployment for more than 130,000 unfortunate people. He was the man who surrounded himself in his Cabinet with mediocre yesmen and who managed to get rid very quickly of any minister who had the temerity to think a bit more independently, by sending him away as ambassador or by passing him over to the judiciary — locally or overseas.

The arrogance of Sir Robert is not even denied by his followers, and his contempt for Parliament shows clearly in his replies to questions without notice, as anyone can read in Hansard.

Not so long ago, he declared a state of war and Parliament was not even asked.

He has never failed to attack anything that did not fit in with his antiquated ideas; the most recent example was his treatment of the Vernon Report.

His abject servility towards the royal family is well known; and it is not forgotten how he, when the Queen came to Canberra, paid her a very crude compliment which would make any woman blush in embarrassment.

"I did but see her passing by and yet I love her till I die"—Sir Robert Menzies welcoming the Queen to Canberra in 1963. A reader complains about his abject servility to the royal family.

He has seen fit to involve this country in a hopeless war where many young Australians will lose their health or their lives; and which, for many years to come, will cause our name to be mud in Asia.

Instead of sending soldiers, it would have been much more beneficial for our industry to send good salesmen to sell our products that would have found a very receptive market.

The Treasurer, who can't think of any other way to "save" our economy except a credit squeeze, seems to believe that trade is flourishing; but I, as a business woman of long standing, could tell him otherwise.

Your editorial was headed: "The Age of Menzies fades away."

I, and many others, feel that it would have been much better for this country if we had never had to live through such an age.

(Mrs) E. KING
Coogee, NSW
14/1/66

PS

THE statement that I was "closely identified with the Movement" (9/2) was completely false. At no time was I ever associated with the Movement. Like all members of the party, I favored establishment of the industrial groups, but when the Movement took over the groups, I strongly opposed this and when the split came I stayed with the Labor Party.

ARTHUR CALWELL
MHR for Melbourne
10/2/67

Politics

All the way  with LBJ

I DO not wish to detract in any way from the natural welcome which is due to the American President.

However, I would question whether, in view of the horrifying plight of Vietnamese children, taxpayers' money should be used to bring schoolchildren under 15 free of cost, from all parts of NSW, to see LBJ drive through the streets of Sydney.

This was not considered necessary when the Queen visited Sydney.

In a recent letter, my nephew in England, who is the leading plastic surgeon at East Grinstead (Queen Victoria Hospital), mentioned the number of children being flown to Europe for plastic surgery — to Switzerland, Holland, France, Italy and England.

The ones he is treating in England are receiving new eyelids.

One boy of 10, with severely disfiguring untreated burns, was picked up between his incinerated parents.

If the cost allocated to bring thousands of our young, healthy schoolchildren to see the U.S. President could be used instead to fly injured Vietnamese children here to this nearer country, they could have the best treatment of any country and all that we have to offer.

MARGARET WATTS
Chairman
Quaker Service Council
Sydney Regional Meeting
Potts Point, NSW
18/10/66

LARGE as it is, President Johnson's entourage of 400 will not include any boot-lickers.

We are supplying these.
LESTER GOODMAN
Manly, NSW
17/10/66

THIS country should continue to do well in the Olympic swimming events in 1968.

The visit of LBJ has shown that we can all qualify as exponents of the great Australian crawl.
JOHN QUINCEY
Windang, NSW
31/10/66

MAY I offer my thanks and appreciation for the cordial manner in which our President was received by the thousands of gracious enthusiastic people of Australia who turned out to welcome him?

When the leaders of free countries meet personally with the proper application of the right principles, it would seem to be a start in the direction of convincing those who would make an aggressive attempt to destroy our way of life that it will not be a profitable adventure for them.

During past meetings and get-togethers, when political or diplomatic discussions have arisen, I have never heard an uncomplimentary remark about Australia.

The courage and integrity of the Australians infuses our people with warm feelings of friendship.

MERLE FORTENBURY
St Louis, Missouri, U.S.
28/11/66

Whitlam's Kennedy touch

WHAT a refreshing approach Mr Gough Whitlam made at his first press conference as Leader of the Opposition.

His statement, "I want you to know what I am for, not what I am against," had the Kennedy ring about it.

It is to be hoped that this new-look Labor team develops into a strong Opposition; prods the present Government into greater action and, if it will not take the prod, then removes it from power.

"Advance Australia where?" is the question we need to ask at this time.

I am sure Mr Whitlam will make a worthy contribution towards a positive, progressive answer to this question.

GEOFF HINDS
West Merrylands, NSW
17/2/67

Politics

A fitting monument for Harold Holt

AUSTRALIA was shocked to learn on Sunday, December 17, l967, that the Prime Minister, Mr Holt, had disappeared while snorkling off Portsea, Victoria. His body was never found.

OUR late Prime Minister, Mr Harold Holt, has been honored by Australian and world leaders and his determination, human-heartedness and enthusiasm widely praised.

As a sportsman of the sea, he had established a contact with fellow-Australians, which was something new and of value in our national life.

If the nation wishes therefore to honor Mr Holt in an enduring and appropriate way, what should be the form of the tribute?

Australia has a conspicuous need for a national institute of oceanography. At present only one graduate department exists specifically for the training of young scientists in this growing and important field of knowledge.

We have ever-increasing interests in our own offshore regions and we stand in an excellent situation geographically to train oceanographers from neighboring Asian countries.

A predominantly training institution attached to a university would be the logical first step towards such a national institute of oceanography.

Such an institution to be named in honor of Mr Holt could be established, granted public and official support.

R. GARTH EVERSON
Kenmore, Qld
29/12/67

Harold Holt

THE influx of distinguished visitors to honor Mr Holt shows the high regard in which he was held by their governments.

In view of this, it is to be hoped that a fitting memorial will be established by Australians.

What could be more appropriate than to create a marine sanctuary covering all or part of the Great Barrier Reef and to name this sanctuary after Mr Holt?

Such a sanctuary would be most appropriate as a memorial to Mr Holt. It would link his name always with the sea which he loved and which eventually took his life. A memorial monument could be erected at Bingil Bay to proclaim the sanctuary.

Apart from its suitability as a memorial, such a sanctuary would have obvious value for conservation purposes, particularly in view of recent events demonstrating the need for some sort of protection for the reef.

BRIAN S. HANCOCK
Hawthorndene, SA
29/12/67

Widow's strength, courage

AFTER having had the privilege of attending the memorial service to our late Prime Minister at Westminister Abbey on January 18, I would without reservation judge this occasion as the time I derived most pride from having been born Australian.

Who among the large crowd will forget the combination of strength and courage shown by his bereaved widow, Zara Holt?

These qualities, so typically Australian, were as conspicuous as her bronzed countenance and even though small of stature, she appeared as a giant among us, her follow countrymen.

I would like to record my thanks for the sobering effect which that day's events had on my sense of proprieties.

TED FORD
NSW Government Office
1/2/68

Zara Holt

Politics

'Ah wouldn't do thet if ah wuz yew, Toledo'

IN *The Australian* (10/1) in an article on Senator J. G. Gorton headed Meet The New Prime Minister, the writer, Alan Ramsey, stated: "He is not an intellectual: he said in an interview once: 'I like my TV with redskins biting the dust, some violence mixed in and a certain amount of sex. I'm not a boor, but I'm not a culture-vulture either'."

Alan Ramsey should have used some extracts from the Hansard report of Senator Gorton's speech in the Senate on October 30, 1967, when he endeavored to disparage the now well-known Vincent Report on television.

He said: "I just speak on my own behalf as a bloke who likes to watch television and, I hope, on behalf of some members of the Australian community who share my choice of television programs. I make one plea. Do not make me look at any more culture than I want to look at.

"I am perfectly happy for those who want to look at Swan Lake, the Edinburgh Festival, or interviews with the Right Reverend Bishop of Bongo Bongo, to have a channel on which they can watch those programs.

"But I want to have a chance to watch men walking down the streets of little western towns, reach for their guns and saying, 'Ah wouldn't do thet if ah wuz yew, Toledo.' I want to have a chance to watch a program about a private eye who gets bashed over the head with beer bottles and telegraph poles, but two minutes later

is perfectly capable of taking on anything that he may be required to take on."

On reading Senator Gorton's speech in Hansard, my association immediately wrote to him decrying his denigration of cultural television subjects (the senator plainly gave **his** interpretations of "cultural" material in his speech), and also strongly protesting against his clear preference for subjects of violence on television.

Senator Gorton has never replied to us. We were apparently dismissed as "culture vultures."

HAL ALEXANDER
General Secretary
Actors and Announcers Equity Association of Australia
Darlinghurst, NSW
31/1/68

Politics

Parliament must be reformed

IT would be a shame if the eruption in the House of Representatives last week should be dismissed as a passing and isolated incident.

It was, in fact, an expression of acute exasperation and of concern being felt by so many MPs (Government as well as Opposition) as they witness the collapse of Parliament as an institution of democratic decision-making for this country.

As it now functions, Parliament has become little more than a windy talking shop. Even here, its role is circumscribed, as last week's events show.

This has largely arisen because the ministry treats Parliament as its personal possession, ignoring the rights of private members regardless of on which side of the House they sit.

Consistent with this attitude, the ministry crudely manipulates the House by abusing standing orders — which have been so tampered with over the years that the institution of Parliament stands humbled and gravely weakened like a Samson shorn of his hair.

As Parliament now functions, the Australian public does not get value for the money it provides to maintain that organ.

Last week's protest must be seen within the context of these grave failings, which are becoming accentuated.

Clearly there is a need for fundamental and deep-seated reform in the structure and manner of operation of Parliament.

It is utter nonsense to expect that a system which was developed in the last century and the one before it, to meet the leisurely pace of change and relatively uncomplicated needs of that period, should be capable of successfully grappling with the rapid change and complex issues which are projected into the parliamentary sphere in this last third of the 20th century.

A priority need would be the provision of standing specialist committees comprised of MPs but backed by full-time expert staff advisers.

These committees would not only be charged with the duty of investigating the complexities and ramifications of legislative proposals, but would go beyond this charter and investigate community needs and propose need-meeting processes for the benefit of the public.

As things stand at the moment, research resources for MPs are quite inadequate. Only the parliamentary library exists for this purpose, and its capacity is overtaxed because of the unfair attitude of the ministry towards its services.

Again, in Federal Parliament, we ought to sit longer than we do. We sit for fewer days than we did 20 years

ago. We sit for fewer days than does the House of Commons in Britain, or Canada, or than does the American Congress.

Federal Parliament could sit on Fridays, with this day reserved for non-Government business, so that the Opposition and private members would have a greater opportunity to initiate matters of public importance.

Again, we would need some guarantees for private members so that their interests would not be swamped out by the organised opposition.

Gagging debate, late night and all night sittings, rushed legislation, crude abuse of the standing orders; all of these things and many others, too, are grave defects apparent in our present parliamentary system of government.

I do hope the public might take an informed interest and develop some concern towards the need for reform in our parliamentary procedures.

Otherwise, they can only worsen and lead to a collapse in the role of our systems of parliamentary democracy, which is the nerve centre of our freedoms and rights.

BILL HAYDEN
Ipswich, Qld
(The writer is the Labor MHR for the seat of Oxley, Queensland.)
17/4/70

Calwell was proved right

THE recent publication of the Pentagon papers indicates that the people of Australia owe Arthur Calwell a deep apology for their rejection of his platform in 1966.

Five years and several hundred Australian Vietnam deaths later, we see

that Arthur and the A.L.P. were right after all.

On behalf of the Australian people I apologise. Their endorsement of this apology will follow at the 1972 federal elections.

JOHN GRAHAM
Mulgrave, Vic
28/6/71

┌─ **PS** ─────────

CONFOUND that Gough Whitlam fellow! Why before we know where we are, we'll have those damn New Guineans demanding a fair go.

R. J. McCARTHY
Cooma, NSW
11/2/70

Politics

It's time — Labor's victory

THE 23 YEAR ITCH

WE, the undersigned, who are not members of any political party, believe that Australia's interests will be best served by a change of government as a result of this election.

Our democratic system works properly only when each of the major parties has the chance to govern. Each benefits from the responsibilities of office. Each gains from the freedom of opposition.

Some of us think the Liberal-Country Party coalition has had a productive as well as long period in office. Others of us are less enthusiastic about its record, especially in recent years.

But we all agree that today, after 23 years in office, it needs new ideas and has problems of long term leadership which can best be worked out in opposition.

Although we do not subscribe to all the Australian Labor Party's policies, we see no over-riding reason for continuing to exclude it from office.

It is Australia's oldest and biggest party. It represents aspirations in our society which cannot be ignored. It has prepared itself for office and needs only a moderate swing in its favor at this election to take power.

If denied office any longer, the Labor Party is in danger of disintegrating as a force in Australia's political life.

We believe a change of government will benefit both the major parties on which the vitality of our political system depends.

The ultimate beneficiary will be the Australian nation and its people.

Prof R. R. Andrew, Dean of Medicine, Monash University; **Prof Macmahon Ball,** Professor of Political Science, Melbourne University; **Prof Hedley Bull,** Professor of International Relations, Australian National University; **Sir Macfarlane Burnet,** Scientist and Nobel Prize winner; **David Campbell,** Poet; **Walter Crocker,** former Australian diplomat; **Prof Manning Clark,** Historian; **Prof R. I. Downing,** Professor of Economics, Melbourne University; **Dr Frank Fenner,** Research Biologist; **Leonard French,** Painter; **Bruce Grant,** Journalist; **Sir Keith Hancock,** Scholar; **Rev Dr J. D. McCaughey,** Master of Ormond College, Melbourne University; **Kenneth Myer,** Businessman; **Patrick White,** Novelist and playwright; **Miss Judith Wright,** Poet.

23/11/72

Politics

New honors

I HEARTILY applaud the decision of Mr Whitlam to drop the New Year's Honors List. Let us have an Australian system of recognition to replace these foreign awards.

J. KEEGAN
Granville, NSW
13/12/72

MY children have asked me to ask you if Gough is going to change the language, too?

JEREMY J. POWER
Coffs Harbor, NSW
18/12/72

ONE hundred days of hard Labor? That leaves only 995 days to go!

(Miss) MARGARET BAHR
Canterbury, NSW
15/3/73

WHAT a pleasure to see a Prime Minister visiting Washington who does not make us cringe when he opens his mouth.

JUDITH LITTLE
Rose Bay, NSW
7/8/73

The first six months

HAVING long believed that the popular Australian attitude was to give a man "a fair go," I am at a loss to understand the continual destructive criticism directed towards the Federal Government since its recent election.

Although the Government has only been in power a mere six months, it has achieved more in this time than any comparable period of the Liberal-Country Party era, despite the fact that they had an uninterrupted run of 23 years to bring about reform and development in aid of the Australian community.

The Liberal-Country Party coalition achieved development only at the expense of the nation. On the eve of its defeat, it had allowed a huge portion of Australian assets, in fact 33 per cent, to pass into the hands of overseas cartels.

Probably the worst aspect of the takeover is in the field of mineral extraction, which has caused severe damage to our ecology by wholesale destruction of rainforests, sand dunes and fauna and flora.

The Labor Government, since it has been in power, has made numerous dramatic moves to reverse this situation.

A few examples of this are the Government's moves to retain Australian ownership of its oil supplies, its vetoing of overseas takeover bids when this is not in the best interests of the country and its recent steps to extend our offshore limit to 200 miles.

We voted Labor in: let's give them a go!

KERRY GORMAN
Norman Park, Qld
18/6/73

Politics

Fraser spells out Opposition role

I'D like to amplify your report (14/4) which emphasises the role of the Liberal Party in opposition.

The Opposition can and does use the machinery of Parliament to highlight the "flippancy and bombastic" nature of Mr Whitlam's attitude.

His attitude should be exposed to the public. However, in a vote on party lines, Mr Whitlam has the numbers if he wants to persist.

The Opposition can only stop it when a general election reverses the situation.

MALCOLM FRASER
Melbourne, Vic
(The writer is Liberal MHR for Wannon, Vic.)
16/4/73

Politics

The sacking of Whitlam

Ultimate in hypocrisy

IN the present national crisis which is fast descending on us, each of the two political groups involved is speaking as if it alone possessed a virtuous regard for constitutional convention and principle. Such an attitude represents the ultimate in hypocrisy!

The Opposition in deciding to deny Supply has blatantly breached an historic constitutional convention for no better reason than to displace the present Labor Government. The short-term advantages of such action may well seem strong; in the long-term, however,

the action is bound to be disastrous.

The Opposition may well come to rue the day when it sacrificed principle for an itch for power at all costs. A shoddy exercise indeed!

Yet Mr Whitlam can hardly, without a blush, assume the role of virtuous mentor and guardian of our constitutional integrity. In the Gair affair and the Cope affair (perhaps in the Cairns

and Connor affairs) he showed a cynical disregard for the constitutional proprieties. In possibly opting for a half-Senate election (which might give Labor a temporary majority in the Senate), he again is merely cocking an eye at possible short-term political advantages.

In view of the recent unpleasant loans affair resulting in the removal of two ministers and the very strong possibility that the Government has now lost the confidence of the electorate, the proper constitu-
Continued next page

Politics

Ultimate in hypocrisy

From previous page

tional course would appear to be for the Prime Minister to submit himself to a double dissolution and an election, and this course would ultimately rebound to the credit of the Labor movement.

It could, of course, result in the decimation of Labor at the polls, but at least it would go down with its flags flying with the remembrance of many worthy reforms accomplished during its term of office and with the thought — which posterity will not fail to record — that it was only done to death by an unconscionable and shabby manoeuvre.

In any event, the result of an appeal to the electorate might not be so unfavorable to Labor. The people can sometimes see where the merits lie.

But apparently it is not to be. Mr Whitlam will apparently approach the situation with an eye to immediate advantages as cynical as that of his opponents. His reluctance to face the electors seems to suggest that he considers his majority in the House is at present as fortuitous as the Opposition majority in the Senate!

So — we will get into a mess through the plain lack of anybody who would measure the position with the eye of a statesman.

Who cares anyway? The public? Maybe, maybe not. Maybe we deserve what we will get: the medicine might even be good for us.

E. I. SYKES
North Melbourne, Vic
(The writer is professor of public law at the University of Melbourne.)
22/10/75

Governor-General had the rights

I CAN no longer stand by without protest and allow various kinds of lawyers to voice their disapproval of the constitutional action taken by the Governor-General, when a situation of impasse had been reached.

One academic even suggested that the Governor-General's powers under the Constitution were never meant to be taken literally! He failed to explain how he knows what was "never meant" in the teeth of the clear words.

The contrary is the case. These powers may be reserved for extreme situations, but are certainly "meant" so that the Governor-General may have the discretion to refer a situation to the ultimate sovereign — the vote of the people.

The position is described in very clear terms in the book on constitutional law by Dr A. V. Dicey, KC, one of the greatest constitutional lawyers of the British Commonwealth. After describing the electorate as the sovereign and explaining the part played by the Crown, and mentioning a case in Victoria of the Lower House going to the people (who changed the Government) when Supply had been stopped by the (elective) Upper House, he emphatically states the powers of the Crown to dismiss a ministry and dissolve Parliament, though the course be an unusual one.

He continues: "On the other hand, there are certainly combinations of circumstances under which the Crown has a right to dismiss a ministry who command a parliamentary majority and to dissolve the Parliament by which the ministry are supported."

The Governor-General, under the present circumstances, clearly had the discretion and responsibility. He exercised it non-politically and with propriety and courage, so that the people might decide.

(Sir) ARNOLD BENNETT
Brisbane
26/11/75

PS

I AM outraged by Whitlam's sacking. What are we? Just one more banana republic! Where has my vote gone? Nowhere! How dare the Liberal-CP parties talk of dishonesty in Labor. They have showm themselves to be dishonest and downright immoral.
(Ms) JENNY MACLEOD
Glebe, NSW
14/11/75

I AM afraid Ms Jenny MacLeod got it wrong in her letter last Friday when she saw Mr Whitlam's sacking as the action of a banana republic. It is, in fact, the action of a banana monarchy.
DONALD HORNE
Woollahra, NSW
19/11/75

Politics

The unthinkable

THREE British — or should I say Stuart? — cheers for Sir John Kerr. He has stripped away the illusion we had that we are a democracy and reminded us that we are, constitutionally speaking, back in the 17th century.

We are the true British stock after all. The decadent, sick Britishers in the UK long, long ago curbed their kings and protector and drew the teeth of their Upper House in 1911.

We all owe a debt to Sir John. He has made us face the unthinkable — that we have a Queen's viceroy who can unmake and make governments much as kings did in the distant past.

DAL STIVENS
Lindfield, NSW
25/11/75

WHEN Charles Blackman destroyed by sawing in half one of his loveliest paintings last Friday, he displayed an integrity sadly lacking in most other artists (painters, writers, composers, etc).

By sacrificing a personally-loved painting, he wounded himself deeply in protest at the sickening attempts at manipulation of "personalities" as a prop to party politics, the sole aim of which seems to be the exploitation of already corrupted powers.

I join him all too belatedly — not by destroying an unpublished book of poems (I lack that kind of integrity), but by heartily wishing the Liberal and Labor parties a plague on both their houses.

BRUCE BEAVER
Abbotsford, NSW
28/11/75

I REALISE now that I must have been stupid and naive, but I confess I once agreed with Bob Hawke's self-assessment that he

should be Prime Minister of Australia. But no more.

As an Australian working in London, I was, this week, unfortunately witness to Mr Hawke's petulant and boorish performance by TV satellite on the prestige BBC current affairs program, Panorama.

It is easy to understand his bitter disappointment at Labor's disastrous defeat, but as a man of no small intellect, he should know that gratuitous, irrelevant and petulant cracks about Pommies is hardly likely to raise his standing in international politics. The immediate result of Mr Hawke's performance was to make Malcolm Fraser, who was on the same program, appear a towering statesman — which, of course, he isn't.

Australia — and the international community — could well do without the likes of Bob Hawke.

IAN D. RICHARDSON
London
18/12/75

THOSE who deem to criticise Professor Manning Clark's tribute to the Whitlam years obviously overlook the fact that 43 per cent of thinking Australians who valued democracy voted for a return of the Whitlam Government, considering these three years to have been the most progressive in our history.

Never before has so much been achieved in so short a time and under such great difficulties. Regrettably, memories are short, for many of the same men who were responsible for conscripting our youth to fight and die in the immoral war of Vietnam have again been elected to government.

(Mrs) THYRA STANNETT
Townsville, Qld
19/1/76

Politics

The aftermath for Kerr

MY wife and I were at the Commonwealth Society's reception last week and we saw the disgusting scene made by the demonstrators and their organisers. It was ugly, crude and went too far.

The great majority of people in Australia are solidly behind the Governor-General. He knows his job and he carries it out with precision.

If certain political extremists don't like it — mob rule and demonstrations will not change it. Our great Constitution ensures that it stays the way it is and can only be altered by due process in Parliament and referendum.

Some of the news media will endeavor now to say that because the Queen is visiting us next year, the Governor-General should resign to prevent embarrassment. Her Majesty cannot be embarrassed by anyone who upholds the Constitution.

But more, perhaps, to the point is the fact that any demonstration of the kind we saw last night would only bring lasting and irreparable harm to their cause and those who organise it.

I was grateful to be present last night, because I felt I was witnessing a facet of Australian history. All our Governors-General in the past have been appointed because they were great men.

Today we have our first Australian Governor-General to become a great man in the position itself. He is the only one to be put to the test of safeguarding the Constitution.

His courage, his devotion to duty and his bearing adorn the task with superb distinction. Well done, Sir

THE SACKING OF ELECTED GOVERNMENTS PRECEDENT

John, and carry on. We're with you.

MICHAEL PARKER
Toorak, Vic
17/6/76

I ARRIVED home a few days ago after living in England for some time. It was as though in jetting across the world, I had somehow travelled back in time at least a decade.

The television and radio told me that some rabble students were demonstrating against Sir John Kerr. Newspaper editorials told me that the students' actions smacked of nazism.

RSL spokesmen pompously condemned the demonstrators while upholding and praising the primary act of violence of the Governor-General — the ripping to ribbons of the Australian Constitution.

Were not the same pontifications delivered by precisely the same sections of society about students and other citizens demonstrating against the Australian involvement in the shameful Vietnam war?

KATHLEEN TAYLOR
Bondi, NSW
17/6/76

Politics

We were shoved, abused and spat on

THERE is one angle of the disreputable incident which occurred outside the Royal Commonwealth Society the other night which has not been brought to the attention of your readers. In view of the increasing violence of our society, I feel that all should be aware of the situation.

On the night concerned, I and my husband had left our taxi and had to approach the building on foot. We were pushed, shoved, abused, spat on and sprayed with a yellow dye.

As a result of this dye, my evening dress and fur stole have been ruined. I must point out that evening wear for ladies of my age and figures takes some skill in devising and is now far from

cheap. I have inquired from my lawyer if I can claim damages from the organisers of the riot, but have been told I cannot.

These people had enough money to charter several buses, which they kept waiting for them at overtime rates for some hours. They brought their children, whom they held on their shoulders to see the fun.

They didn't hesitate to attack several guests, long before the Governor-General appeared. The fact that we were wearing evening dress appeared to infuriate them.

If the people who organised these outings had to pay for the damage they caused, they might not have the money to spend on transport

to get them all over the country.

I shall continue to attend legal gatherings where and when I wish. I do not dispute the right of peaceful assembly, but the mindless violence of the other night should be a warning to us all.

ANNE CLEMENS
Toorak, Vic
17/6/76

AUSTRALIA '76 — the knighted and the benighted.
JAMES BARNETT
Stanmore, NSW
17/6/76

Cynical contempt

THE Anglican and Catholic archbishops of Perth in a recent joint statement warn of the peril to society "when hatred and vindictive bitterness manifest themselves in violent action under the guise of furthering a just cause." The archbishops, of course, are referring to the anti-Kerr demonstrations.

I agree wholeheartedly with their graces in deploring the use of violence. In the political crisis leading to the Whitlam Government's dismissal last year, however, I sought in vain for any ecclesiastical censure of violence done to the parliamentary and democratic processes. The over-weening ambition and ruthless determination of our present political masters in grasping for power at any price escaped condemnation from the two archbishops.

Can these gentlemen not see that the present violence has its roots in the amoral activities and cynical contempt for due political process displayed by the coalition when in opposition?

Any perspicacious prelate could surely have recognised the danger inherent in the political debacle of last November. If only some of our religious leaders would exercise their prophetic function at times other than when the peace of the non-Labor Establishment is at risk, their credibility might rate higher in the community at large.

In view of this, the ecclesiastical duet in the West does not impress me in the least.

K. V. BRANNELLY
Kensington, NSW
27/7/76

┌─ **PS** ─

MR Whitlam is really bitter about the Treasury not telling him that things were going badly, businesses going broke and people becoming unemployed (news report 23/11). Perhaps they assumed that he, like all other Australians, already knew about this.
D. H. BISCOE
Hobart, Tas
28/11/74

I TAKE issue with your editorial, Whitlam the Great? (3/12), regarding Mr Whitlam's lack of humility. He has learned humility and is now perfect — he is the first to admit it!
I. B. NANKERVIS
Pymble, NSW
14/12/74

AMERICANS elected Richard Nixon, ignoring his past record. Australians have elected Malcolm Fraser.
S. W. DYER
Woden, A.C.T.
17/12/75

Politics

WE ALL DID OUR BIT— TAMIE LOOKED AFTER THE FLOWERS, I ARRANGED THE SEATING... GOUGH ORGANISED THE 21-GUN SALUTE....

Future consequences

THERE has been much protest about the nature of protests against Sir John Kerr. Much of this has been on the grounds that they are backward-looking and that they occur in his presence.

On behalf of a group of concerned citizens, we have hired the Sydney Town Hall for September 20 at 8 pm for an occasion that is not open to these criticisms. It is to be a formal public meeting. It will be a protest, but it will be concerned not with the past but with the future consequences of the Governor-General's actions of last year. The Governor-General is not expected to be present.

Would those who have attacked previous protests also protest against this?

**DONALD HORNE
FRANK HARDY**
Woollahra, NSW
14/9/76

Come back, Gough . . .

WHO among those who voted out the Whitlam Government on December 13, 1975, would now categorically deny the conspiracy theory, in the light of the allegations published on April 28 regarding CIA activities in Australia during the year of Whitlam's dismissal? There were those of us who suspected it and said so. There were those of us who suspected that a Fraser Government would be greater economic mismanagers than their predecessors. How long will it be before the electorate wakes up to the way it is manipulated? Come back, Gough, most is forgiven!

R. A. WATTERS
Jakarta, Indonesia
9/5/77

PS

I LIKE the name Mr Fraser has chosen for the super spy force — Office of National Assessments or ONA. A popular contraceptive on sale in Britain has the same name. Could this have something to do with what Mr Fraser is trying to do to the country?
DICK HOPKINS
Woy Woy Bay, NSW
11/5/77

Politics

Menzies: A golden era recalled

ON Tuesday, Sir Robert Menzies celebrated his 83rd birthday. In spite of the frustrations of infirmity, it must have been a great celebration, coming so soon after the massive victory at the polls of the party he founded in 1946.

But he ought perhaps to feel particularly gratified because, I believe, the Australian people were thinking not so much about the merits of leaders, or of this or that tax, but about their general desire to return to the golden days of Sir Robert Menzies — days of security and stability and law and order, when you had a much better chance than now to spend your own money, put a worthwile sum aside for old age, start up a little business, create a great one.

A few months ago, an opinion poll found that Australians, when asked who was the greatest living Australian, most frequently named Sir Robert Menzies. That was a remarkable result for a man who has been out of public life for 12 years.

Our political commentators should have seen that poll as a warning of how deeply Australians value the principles which Sir Robert represented and how they yearned for the confidence which he inspired, not only at home but also throughout the world, in a great future for Australia.

LADY McNICOLL
Yarralumla, A.C.T.
22/12/77

Nineteen guns and a piper's lament,
Sounded Sir Robert's knell,
Family and nation and overseas friends
Paid respect at a chieftain's farewell.
Goodbye to a man who has lived a full life,
Who has struggled and worked and succeeded,
An Australian who led us through progress and change
And gave the stability needed.
The birth of the Holden, the war in Korea,
Communist Petrov's defection,
Immigration, Olympics, a tour by the Queen,
All aided by Menzies direction.

"Let us now praise the famous"
and remember the worth
Of a worker to Liberal plan,
Grand, eloquent, patient,
home-loving, astute
Sir Robert — the leader —
the man.
HEATHER MORRISSON
Bundaberg, Qld
26/5/78

Menzies: His record was frayed

NOW that the captains and the kings have departed and the echoes of the dirges and the eulogies have faded away along with the quite extraordinary extravagances in the reportage of the event, it should not, I imagine, be considered tasteless or improper to consider a second opinion on the man and his times.

A gifted public speaker with a turn of wit and repartee, he was a consummate party politician and master electoral strategist. But where were any discernible gifts of statesmanship?

In the diastrous Suez affair he acted as a messenger, not a negotiator, between Eden and the Egyptians, thus lowering the prestige in international eyes of the Australian Prime Minister's office.

He committed the lives of young Australians to the Vietnam maelstrom, even then considered by millions here and in the U.S. to be the result of one of the most tragic misreadings of foreign events in the history of human conflict. Now everyone knows.

He was a cold war warrior who once predicted we had only three years to prepare for a hot one. And that at a time when the whole world yearned, with many actively working, for peace.

At home, the record was equally frayed.

Inheriting a potentially booming post-war economy, he presided over a burst of monetary inflation not experienced before or since.

He set up the Petrov commission, generating an anticommunist hysteria that, though electorally useful, uncovered not one traitor and unearthed not one treason.

One could go on. But let the departed rest in peace — once the balance sheets have been drawn up.

J. R. SHERIDAN
Campbelltown, SA
26/5/78

Politics

Don Dunstan says thank you

I HAVE been deeply touched by and grateful for the very many thousands of letters which I have received from people in all States, including letters from many people who have said that they were not of my political persuasion, but nevertheless wished to express appreciation of my service to politics in Australia and their regret at the decision which I have had to take.

All those who provided their addresses will be answered by my secretary.

I hope that they will appreciate that my doctors have been quite adamant that I may not do this myself, but I can assure them all that I have seen every letter and have been deeply touched by their kindness.

For those who did not provide their addresses, I hope that this letter will serve to express my thanks.

DON DUNSTAN
Norwood, SA
2/3/79

Don Dunstan

PS

WHAT we see on TV is "not the real Bill Snedden," according to his special advisor, Mr Tony Eggleton (19/2). Could we ask Mr Eggleton to explain to us viewers, then, which Bill Snedden is it that didn't lose the last election?
D. MARTIN
Frankston, Vic
28/2/75

WE need not be too sorry for Malcolm Fraser. He suffered only from the attention of a few half-baked students and unionists. Whitlam, on the other hand, has recently experienced not only an earthquake, but also a landslide!
T. W. STANIER
Sandy Bay, Tas
30/8/76

AFTER a most shameful week in Australia's history, I can't help marvelling at the gall of union spokesmen who accuse the Government of union-bashing. While a single

Bob Hawke

union holds the entire community to ransom, there's no doubt in my mind as to who's bashing whom!
ROSEMARY SINCLAIR
Bendemeer, NSW
20/5/77

WE know now that promises were made to be broken, but what about boasts that were apparently made to be forgotten? Some time ago, Mr Anthony offered to eat his hat if interest rates did not drop as forecast. In case he now regrets his extravagance, I can offer him a tasty

English tweed hat, even an old Australian slouch and will guarantee to provide sweet and sour sauce.
PETER YELDHAM
Avalon Beach, NSW
4/6/79

BULL**** snarled Mr Hawke when pressed to add his piece to the speeches of the other two, equally literate, members of the recently conceived A.L.P. troika. Though hardly novel, the utter brilliance of the exclamation as a comprehensive reply to all and everything with which a good socialist disagrees and, in particular, to anything subscribed to by the present Government, sets the gathering agog. There in the flesh before the now-inspired audience is the epitome of what is required of a future Labor Prime Minister of Australia.
HUGO HUGHES
St Lucia, Qld
16/9/80

Miscellany

Dear John, it was a disaster, my dear, a disaster

I WOULD like to thank that wonderful Mr Hallows for his advice in last Saturday's *Weekend Australian* on how to cook a real ethnic "barbie."

We "barbie" quite a lot and, indeed, whose thoughts don't turn from Vesta when we are having this lovely weather in Sydney. Anyway, I thought I'd be a devil and try one of Mr Hallows' shishkebabs from Turkey (isn't it interesting where he's been).

I asked Gail and Dave and their 12-year-old Trent for Sunday and sent Geoff up to get the meat, charcoal and Jiffies, and our boy Brian up to the pub to get the Retsina, he's 18 so he can go in, and I went up to Frankenstein's supermarket to get the olive oil. We already had half a cask of red wine for the soaking from Nan's birthday.

"Mr Hallows said be sure to get entrecote of beef," I said to Geoff.

"What's that?"

"I don't know, but Graham up the shop'll know."

"What sort of snags you want, thick or thin?"

"No snags," I said. "Mr Hallows doesn't think they're nice."

"Bloody Hallows sounds like a . . . ."

"Geoffrey," I said. "It doesn't hurt to be a bit different for once."

Well, where do I go from here, I thought, when Brian came back without the Retsina, a flagon of white and a split lip, and Geoff said Graham didn't know what an entrecote was either and came back with 2 lb of barbie steaks and a couple of pounds of thin sausages.

I had already cut up some wire coat hangers with the clippers though, so I thought come what may, we're having shishkebabs.

I'd got the olive oil all right and the garlic, but the Greek oregano was a bit hard. Actually, they didn't have the Italian one either, so I got a nice little bottle of mixed herbs. To go with it all, I got some ethnic coleslaw from our local deli.

I cut up all the meat and some of the sausages (didn't see the point in letting them go to waste) and soaked it all overnight, OUTSIDE the fridge, Mr Hallows. The blowies went mad.

Well, talk about laugh on the Sunday! Gail and Dave came at 11 and they're a couple of cards I can tell you.

The boys had a bit of trouble getting the charcoal going, but after a few beers nobody minded lunch a few hours late.

I had threaded the meat on the coat hangers and took it out all dripping with its lovely olive oil and burgandy to Geoff and Dave.

"Where's the snags?" said Geoff.

"On the shitskebab," said Gail. Well, that just broke us up. You can see what I mean about her. She's a scream after she's had a few.

I had the electric fan ready, just like Mr Hallows said, for the fire. I ran it on an extension cord from the laundry and when the lovely meat juices started spitting into the flames, I gave it a blast on medium.

Well, of course I knew something would go wrong! When Mr Hallows' shishkebabs hit that fan, all hell broke loose.

We had dinner all over the patio. Trent's T-shirt was completely ruined (but we managed to scrape it off him before it stuck to the burns), Gail's tovar was singed and Geoff, dashing up to the laundry, tripped over his thongs and broke his index toe.

I might tell you I was feeling a bit let down while we were waiting in the Outpatients, but after we'd got back and got little Trent to bed, there was still a bit of sun left, so I got the rest of the snags, Gail buttered some bread and good old Dave went up the back and chopped some wood.

But we tried, Mr Hallows, honestly we did.

ELIZABETH BROOKER
Wahroonga, NSW
27/8/77

Miscellany

Granville disaster

WE will long remember the Granville train disaster and all the personal grief, suffering and sadness that it brought without warning upon so many people, particularly close relatives and friends who have lost their loved ones, or are still gravely concerned for the injured.

Disaster strikes mostly without or with little warning, as Red Cross throughout the world has experienced and it is a time when all sections of the community rally as a united force to assist wherever their services or particular qualifications can be used. The Granville disaster was no exception.

Those who worked so untiringly at the scene of the disaster deserve the highest praise, working in some instances to the point of exhaustion.

Red Cross Blood Transfusion Service played a major role in providing blood to the scene of the disaster and to hospitals treating injured victims.

As chairman of the NSW Division of the Australian Red Cross Society, I wish to publicly thank on behalf of Red Cross the thousands of people who reported during this week at various centres to donate blood to help save the lives of the injured.

Never before have we experienced such spontaneous public response to a call for blood donors. Hundreds of these donors stood in street queues for many hours awaiting their turn to give.

MARGARET E. WADDELL
Chairman
NSW Division
Australian Red Cross
Society
Sydney
27/1/77

It's the tie that binds

CONGRATULATIONS to Janet Hawley and her campaign to gain acceptance of civilised dress for Australian men. It is refreshing indeed to have a woman pushing male liberation for a change; the bras have been burned, now for the ties!

The CBOA has for a number of years been campaigning to get bank officers out of that useless piece of material known as the tie. In this regard, we do point out an inaccuracy in Janet Hawley's article (4/1). Despite the reported statement of a Commonwealth Bank "spokesman," managers have only very limited discretion concerning male dress and removal of ties is authorised only under very narrowly defined conditions.

Not only is the tie a northern hemisphere anachronism — "neither use nor ornament" — but it is also a practical example of discrimination against men. How many women bank officers are required to wear ties? None.

Generally speaking, there is also little doubt — based on evidence which the CBOA has obtained from the University of Sydney and Health Departments — that the removal of ties creates a physical and psychological atmosphere conducive to increased efficiency and productivity.

KEVIN WALSH
Assistant Federal Secretary
Commonwealth Bank
Officers Association
Sydney
7/1/77

PS

YOUR report (11/8) of a dramatic increase in the number of births in New York exactly nine months after a general breakdown of television and electric light services suggests that most people prefer watching television to making love. Perhaps we could stop the population explosion by giving television and electricity to people in less affluent nations; this would also cause less religious controversy than traditional methods of birth control.

ALAN BELLET
O'Connor, A.C.T.
18/8/68

YOUR report (7/12) of the Whitlam-Snedden confrontation and the 34 economists only proves the point made by George Bernard Shaw that "if all the economists were laid end to end, they would never reach a conclusion." This is as true today as it was 50 years ago.

C. G. HEARN
Woomera, SA
14/12/73

Miscellany

The great stomach disaster

IT was, of course, with tremendous interest and enthusiasm that I read of our Prime Minister's diet and keep-fit program, for I had noticed with regret a considerable thickening of his and Mr Whitlam's girth. Perhaps they could get fit together and solve their problems while doing push-ups.

But while we are all utterly fascinated at the thought of Mr Fraser doing. his 5BX in between running the country and eating grapes at high-level functions, I do not think this piece of news is shattering enough to spur the rest of the country into getting fit.

The state of the Australian stomach is like our economy, a national disaster and as such should be given top priority. We have active unions fighting for more pay, shorter hours, longer holidays etc, but what they don't seem to realise is that soon there will be no one left to enjoy it. They'll all be in hospitals, or the cemetery.

Might I, in my humble way, suggest that instead of being regaled daily that almost everything we eat and do will lead to a heart attack (it is so depressing), something constructive is done.

All governments could flare the path by having keep-fit classes in place of their five tea-breaks, a special class being established for Cabinet; it being a well known fact that tensions as well as obesity lead to heart disorders and the increased pace of the circulatory system encourages clearer thinking.

The Government having taken up the cudgel, who knows, industry and private enterprise might follow. Free classes at every town hall (they're not used much anyway) for mums should be established; and the best of British luck to the instructors if they bring their kids.

There might just be, dare I even suggest it, a television station avant-garde enough to run an evening program for those who missed out during the day. (It couldn't be much duller than some of the ones we are expected to watch until the ratings start.)

There are a great many people like myself over the age of . . . well the age doesn't really matter, dears, who would like to get fit if there were someone to jolly them along. We don't all have the mental discipline of Mr Fraser or "Jog Along Lynch."

I feel the ideal station to lead this festival of fitness would be the ABC — a little exercise might release enough energy to alleviate their weighty problems.

Finally, a sobering thought for our bronzed Anzacs; the sex act is equivalent in energy expended to an 8km hike over rough terrain and the mere thought of a 32km trek is enough to give most of us palpitations. So unless we follow, however falteringly, in the steps of our beloved Prime Minister, it will be a case of:

"Make the most of what ye yet may spend
Before ye too into the dust descend."

SUE BECKER
Wahroonga, NSW
8/2/77

The day we drank the Birdsville pub out of rum

I REALLY must take issue with your correspondent's statement that there is ". . . no accommodation in Birdsville for the weary traveller" (31/8). The Birdsville Hotel is alive and well — or it was last May when my wife and I stopped overnight for the first time in 22 years. Taffy Nichols runs a clean and hospitable pub. The food was good, the plates well-heaped, the beds comfortable and the washing machine worked. Furthermore, bartender Murray gave us the very last two Bundaberg rums in the place (Brownies, he called them), which lets us say we drank the Birdsville pub out of rum — a fine story, even if one without much substance. How many barmen in western Queensland (or any similarly dry place) would do that?

No accommodation indeed! The whole town, all 1000 yards of it, from the A.I.M. Hospital to the police station (and that includes Brookes' store and the pub) were accommodating and friendly. It won't be another 22 years for us.

(Dr) F. H. BAUER
Winnellie, NT
8/9/78

Miscellany

Lang Hancock calls for taxpayers' revolt

Lang Hancock

CONGRATULATIONS on your efforts to help bring to public notice the many-sided monster, taxation, which is devouring at will all enterprising Australians, and to awaken us to the destructive effects of over-government and government wastage.

Increasingly, people from all walks of life are beginning to realise that a person should be rewarded — not discriminated against — for initiative, effort and achievement. The taxation monster feeds off the end result of these, namely the reward. In doing so, the taxation monster erodes and destroys the desire many people have to produce worthwhile results.

The solution does not lie in the comfortable alternatives of joining the bureaucracy (one in every three Australians now employed has done so), or the ranks of the subsidised unemployed. (The remainder are forced to "produce the goods" and, at the same time, pay the cost for the others.)

The solution does lie in immediately reducing and, for the most part, finally eliminating the army of bureaucrats and their pet programs.

Most importantly, by placing the taxation monster on a starvation diet — and giving people a new lease on life — capital would be attracted,

new business opportunities and new jobs would be created and incentive and productivity would return.

It's time for a Californian-style tax revolt and time for all of us to make our governments realise Australians have had enough of paying higher and higher taxes.

Congratulations to all those individuals and heads of organisations who are taking a tax stand, for without people taking a stand, the taxation that we all pay will only get worse and the Government's power, size and resulting wastage will get bigger and bigger.

Instead of the present Constitution Convention being entirely barren, it could call for an amendment to the Constitution to prohibit any government or official from increasing existing taxes, or imposing new taxes unless the move had the prior approval of the people at a referendum.

May I suggest to your readers that they all write letters to their State and federal MPs, also to their local government, asking these people for details of what they are doing to cut down taxation and government wastage and if they are doing nothing, then ask them to resign.

LANG HANCOCK
Perth
3/8/78

PS

That's entertainment

Movies

The rebirth of our films

AS major financier behind the totally Australian feature film 2000 Weeks, may we congratulate Mr Laurie Thomas' attitude towards the rebirth of a film industry.

The relationship between gaining finance for a film and subsequent distribution of the end product does — and probably will always — have an element of chance.

But in re-establishing a thriving film industry within Australia there is one other major factor to be considered. May we explain by example:

Our decision to take the risk in providing the major percentage of the finance and production facilities required to make 2000 Weeks was not tempered by distribution possibilities alone.

The major reason was to give the opportunity to actors, technical crews, production personnel — and a young director (Tim Burstall) to gain the experience so vitally necessary for them to make the box office successes in the future.

Mr Thomas wrote: "Another thing 2000 Weeks emphasises is that the future must lie with the independent producers like Burstall."

In principle, we disagree with the terminology used, which is slightly astray. Burstall acted as director, not producer.

As chairman of Senior Films, I act as producer, but my company supplies the production services.

No one man can hold the key to the future of films in Australia.

But far-sighted film production companies with the financial means to support creative film people and to provide the necessary skilled technical crews, to the point where the product is made available to the distributor, can do so.

That is what happened with 2000 Weeks. It will happen again both through our own efforts here at Senior and through similar companies with aligned enlightened farsightedness in Australia.

D. J. BILCOCK
Chairman
Senior Film Productions
St Kilda, Vic
21/10/68

HOW can Australia begin to think of establishing a film industry when its repressive 19th-century censorship forbids the entry of important films even for study purposes?

It is a matter of urgency that young film makers be allowed access to the best of new cinema if our film sensibility is not to become hopelessly dated, left behind at the level of middle-aged public servants.

This problem is bound to become more acute, as serious film makers today look to every aspect of human activity for film material. They will no longer be comprom-

Taboos must go

ised by the traditional taboos. Film makers must be as free as writers to question morality, society, the status quo.

Even in recent films where the sex act is explicitly shown — as in I Am Curious (Yellow) by Vilgot Sjorman, where it is woven into the powerful social and political commentary — the events are handled with a directness and candor which pre-

cludes embarrassment or disgust.

I saw this film in a large country cinema in Holland, with a general public audience and they didn't turn a hair. Why should they? It was an experience reasonably familiar to all of them.

After film-making in London for four years, I recently returned to take up a fellowship at the Australian National University, but I am appalled at these unfamiliar restrictions on my freedom to see the films needed to keep in touch with important overseas work.

ARTHUR CANTRILL
Canberra
11/6/69

Movies

We need foresight, not another sop

Piddling incentive

IN her article, aptly headed Where's The Wild Applause For That Film Grant? Miss Sylvia Lawson has expressed very well the feelings of the majority of people who want to make films in Australia.

In ignoring the main issue and handing out a sop, the Government has made another sidestep in line with the prevailing policy of seeming to patch and mend for political expediency, instead of building for the future.

What is urgently wanted first and foremost to make films in Australia is the establishment of a government borrowing fund — not a subsidy — and submissions to this effect have been made to the Government for years now. This borrowing fund is vitally necessary because the accepted and traditional source of investment in film production — that is, from distributors — is not available in Australia.

In allocating public money for the formation of a school and for experimental films, the Government is putting the cart before the horse — the Government-sponsored drama and ballet schools were established after professional drama and ballet companies had been established, not vice versa.

Viable and continuous film production is not only a matter of importance to the 15,000 people represented by the Australian Film Council; it is also a matter of national importance. It is more than time that our films were shown on the screens of the world. They would do more for Australia than all the

embassies or tourist bureaus and every politician and businessman knows that trade follows the film.

The Council for the Arts Film Committee recommended to the Government that a borrowing fund of $1 million should be set up. The Vincent Report recommended this, the Willis Report recommended it, Williamson Powell International Films, in conjunction with Actors Equity, the Musicians Union, the Writers Guild and other responsible associations recommended it and the Australian Film Council will continue to recommend it.

JOHN McCALLUM
Artarmon, NSW
20/8/69

PS

RON Randell, speaking on an Australian film he proposes to make, was reported to have said: "Perhaps we will have one of our Aborigines talking about his nickel shares — but whatever we do we will strive for realism." Ha! Ha! Ha!
E. COX
Hamilton, Qld
10/4/70

THE more I see, hear and read about the film, They're a Weird Mob, the more I am becoming convinced that if this film gets loose on the screens of the world, it will make this country and its people the laughing stock of the world.
W. O. RANKIN
South Brisbane, Qld
2/9/66

THE $5000 annual Australian Film Development Corporation award, just announced, for the best Australian feature-length film suitable for cinema distribution is about as useful in the life-saving sense to the industry as tossing a jellybaby to a man dying of starvation.

If the award were to be given for the best screenplay or direction, fair enough. But $5000 to be awarded to the production company concerned "to help it with future productions" makes the amount piddling in the extreme.

The Minister for the Arts, Mr Howson, deserves a special award himself for what must surely be the punchline of the year — "I hope this (the award) will stimulate private investment in national productions and lead to a greater continuity in production and employment in the industry."

Those of us who have suffered the soul-destroying frustration of managing to raise sufficient private investment to produce an award-winning film with wide overseas acceptance, only to find no outlets whatsoever at home in Australia, would love to know how a tiny and insignificant annual carrot of $5000 is going both to entice our industrial tycoons and provide work for our skilled technicians.

I have in front of me a detailed budget for just such a film in length and type as required for the $5000 award. The budget totals $81,000.

REG BARRY
Mt Waverley, Vic
14/4/72

Movies

Writer-knocking is condemned

PIP James *(The Australian, 11/4)* quotes visiting English actor Robert Powell as being bitter about the worldwide "American cultural dominance."

He is quoted as saying he finds Australia an exciting place to make films and "the energy, the vitality and the talent are phenomenal here. My Brilliant Career is a wonderful film."

He is quoted as saying there is nothing wrong with the industry that good scriptwriters wouldn't fix.

Evidently the "talent" Mr Powell discovered here did not extend to the local scriptwriters and the inference is that all we need to make our industry perfect is new scriptwriters.

In that one keeps being told every good film is based on a good script, one wonders how Sunday Too Far Away, Picnic At Hanging Rock, Caddie, The Devil's Playground, The Last Wave et al, of which My Brilliant Career is only one, have managed to gain us so much kudos overseas.

Were these films all successes — at least in the eyes of overseas film buffs — inspite of their scripts?

Maybe one should get used to this writer-knocking. After all, the writer is the invisible member of the creative team and the obvious bunny.

But what Mr Powell doesn't seem to realise is that in repeating this hoary old furphy, he is encouraging the very things he claims to abhor — foreign cultural dominance.

Already the invasion of the Australian film industry has begun and the result of this importation of the third and fourth rate (what other writers would come for the money offered?) will be the emigration of the local first rate.

The appreciation offered Australian writers overseas is very tempting. In fact, if this unrealistic "inferiority" nonsense gains much more credence, Australia may wake up one day to find itself, once again, with no film industry.

Of course, films will be made here — kangaroo westerns, pornography and violence, all nationalistically unidentifiable except as part of the multinational plastic limbo whose "culture" is based on the sacred creed of the fast buck.

If anyone thinks this is a far-fetched vision of the distant future, let him find out where much public money is going even now.

Australian writers are the cornerstones on which the Australian film industry is founded. Without them it would cease to exist.

ELEANOR WITCOMBE
Hunters Hill, NSW
29/4/80

We can laugh at ourselves

I AM relieved to see that the first Robert Menzies scholar, Mr Aly Eyiam, thinks that the film, Adventures of Barry McKenzie, has set Australia's image back a mere 10 years in London. Most Australian critics claim that our crash hot international status was retarded 30 years, but then I suppose that Mr Eyiam's judgment — being that of a Robert Menzies Scholar — would be the more accurate assessment.

No doubt we can expect a report of further shattering damage after the London release of Barry McKenzie Holds His Own next March.

It still surprises me that a couple of innocuous comedy films could cause such reactions. It's not as if Barry McKenzie is even slightly interested in damaging any aspect of Australian society (compare, say, Easy Rider); in addition, he embodies all the traditional virtues — mateship, family values, patriotism and integrity.

He may be fond of the amber fluid, but even the most rigorous Robert Menzies scholar would find it hard to maintain that this addition is foreign to the Australian Way of Life.

I think that the English see the Barry McKenzie films as a sign of Australia's maturity. They are proof we can laugh at ourselves.

BRUCE BERESFORD
Turramurra, NSW

(The writer is the director of Adventures of Barry McKenzie and Barry McKenzie Holds His Own.)
2/1/75

That's Television entertainment

A sad outlook for our TV writers

LET us hope that Mr Francis Evers' rousing article on the position of Australian scriptwriters (9/1) will stimulate some action from those who have the power to change this state of affairs.

Not simply because we ask for the right to be allowed to earn a living in our own country — though this is a very real need, heaven knows! — but we feel that Australians, sometime, are entitled to see their own national way of life, their history and their character, reflected in the television drama that is shown on their screens. Apart from one series showing in Melbourne, there is no Australian drama at all showing on our commercial television stations — although 70 per cent of viewing time on these stations between 7.30 pm and the time stations close is occupied by imported drama, American and English.

The Writers' Guild has put forward a proposal to encourage local productions, which would involve commercial stations in devoting as little as 1.3 per cent of their total viewing time to locally written and produced drama and documentary. This would give writers and actors here a chance to earn a living, would allow them to develop through continuing work, would allow a television drama set in their own country — but the Postmaster-General has replied that he is not convinced that this is in the best interests of television program productions.

We can only hope that the Government will soon implement a plan that will serve the interests of Australian television. It will have to happen soon, if the flow of actors and writers out of this country is to be halted.

I have just returned from London, where I have seen at first-hand the angry disappointment of our writers and actors living there. Almost without exception, they are doing well in London — very well — but many of them would like to return to live in their own country, to put their experience to use in local television or films. But they know they can't do this, because there is no work for them in Australia.

How sad that markets do not exist for us in Australia; how sad that there is no support for us in our own country.

RICHARD LANE
President
The Australian Radio,
Television and Screen
Writers Guild
Sydney
13/7/65

Sacred cows

SO the Mavis Bramston Show is to be censored because one bishop sold his Ampol shares and a few ministers asked their congregations to protest. Have the churches now become guardians of our morals to such an extent that they can dictate policy to the TV stations?

For the first time, we've been given the opportunity to enjoy a TV show that, no matter what its faults, does at least endeavor to give us a little humor and demolish a few of our "Sacred Cows" at the same time. I really don't think that this will harm us in any way — why with a little bit of luck it could give us a more realistic attitude to life.

As far as I'm concerned, I'll stick to Ampol if Ampol stick with the Mavis Bramston Show.

GREGORY BROOK
Ballarat, Vic
2/4/65

PS

IF Mr Hawke of the ACTU wants his nose bloodied, let him just once use the term Royal Apartheid Air Force (This Day Tonight, 23/6) in my presence.
W. K. HOLDSWORTH
West Burleigh, Qld
(The writer was a flight-lieutenant with the RAAF during World War II.)
2/7/71

Television

Color — a luxury we can forgo

I HAVE been most disturbed by recent news items which indicate that the Commonwealth Government is giving serious consideration to the introduction of color television in Australia.

While I agree that television as such is a most useful medium of communication, I consider that **color** television is a luxury which we could well forgo. To introduce it would be evidence that we had a most peculiar and self-centred set of values.

The many millions of dollars which the introduction of color television would cost could, I believe, be spent more usefully on increasing aid to under-developed countries, or on education or social services within Australia.

I hope that other Australians will join me in this protest by writing to the press or to MPs now, before the Commonwealth Government has spent so much on conversion preparations that it feels obliged to introduce this expensive luxury.

JOHN C. N. GOOCH
O'Connor, A.C.T.
26/11/68

Blue shows and the red menace

ONE must agree with all the technical reasons for the early introduction of color TV to Australia advanced by Mr G. A. Taylor. But he misses the real reasons why the Government is blocking its introduction.

As I understand the principle of color TV, it employs the blending of the three primary colors.

Now as you know, the average, overprotected, ill-educated Australian has to be saved from blue shows, the red menace and the yellow hordes.

The Government, therefore, with due concern for the taxpayers, wishes to prevent us from wasting our money buying very expensive color TV sets for viewing only grey material.

P. M. BAMFORTH
Heathcote, NSW
15/11/68

PS

HOW very apt and utterly predictable that our "land of the moron" should choose a horse-race to launch the era of color television. And how ironic that the chairman of our so-called Broadcasting Control Board is willing to ignore the wishes of the Minister for the Media to ensure that we can enjoy this "colorful" racing spectacle and yet, year in and year out, allows commercial television channels to poison the minds of our children with endless hours of cartoons, give-aways and "competitions" hosted by mindless morons — all in the name of children's television. And how sick and depressing it all is.

D. SCOTT-LUMLEY
South Yarra, Vic
7/6/74

Moral choice

THE choice whether or not to indulge in the indolent non-participant super-luxury of color TV is coming to the people of Australia several years later than it did in the U.S., Europe or Japan.

In those few years there has been a tremendous increase in our awareness of the limits to the resources on this planet, of the part that every advance in technology plays in accelerating the destruction of those resources, and of the appalling inequalities of their use between peoples.

(Barbara Ward points out that a child born in the U.S. will put 500 times the demand on world resources of a child born in central Africa or India.)

The Club of Rome recently stated: "The energy crises is the first of a series of predictable events . . . Nothing will be as before and there is no longer any excuse to pretend ignorance of the menace ahead of us, of the profound wrongness of the present direction in which humanity persists in moving, by inertia or by narrow motivation."

There is need to call a halt somewhere to the continuing greed in the affluent countries; and for Australia now, color TV presents a challenge line.

There is, for each individual, a simple alternative to buying a color TV set. The estimated total cost of $800 to $1000 can be donated to Austcare or Freedom from Hunger for the starving people in Africa.

So we each now face a moral choice. Our individual decisions will be difficult to hide. There will be no need to mark the houses. Visitors do call. And children talk.

G. LOFTUS HILLS
Lower Plenty, Vic
8/6/74

Television

Just token Australian content

THE recent assertions that Australian television is "the best television in the world" and that a 75 per cent Australian content would "largely ignore viewers' likes, lower art standards and promote sloppiness in Australian productions" are simply untrue.

Do you realise that today's TV programs are predominantly tired re-runs of old programs? In two recent weeks in Melbourne, the combined TV stations showed 110 movies, of which no less than 106 were "repeat" programs. According to my desk calculator, that is a cool 96.36 per cent!

This system of multiple repeats — perhaps derived from the philosophy of the TV advertiser — is also applied to almost all the imported comedy series seen today and is the standard rule in the case of children's cartoons.

The quality of Australian films and TV productions cannot be assessed by studying cheaply made handyman and gardening features which are promoted by the networks as a token gesture to Australian content.

Why have the majority of the 400 or so films listed in the catalogues of the Sydney Filmmakers Co-operative, or the Melbourne Vincent Library never been seen on national television?

If the recent productions of the young filmmakers of the Australian Film and Television School are good enough to show to an international audience at the Australia 75 festival of arts and sciences in Canberra next month, why cannot they be seen on commercial TV?

It is the network's lack of support of young film-makers which is preventing the cost of Australian film production from dropping even lower.

The great Australian film pioneers of the '20s — such as Longford, Hurley and the McDonald sisters — were "bludgeoned into creative silence" by American and British film chain monopolists.

If public support is not given to the Federal Government's bold initiative at Terrigal to promote the showing of Australian films and video productions to TV audiences, history will inevitably and tragically repeat itself.

BASIL GILBERT
Parkville, Vic
(The writer is lecturer in the history of art at·the University of Melbourne.)
19/2/75

Our history is worth exploiting

THE comment by Reg Barry (Letters, 22/4) on Australian period drama for TV — "We just do not have the history, nor the background to exploit . . . we have a surfeit of galloping-through-the-gumtrees sagas and gold-rush epics, but how long can that last?" — cannot go unchallenged.

I would have hoped that the "cultural cringe" of Australians towards their heritage would not have manifested itself in one of our leading TV writers. It has always staggered me that so little attention has been given by Australian TV and film producers to the enormous potential for exciting, and dare I say it, "educational" TV programs on our rich and diverse history.

Ben Hall and Rush are just two fine examples of what can be done, but the potential is still untapped.

Where are the writers and the producers to recreate on screen the establishment of the first colony at Sydney Cove, the Irish convict rebellion, the Rum rebellion, the story of Macarthur and Macquarie, the sagas of those who battled the elements to establish Australia's pastoral industry, the explorers. Eureka Stockade, the appalling treatment of the Aborigines, the great shearers' strike of 1891, the battle over conscription, the Lang dismissal, Australia at war and so on, just to mention a few.

I have heard rumor that Marcus Clarke's epic novel, For the Term of His Natural Life, is to be made into a film. Great!

Has anyone thought of making a film on that most controversial of figures, Billy Hughes, or the fascinating struggle of the life of John Curtin?

Australia's history is as rich and diversified as the United States'. It is up to our TV writers and producers to get off their backsides and use their imagination. To paraphrase Mr Barry: "We get the TV writers and producers we deserve."

B. COHEN
Labor MHR for Robertson
Gosford, NSW
26/4/76

That's entertainment

The ABC has failed miserably

FOR years I've been under the misguided impression that television in Australia should be led by the ABC.

I think this impression is a carry-over from the BBC — Steptoe, Call It What You Like, The Rag Trade and Hancock.

This is not true in Australia, even though the ABC consistently imports overseas producers and copies overseas shows.

The blunt fact is that in Australia the ABC fails miserably and the lead has been taken by commercial stations or production houses which operate on a fairly small but successful budget and format.

Their ratings are high and their contributions successful — Mavis, McGooley, Homicide, Pick-A-Box and even Showcase.

What has the ABC achieved by itself and its gargantuan collection of staff, studios and equipment spread throughout the nation?

On the ABC early on a Friday night — peak time, actually — you can watch How to Build a Boat and its exciting sequel, How to Sail a Boat.

Not long ago, Mr Duckmanton became general manager and many newspapers reported a new look for the ABC.

It's been a year now and, frankly, I preferred the old look — the ballets, operas, historical dramas, Lorrae Desmond.

So far the new look has comprised Nice 'n Juicy (now scrapped), Australian Playhouse (a thundering bore), Be Our Guest (the bomb of the year, now under the title of Something Else, which is still something terrible).

Soon the ABC will again present an old favorite, Eric Jupp and his orchestra, but the presentation will be the same — a collection (or gaggle) of musicians of assorted shapes and sizes, sitting among microphones, cables, and music stands.

Behind will be a weird contraption which the ABC loosely calls a set.

Perhaps there will be a lone singer stuck in a corner.

This format was discarded soon after television began, because it was decided it was "radio with pictures."

Will the ABC get out of its rut — or will it wallow, continuing to set television back a hundred years?

CHARLES BURNETT
Woollahra, NSW
20/3/67

To the barricades . .

I APPLAUD Kenneth Hince's attack on the ABC's "piddling personality cultism" as evidenced in its music programs (The Australian, 9/1).

I would add that, through its "personalities," the ABC seems to have abandoned the barricades and to be contributing to the debasement of the language and the Barry Humphreysisation of poetry.

In a recent program I heard a "personality" use the deathless phrase: "We didn't used to be able to play that." Mediocre pop singers are great "talents;" the merely average are "fantastic" — while the ultimate accolade for, say, Cilla Black, is "absolutely fantastic."

On January 4, I heard a "personality" describe a ham sandwich as "fabulous" — three times.

The tragi-comic ineptitude of the Hospital Hour man and his doggerel are surpassed only by the between-records inanities on traffic and the weather of the lady who rides the air-waves in Sydney on week-day afternoons.

To the barricades, Kenneth Hince — I'm with you!

PATRICK CONNOR
Epping, NSW
9/1/71

The ABC

Sack the lot — start again

BEING the biggest might be a selling point for banks, but has its drawbacks for a creative organisation.

Most of the ABC's problems can be attributed to sheer size. Management has lost effective contact with creative staff and is driven to try to rule by anonymous decree.

The production staff, for their part, tend to operate in self-indulgent, quarrelsome little fiefs — each seeking as much as it can get for itself without regard for the good of the whole and without any true sense of fiscal responsibility.

It is natural for any good, aggressive producer to fight for what he thinks he needs in terms of budget, staff, technical facilities and air time. But the ABC producer, unlike his commercial-TV counterpart, does not have to be concerned with a final reckoning in terms of his company's balance sheet.

The best producers, of course, are concerned that the dollars they spend bear some relation to potential audience. But they are surrounded in each department by a damaging percentage of has-beens and never-beens who either waste precious program dollars by doing nothing, or waste even more by trying to do something.

But the organisation has reached a point of size and bureaucratic rigidity where it is simply incapable of weeding out the drones.

One solution might be to sack everyone and start from scratch with just three people; a program manager, an accountant and an engineer.

Rather than producing its own programs, the ABC would offer contracts to independent program packagers in public affairs, drama, education etc. Many of these packagers, of course, would probably come from within the old ABC production units.

For example, producers from Four Corners or Torque or Certain Women would simply set up their own companies, recruit the staff they want and work out a competitive price for the kind of format they offer.

At the same time, programs would no longer have to carry the huge administrative overheads imposed by the whole Public Service infrastructure of assistant general managers, controllers, State managers etc.

The packaging concept would also offer a valuable spin-off for the whole issue of support for the arts. Instead of various councils and boards dishing out hundreds of thousands of dollars in grants for projects that will never see the inside of a TV screen, the ABC would serve as a genuine new market for talented film and program makers.

Any program packager who didn't meet ABC standards in one contract period would not be invited back.

Many of my ABC friends will be quick to say what an unworkable idea this is (e.g. what would we do about News? Answer: it would be an exception).

But it would be interesting to read their thoughts as they looked around their departments, considering how much money they would really need to produce their current program as a competitive package — and which of their colleagues they would choose to do it.

GERALD STONE
Producer Interviewer
TCN 9
Willoughby, NSW
(Mr Stone formerly worked on ABC-TV current affairs).
6/4/76

PS

THERE must be thousands, like myself, who are laughing their heads off at the anguished screams of conservative politicians about ABC "bias." For the first time in living memory, the Labor Party is getting a reasonably fair go from the media; and these spoiled darlings hate it.
LARRY DRAKE
Rathdowney, Qld
28/8/72

THE intended ABC presentation, in February and March, of an Elgar 3 Concerts Festival featuring eight of Elgar's best-loved works without featuring his Pomp And Circumstance March is akin to Digger Revell failing to perform My Little Rockers Turned Surfie! Figs up their noses!
PHILIP ASPDEN
Jervis Bay, NSW
20/1/81

The ABC

To hell with ratings!

IF she is not very careful, the ABC will soon be falling into t' e same cultural quagmire in which most of the commercial radio and TV stations in Australia flounder.

Surely the ABC's charter clearly states that the purpose of the commission is to provide an alternate; an alternative to the "flash, bang, wallop," over-commercialised "talk-like-an-ocker," Top 40 and "kitchen-sink" broadcast.

It appears Aunty is worried about not having a large enough audience, so for the sake of ratings she is prepared to lower her standards and "prostitute" herself.

Australia looks to the ABC to set high cultural standards, not plunge headlong into the abyss of everyday commercialism.

The ABC has enough problems with her budget cuts. Budget cuts are fine if the hangers-on and bludgers are axed, but unfortunately it is the creative element within the ABC which seems to suffer.

Already the ABC's Sydney Show Band has been eliminated; next it will be the Sydney Symphony which is trimmed and heaven knows they need encouragement.

Let's leave Aunty on her pedestal. Let's take a leaf out of the BBC's book and maintain the highest standards of fine music, news, current affairs and feature broadcasts. The ABC has the necessary finance and facilities.

If she doesn't stop trying to sell herself to the masses, she'll become just another station on the dial.

The ABC should retain her gracious image of sophisticated, intellectually stimulating entertainment. There are, however, minor signs that the decay has started.

If going after ratings means the ABC lowering her standards and losing her individuality, then to hell with the ratings.

G. BENNETT
Eastwood, NSW
4/3/76

Channel 2 for deja vu

MAY I enlist the support of your paper to persuade the ABC to stop repeating programs on TV.

This evening (20/1) on Channel 2 between 6.30 pm and the close of transmission, only one program is not a repeat and it goes deeper than that.

One program is The Best Of Peach's Australia, which is itself a repeat of a program already presented twice. Since the original program was made in 1976, it is now in its sixth year on television and I have seen each episode four times.

Without any warning, even Weekend Magazine is now entirely repeats.

To cap the lot, in honor of Australia Day, we are now going to have Australia Week. Previews reveal that once again we are to be bombarded with repeats. Patriotism is indeed the last refuge of a scoundrel.

If the ABC is interested in a catchy slogan may I suggest: Channel 2 for deja vu.

R. WEBB
Gympie, Qld
27/1/81

'Orrible, ain't it!

AS one who worked for many years for the ABC, I wish to endorse the letter written to your paper (29/9) by Richard Turner, of Mt Waverley, Victoria, concerning some of the speech emanating from the ABC.

A number of ABC announcers are, in my opinion, semi-literate, possess insufficient general knowledge to be able to carry out their duties, such as news reading, competently and are grossly overpaid for their inefficiency.

Surely, "top-paid" news readers should know a smattering of the French language, when not speaking American, as the majority of announcers appear to be doing. Long Es when there should be short ones and vice versa is one of the many sins which are, apparently, the order of the day.

Why do they not study either the Oxford-English dictionary or the book on spoken English, provided by the ABC.

I suppose one cannot blame the young people of today when most of their school teachers say "haitch" instead of "aitch."

'Orrible, ain't it?

CHARLES PECKOVER
Noosa Heads, Qld
14/10/76

PS

THANK goodness ABC radio and TV went on strike. After listening to the commercial stations for 24 hours, one realises how good the ABC is.

Z. McLEOD
Elizabeth Bay, NSW
6/12/76

The great debates

Death sentence

Ronald Ryan was the last man hanged in Australia. He was executed at Melbourne's Pentridge Jail on February 3, 1967, convicted of having murdered prison warden, George Hodson, while escaping from Pentridge Jail in December, 1965. Ryan's execution caused a bitter controversy through Australia.

The mark of immature society

SIR Henry Bolte and the Executive Council of Victoria have had to make what must have been an agonising decision.

They deserve our utmost sympathy and the support of our constant prayers.

We, the people of Victoria, cannot stand apart from them. They represent us and their decision is ours, for which we are all responsible.

Capital punishment reflects the attitude of our society in general to violence: violence is the mark of an immature society and the increase of violence among us is an indication that we are becoming a less, not more, mature society.

If Ryan is executed, many of us will feel ashamed — not so much of the Government, but of ourselves who allow (and even encourage) the sort of society where such methods of retribution are still possible.

But I and many others believe that though we may still deserve thus to be put to shame, capital punishment is now outdated.

The commutation of every capital sentence in Victoria since 1951 is an indication that the Government reflects a public opinion which is coming round to the same belief.

We know much that our fathers did not know, including the established fact that capital punishment is no deterrent.

But even if it were, we appreciate now what the prophets and preachers have been telling us for years; that no man's life, however bad he may be, may be taken away as an example to others.

Each is an end in himself.

The executed man may have a second chance in the life beyond death, but society has no second chance; an execution can only mean that we refuse to accept the responsibility so clearly laid upon us, and if carried out we would be left in a morally weaker position than we were before.

(Dr) FRANK WOODS
Anglican Archbishop
of Melbourne
6/1/67

PS

WE would like to wish Sir Henry Bolte and the Victorian Cabinet a Merry Christmas and a topping New Year.
TONY MORPHETT, NEIL SHARD, WILLIAM PINWILL, RICHARD ZOELLER, S. STERN, JOHN HEPWORTH, LACHLAN SHAW, PAUL ORMONDE, B. S. SOHDA
West Heidelberg, Vic
28/12/66

Death sentence

What of the victim?

PATRICK Tennison (*The Australian*, 28/12) castigates supporters of hanging as emotional — then proceeds to quote at length Hugh Buggy's harrowing accounts of hangings.

Yet the impact of these would be completely lost if they did not trade upon the emotions!

If justice were to be done in this matter, these accounts should be balanced by reports of the last moments of the murderers' victims.

The utter injustice of murder is that the killer is always given a fair trial, his victim none.

When Tennison sneers at our being emotional, he misses the cardinal point: that we, the myriad laymen, are emotional, even though we may hide it.

Man is an emotional animal.

Our being emotional is the price we pay for possessing the five senses, for being human.

If we were not so, the matter of crime and punishment would be irrelevant.

So long as we fear hanging — and the sane majority do — it is a deterrent. Fear, righteous fear, is not to be sneered at.

Of course, some lawyers decry hanging.

There is always the chance that an unhanged killer will provide further work for the legal profession, a number of whose members, like the police, would be destitute without crime.

And some politicians oppose hanging. Their brave opposition is such a useful, emotional vote-catcher.

There are none so blind as will not see the close connection between the low frequency of hangings and the escalation of killings, bashings, brutality, cruelty to children and general lawlessness in these "enlightened" days.

Perhaps prosperity, affluence and a general softening of outlook is to be blamed.

To quote Dickens, "Hunger is a great sharpener of the intellect."

DENNIS HODGKINSON
Launceston, Tas
31/12/66

PS

IN the Masses I have said since last Wednesday, I have been praying for Ronald Ryan and also for the dead Pentridge warder, George Henry Hodson and those who were dear to each of them. Even more earnestly I have prayed for those who, having the power to choose between life and death for Ryan, rejected the well-argued appeals of so many wise and enlightened members of our community. They are surely the ones most in need of prayer.

(Fr) M. E. COSTIGAN
Glen Iris, Vic
30/1/67

IT is a pity all those who vociferate so quickly and loudly against the hanging of a hardened criminal do not search their conscience when they remain silent at the incineration of innocent children in Vietnam.

HARRY SOBOTT
Ringwood East, Vic
28/12/66

One life cannot pay for another

AS a member of the teaching profession, I am concerned about the moral and intellectual development of our society.

I am appalled by the recent decisions made by the authorities in the case of Ronald Ryan and hope that this State of Victoria will show itself in a better light before it is too late to revoke its decision.

Capital punishment is useless and senseless.

The murder committed by Ryan was that of a desperate man. It was not premeditated.

One life cannot pay for another and we would be guilty of a second murder.

Certainly, for public safety, Ryan should be kept well locked up.

It is every society's obligation to pay for the upkeep of its jails and their inhabitants who are morally ill, as it is to pay for its hospitals for those who are physically, or mentally ill.

To make matters worse, the decision by the Government to carry out the sentence was made during the Christmas season in a country professing Christianity.

It was also decided upon after the elections and by ballot. What kind of a nation is this?

A lottery system is used to determine which men go to Vietnam and now a vote has been taken upon a man's life.

We seem to have only progressed from "two-up" and racecourses to some kind of parliamentary Russian roulette — as grim, but more cowardly.

(Miss) A. RANDALL
Newport, Vic
31/12/66

Death sentence

Majority favored Ryan's execution

THE heading of your leading article for Friday, February 3 — A Black Day For Australia — shows how ill-equipped you are to understand, or at least to shed light upon, a subject of concern to the public.

It would, indeed, have been a black day for Australia had the near-monopoly press of this country — for reasons that have mystified numerous people — bulldozed the Victorian Government into letting Ryan escape the justified penalty.

Your statement that "logic, public feeling and human decency have been beaten this time" is impertinent and it implicitly insults more than half your readers.

A fact that you have chosen to disregard is that any proper canvass of public opinion in Victoria would have shown a substantial majority in favor of execution.

And this for a very good reason — a reason that apparently has also escaped your attention.

J. E. PYKE
East Hawthorn, Vic
9/2/67

A tribute

AS one of the large number of Victorians who are convinced that Cabinet was right in the Ryan case, I wish to pay my tribute to Cabinet's steadfastness in carrying out the terrible duty imposed on it by the law.

Weaker, smaller men would have bowed to the whipped-up storm of abuse and misrepresentation.

It is to our leaders' credit that they put conscience before political popularity and hundreds of thousands of Victorians now honor them for staying faithful through such an ordeal.

R. T. CORRIE
East Kew, Vic
9/2/67

Macabre breakfast session

SO Sir Henry managed to fit in his grisly, macabre little breakfast party after all.

Perhaps he feels the gods will be appeased for another 16 years now.

So much for the theory of the civilised State: in one brutal moment a society is transported far back in time.

The ritual is exactly the same, but the event is rather more obscene now because the participants are paying lip service to another philosophy, even as the rope tightens.

I wonder if, up on the hill, Pontius Pilate washed his hands before sitting down to breakfast.

But at least it is all done properly — with dignity.

The medical man ensures there is no injustice by pronouncing the murderer officially dead and in the same instant God's servant clutches another soul for the Church.

The whole gruesome event has possibly given a perverted minority the opportunity to indulge in morbid curiosity at others' misfortune.

Patrick Tennison's disgusting little piece, Death of Ronald Ryan (*The Australian*, 4/2) must have finished off their day nicely.

Most certainly it has degraded society and driven another nail in the coffin of man's dignity.

My seven-year-old son, on hearing that there was to be no reprieve said, "I think the judges are all murderers!"

Ah well, perhaps there is some hope for the soul of society after all.

MILES WOHLERS
Parkdale, Vic
9/2/67

PS

SIR Henry appears to have made much of Ryan's intractable nature. I feel that the condemned and the Premier shared much in common. Perhaps it is one of the perverse jokes of nature that the one should be killed to the greater glory of the other.
NIGEL SINCLAIR
Burdekin, Qld
9/2/67

LIKE you, I trust that Sir Henry is satisfied: the return to the dark ages has shocked not only thinking people in this country, but throughout the world. I hope that all those who so strongly opposed the hanging will continue to work until this archaic and morally indefensible law is removed from the statute book.
R. A. CHAPMAN
Box Hill South, Vic
9/2/67

Death sentence

I still remember the day

DRAW a graph to a historical time base, from the time of Nero, past medieval torture, past mass hangings for petty theft not so long ago, past the death penalty for murder and treason only, to its final abolition, already reached in most of the more civilised states and countries — and even Sir Henry must realise that the inevitable is only a matter of time.

My concern is not one for the murderer, but for a society still employing man to hang fellow man by his neck unto death.

Brought up by a father who only despised the hangman more than he despised the murderer, I can now — a generation later — assure my own children that the days of the hangman are counted.

But thanks to our Government they will be able to say to their own children, "I still remember the day when they hanged a man in Melbourne.

"The name of the Premier then was Sir Henry Bolte."

RICHARD SELIGMAN
Essendon, Vic
30/1/67

A doubt?

THE committee of the Council for Civil Liberties opposes capital punishment, a barbaric practice abandoned by most of the civilised countries of the world.

In its view, there is no evidence to show that capital punishment is effective in reducing the number of murders, which, in fact, have not increased in those countries which have abandoned it.

The British Royal Commission on Capital Punishment warned against the acceptance of "exaggerated esti-

mates of the uniquely deterrent force of the death penalty."

One strong argument against capital punishment is that if a man has been wrongly convicted, the mistake cannot be rectified.

In the case of Ronald Ryan, the letter written by Mr Opas QC to the Chief Secretary raises a disquieting doubt that he may after all be innocent.

A. K. STOUT
President
Council for Civil Liberties
Sydney
30/1/67

Retaliation

AS I await the birth of a child, what should have been a time of joy for me has been turned to a time of horror with the thought that Ronald Ryan will be hanged in my name while I strive to produce a new life.

We claim to be a Christian community — Sir Henry Bolte would object to being called anti-Christian.

Yet the basic laws laid down by Christ were the Ten Commandments, including "Thou shalt not kill."

How can the community accept such blatant denial of a basic Christian principle?

That Ryan was unfortunate enough to have the opportunity to kill and took it, is no excuse for retaliation of this sort.

Instead, attention to prison reform and security is the duty of the Government.

But it is much cheaper to kill the culprit legally and pretend the same thing will never happen again.

It's a fine way to celebrate Australia Day.

(Mrs) J. A. BEACHAM
Birchip, Vic
30/1/67

Sir Henry Bolte

Black tie gesture

THE Government of Victoria has decided to hang Ryan.

This action, in the face of contra opinion by the more civilised in church, professional and press opinion circles, will reduce all of us in Victoria to the ranks of barbarism.

"No man is an island unto himself . . ." Let those of us who feel deeply about this and who are frustrated and impotent to prevent it, wear black ties tomorrow.

Not only for Ryan, but for all in Victoria.

Such a gesture, while ostensibly futile, would at least set the wearers apart from the successors, in this respect, of Ghengis Khan, Hitler, Stalin, Mao, Ho Chi Minh and the leaders of some of the less enlightened American states.

ALLAN TAYLOR
Canterbury, Vic
30/1/67

The great debates

It's wrong to send Australians

I DEEPLY deplore the decision of the Australian Government to send an Australian infantry battalion to fight in Vietnam. It not only contributes nothing to the solution of the problems of South-East Asia, but makes the findings of such a solution more difficult. It is fraught with very grave consequences for future generations of the Australian people.

I am in agreement with the vast body of public opinion throughout the world which recognises that the struggle in South Vietnam cannot be resolved by military measures and that only a negotiated settlement can bring an end to the insensate slaughter of many innocent people.

The emphasis placed on military measures by the decision of the Australian Government has made the initiation of negotiations more difficult, in that firstly it will help to destroy any hope that North Vietnam could continue to maintain its independence from China and will thus strengthen China's hand (it is nonsensical to think that a battalion of infantry sent by a nation numbering 11 million people will "soften up" a dictator who can command the military potential resident in a nation numbering 700 million close to the combat area); and secondly it will still further reduce the possibility of Russia's using its influence in furtherance of a negoti-

ated settlement. The Australian Government's decision will therefore prolong the agonies of the people of South Vietnam.

The inability of the United Nations to take a lead in the negotiations is in some measure the consequence of the Australian Government's refusal to support the admission to that body of the People's Republic of China.

The sooner our Government reverses its attitude in this respect, the better will be the chances that China will beome less intransigent than she is at present.

JOHN J. DEDMAN
Yarralumla, A.C.T.
6/5/65

AUSTRALIANS must be gravely disappointed at the unexpected secrecy of the Government's first conscription lottery draw.

The most disturbing feature of this secrecy is that it provides an almost impermeable cloak for the corruption that will inevitably surround the intake.

Under these conditions, it is hard to accept as sincere Sir Robert's assurance that the system is not open to corruption.

The new Minister for Labor and National Service has said that the dates drawn are to be kept secret to discourage those not already registered from alter-

Conscription corruption

ing birthdays. (He added that birth records were not being checked). If we are seriously to believe this, any 20-year-old could avoid all risk merely by adding a year or two to his age.

Having noted your defence correspondent's paternal warning to conscripts against playing hookey, might I ask a further question of him. If it is, in his words, unjust for the army to make a unilateral altera-

tion to a service contract, is it not a far more grievous injustice for men to be conscripted with the protection of no contract and where the conditions of service are not only unilateral but subject to alteration at the whim of a few politicians?

It seems that Captain Robertson's idea of democracy is rather quaint if he can pretend that conscription has been introduced "by democratic processess" when those to be conscripted have no vote and when the issue was not put to a referendum.

GEORGE ATKIN
Armidale, NSW
18/3/65

Vietnam war

The law of war

YOU published in your issue of April 26 a photograph which purported to be of a prisoner taken by the South Vietnamese being subjected by his captors to questioning accompanied by violence. Your caption stated that such prisoners were sometimes thrown out of aircraft by their captors. From time to time, photographs and reports to similar effect have recently been appearing in the Australian press.

I am not in a position to assess the genuineness of such photographs, the truth of the allegations involved, or the source from which they emanate. If they are true, however, we ought all to be voicing the most urgent protest against such flagrant violations of the law of war.

Under the Geneva Prisoners of War Convention of 1949, Articles 17-18, the prisoner of war is bound to give only a bare minimum of details concerning his surname, rank and number etc; is not to be subjected to torture; is to retain his articles of personal use, identity documents, badges of rank and other decorations.

Such prisoners are to be evacuated as soon as possible to an area where they will be out of danger from combat operations unless this is impossible because they are sick or wounded; and pending and during evacuation they are to be humanely treated, properly fed and clothed and to receive proper medical attention (Articles 19-20).

The public is accustomed to wartime allegations made by each side against the other of atrocities and outrageous violations of international law. We take them usually with mixture of feelings; pity and indignation at the cruelty of war, doubt whether one side is worse than the other; and sad resignation to the fact that organised violence inevitably brings lawlessness and immorality with it.

The reports recently appearing, however, demand, in case they are true, a more vigorous reaction. If they are untrue, they should be repudiated by the authorities concerned. If they are true, the authorities should be called upon to desist immediately from practices which can only undermine further our generation's tenuous hold on the principles of humanity.

JULIUS STONE
Challis Professor of
Jurisprudence and
International Law
Sydney University
29/4/65

£100 offer for children

THE offer of Mr Morris West (*The Australian*, 30/6) to pay for two children, victims of the Vietnam war, to be brought to Australia, should evoke deep admiration from those who are concerned for these children.

Yes, Mr West's offer has inspired at least one other to follow his lead; so I, the undersigned, hereby make an offer of £100 (perhaps more if required) to any one organisation willing and able to carry out this project.

I would like, if possible, to see children of the enemy, or of North Vietnam, brought here — not because of any ideological bias and not because I would deny any child in need, but because in the action we support against these people, we are more directly responsible for the plight of these children than those in South Vietnam.

In our anxiety to protect our own hearths and homes, we would render the enemy's children homeless; but Christ said, "For if you love those who love you, what reward have you?" (Matt 5:46).

I have not made my offer publicly to display piety before man, but in order that it may make others compare the meagre sums contributed to the cause of mercy and peace with the vast sums (billions) spent to destroy life and property that belong rightly tó God .

May Mr West, as a reward for his gesture, hear the voice of our Saviour say, "Inasmuch as ye have done this unto one of the least of these My brethren, ye have done it unto Me."

(Pastor) W. D. BRYCE
Baptist Minister
Kingaroy and
Nanango, Qld
8/7/65

PS

I AM most surprised and very disappointed that the young men of today lack the courage to refuse compulsory army service. We are a very long way from the white feather days when a man was judged a coward if he did not volunteer to become a piece of cannon fodder. Today, it requires courage and strength of character to say, "No, I will not be a soldier — I would rather go to jail." Are the sons and grandsons of our brave Anzacs really so gutless?

(Mrs) M. FORRESTER
Woollahra, NSW
14/5/65

Vietnam war

Cowardly?

YOU get called up. You decide you'll have to "make the best of it."

You put on a uniform and get ordered round as though you had no mind of your own. You are trained to kill and when you're sent away you kill, or are killed the way you're told to.

And everybody says how brave you are.

OR:

You get called up and you decide you're not going to be forced into killing peasants in a foreign country just because their politics happen to be different from yours.

You burn your draft card. You lose your job, you're asked to find another flat, you get poison-pen letters, you're the open mark of every dirty insult that can be hurled at you.

And people say what a coward you are.

ESTHER ROLAND
Kenmore, Qld
20/4/66

Appalled

AS the mother of a son who may be called up to go to Vietnam, I am appalled by the article in your newspaper by Jimmy Breslin (12/10), in which he describes how a young American machine-gunner unemotionally chews on a chocolate cracker and explains what a small spool of wire is used for. If Christians can watch dispassionately while American-trained Formosan mercenaries thread the wire through the hands and cheeks of Viet Cong prisoners so that the "gooks" sit quietly in a helicopter when wrapped up like that, what hope can there be for the world?

What has become of the Red Cross?

(Mrs) EVELYN MURRAY
Salisbury, SA
26/10/65

Picture says it all

I BUTTERED the toast, took the top off my freshly boiled egg and began breakfast.

The folded paper lay in front of me and I glanced at the picture (reproduced above).

I saw another woman. While I sat comfortably enjoying my first meal of the day, she crouched in fear.

My children were warm in their beds, too early for them to get up; this woman's children clung to her in the undergrowth, looking fearfully at the horror ahead.

My husband had just left for work, warmly clad and secure; her husband? Perhaps he lay broken and torn on the ground ahead of them; perhaps the blast of the falling bombs, or the jab of a bayonet had driven them into the open field.

The baby hung limp in her arms. Alive? I don't know.

Our lives are only six hours flying time apart. I live in a country where men go out to war and her home is their battlefield. Vietnam!

Perhaps if I didn't look at the picture, if I turned it over, after all, she lives away up there and what could I do . . . I didn't start the war . . . I didn't vote in the Government which condones it.

(Mrs) ESMA BROCHBANK
Cabramatta, NSW
4/9/67

Vietnam war

Moratorium: for and against

MAY I, through your paper, even at this late stage, ask the directors of the Vietnam Moratorium Campaign, with whom I have every sympathy, to adopt a more constructive policy?

I am unrepentant in my opposition to the Vietnam war but the "Call for a Vietnam moratorium" reads in part: "The only way to stop the war and retrieve the last vestige of national self-respect is by a total and immediate withdrawal of Australian and all other foreign troops from Vietnam."

With this, I cannot agree. We are in it up to our ears, but there are less ignominious ways of crawling out. The statement not only ignores the realities of power politics, but is incorrect on two counts. Total and immediate withdrawal of Australian and all other foreign troops, desirable as this may be, will not stop the war. The adoption of an isolationist policy by Australia towards South-East Asia will not retrieve the last vestige of national self-respect.

To leave South Vietnam in the hands of a corrupt, autocratic government which will be equipped with American arms means that the first victims will be the liberal section in the south. The war will continue to a bloody conclusion, of complete exhaustion.

It would not only save the face of our rulers, but even save lives if a force responsible to the United Nations could be established in Vietnam, seeking an armistice and keeping, as far as possible, the peace. To this force, Australia, however reluctantly, would of need contribute. Whether the great powers (and Australia) like it or not, the machinery and the charter of the United Nations provide a procedure for the settlement of such a situation as exists in South-East Asia. It is just that any great power — or any minor power such as our own — will seize on any duck-bottomed piece of power politics sooner than give any opportunity whatever to an international force.

You've got to be realistic and constructive about this thing. Even a pacifist such as myself can see that.

KYLIE TENNANT
Hunters Hill, NSW
21/4/70

I APPRECIATE the quandary of the university authorities as regards dealing with lecturers cancelling classes to participate in the moratorium.

However, Mr L. Chipman seems to have overlooked several vital issues in his letter (5/5).

First, the moratorium is not just another political demonstration, but an expression of moral disapproval of the senseless and sanguinary slaughter in Indo-China. Another very dubious assumption of Mr Chipman is that universities should not take a stand on the moral issues of the day.

The Vietnam conflict is no longer a mere "bush war," but possesses all the potential of escalating into a world-wide conflagration. How can academics afford to remain silent when a global conflict may be just around the corner? Furthermore, the fact that most Australians are apathetic towards the conflict does not absolve thinking individuals from outwardly committing themselves and showing their alarm by participating in the moratorium.

The university and its academics do not jeopardise their autonomy by supporting the moratorium, but, in fact, assert their independence by having the courage to openly commit themselves to the moratorium: It is more than another hair-brained political gambit.

P. C. MAYER
East Brighton, Vic
8/5/70

Magnificent welcome home

SYDNEY was magnificent in its response to the returning troops from Vietnam last Friday.

The warmth and spontaneity of the welcome was something that will be long remembered by those who took part in the march through the city.

After their 12 months' duty in Vietnam, the members of 5th Battalion, Royal Australian Regiment and elements of other units from Vietnam in the march appreciated the heart-felt response from Sydney people.

On behalf of the officers, troops and myself, may I convey through your columns my thanks to the people of Sydney for their wonderful welcome.

(Maj-Gen) J. W. HARRISON,
Sydney
18/5/67

Vietnam war

Why the moratorium is wrong

THE 10 Liberal MPs in their recent statements, attacked in your editorial (27/4), express not only their sentiments but those of the Liberal Party and, I believe, the sentiments of a vast majority of Australians.

The words they used may have been a bit stronger than I would have used, but the meaning was quite clear; they express the fear that the well-wishing, would-be humanitarians were being used by the Communist Party to achieve their own political ends and to frustrate the cause of freedom in the non-communist world.

It has become fashionable in some quarters to shrug off any anti-communist statement, no matter how mild or rational, as the ravings of right-wing ratbags. The Liberal Party is, and always has been, opposed to communism whenever and wherever it exists in the world. Vietnam has been claimed by the communists here and abroad to be part of the communist plan for world domination. The Chinese Defence Minister, Lin Piao, has described the insurgency in South Vietnam as "the test tube of national wars of liberation."

One has only to look to the Communist Party newspaper, Tribune, to find the evidence of direct Communist Party participation in the Vietnam moratorium. If this is not fifth-column activity, then what is it? Surely it is common sense to examine carefully the implications and motivations of the total campaign when one finds key office-bearers of the Communist Party holding important positions on the moratorium committee.

If we were to do as the moratorium organisers demand and withdraw from Vietnam immediately and urge the United States to do the same, the South Vietnamese Government would, in all probability, collapse. This would mean the systematic murder of an estimated one to three million Vietnamese; hardly very humanitarian on our part. We have only to look at the Hue Tet massacre by the Viet Cong for verification of this. Australia is committed to a phased withdrawal based on the progressive Vietnamisation of the war.

The moratorium, far from ending the war, will only make it more protracted as our resolve to stand against aggressive communism is seen by the communists to be weakening.

PETER FITZ-GIBBON
Sydney

(The writer is president, NSW division, Young Liberals.)

1/5/70

The Red menace at home

IF Sir William Yeo is correct in his estimate that 90 per cent of people who take part in anti-war protest marches are communists (*The Australian*, 25/10), then things are more serious than we imagined.

Since 10,000 people took part in the October 22 march in Sydney, by Sir William's arithmetic there are at least 9000 communists running loose in the city at this very minute.

It's frightening to think that in other States, which do not enjoy the protection of Sir William's eternal vigilance, communism is doubtless even more rife.

And it seems incredible that we are sending more troops to Vietnam when we obviously need them right here to protect us against the Red menace at home.

If things get much worse, we'll have to ask the Americans to send "military advisers" to NSW.

LEONARD TAPPER
Balmain, NSW
3/11/67

┌─ **PS** ─────────┐

STILL another unpeaceful Armistice Day. Prayers for the dead — napalm for the living.
(Mrs) **MARIA BARNETTI**
Enmore, NSW
11/11/68

└──────────────┘

Peace gooks

SO Congressman George Miller of California thinks that only gooks and universities are bawling about peace.

As one of the gooks who resigned from an executive position in the Liberal Party because of our mentally and spiritually bankrupt policies in Vietnam, let me warn Mr Miller that before very long it may well be the people of his own so-called democracy who will be bawling for peace.

If we gooks don't speak up against the current satanic thinking, it may be that they have sown more than we can reap.

KEN NOLAN
Chadstone, Vic
2/3/66

Vietnam war

Black Friday for the peace marchers

SEPTEMBER 18 will go down as Black Friday in the annals of the right to peaceful assembly in Sydney. Violent and unprovoked police action made a mockery of the formal right.

The Council for Civil Liberties had a number of observers at the moratorium march. Their reports made the following points:

1. Violence came not from the demonstrators, but from a number of policemen who pushed, punched and kicked pedestrians (including some who were not involved in the march). The breaking of a shop window in Elizabeth Street was entirely due to such police action, according to one CCL observer, who is a solicitor.

2. The police deliberately prevented the marchers from exercising their rights as pedestrians to walk along George Street on the pavement to the Town Hall. The marchers made no attempt to occupy the roadway, or the pavement on the other side of the street.

3. Many policemen wore number-plates, but most of those who attacked the demonstrators did not. It is difficult to believe that the difference was accidental.

4. Senior police officers brushed aside complaints. Indeed, anyone with the temerity to complain was likely to be arrested.

A royal commission is needed to examine the facts of what occurred. Otherwise, the same sort of thing is likely to recur, to the disgrace of the city of Sydney.

KEN BUCKLEY
Vice-President
Council for Civil Liberties
Sydney
23/9/70

Ashamed

SITTING in my consulting room reading Mr Brass' indictment of the Vietnam war, I am not ashamed to admit I was moved to tears.

As a young medical officer attached to a fighting unit in World War II, I was proud of my uniform, my nationality and believed that our country's stand was right.

I worked in surroundings where it appeared to me that death and destruction were on a grand scale and in the practice of my profession before the war and subsequently, have been no stranger to human suffering.

Mr Brass' last paragraph is the most terrible thing I have ever read. The monsters of My Lai are at one with the Beast of Belsen.

I am filled with a personal sense of deep shame.

Let us salvage what remains of our national pride by insisting that our troops are withdrawn from this theatre of war immediately.

SURGEON
(Name and address supplied)
9/12/69

Thanks from a GI visitor

A WEEK ago I had the opportunity and privilege to visit Sydney on my R and R leave.

I am an American GI serving in Vietnam with the 1st Cavalry Division.

I know of no better way to thank so many people than by writing to your newspaper. I speak not only for myself, but for my comrades also.

One cannot thank people for kindness because kindness comes from the heart and the people of Sydney come by it naturally. All were more than kind.

A city doesn't make itself beautiful; it's the people who are the ones who make it.

From the beaches of Manly to Bondi through the parks, waterfront and along the streets, the people were like nowhere else on earth.

When I left Sydney it hurt and I hated to leave. It was like leaving home all over again, a home away from home.

I would like to express again to all the people of Sydney a hardy Yankee thanks to a lot of great people in a great city of a great country.

SP-5 DARREL SOMERVILLE
San Francisco
17/4/68

Vietnam war

A denial of rights

THE announcement by Mr McMahon that "combat" troops will be withdrawn from Vietnam and that the period of national service will be reduced to 18 months will make no difference whatever to the stand of the Draft Resisters Union against conscription.

We remain as implacably opposed to conscription as ever and will continue to refuse to comply in any way with the National Service Act.

We regard the changes in the Act as an admission by the Government of the growing opposition to conscription. However, we will only be satisfied with the total abolition of conscription in any form.

The Government has shown itself to be so wrong in Vietnam that we feel it must be denied the use of conscription in any future wars which it desires, or is pressured into waging.

13 RESISTERS
Highett, Vic
6/9/71

Resisters condemned

IN the wake of the glorified treatment doled out to Australian draft resisters by the Labor Government, how refreshing it was to hear both American political parties reassert the hard line for their draft resisters.

In his recent address to the nation, President Nixon stated, unequivocally: "We cannot provide forgiveness for them. Those who deserted must pay the price and the price is a criminal penalty for disobeying the law of the United States."

The opposition Democratic party has voiced similar sentiments. And I'm all with them.

Why should those who chose to opt out when the going got tough be blessed with the freedom and prosperity gained with the sweat, the blood and the lives of their brothers? They made their choice and now they must suffer the consequences.

How different it is in Australia! Here we reward our law-breakers with amnesty, a pat on the back and a suggestion of compensation!

MARTIN KITCHENER
Dulwich Hill, NSW
15/2/73

Bombing halt applauded

WE wish to applaud the actions of Mr Whitlam, Dr Cairns, Mr Clyde Cameron and the leaders and members of the maritime unions who, by expressing Australia's opposition to the American terror bombing of Hanoi and Haiphong, have contributed to bringing about its cessation.

By their actions they have placed Australia with those nations seeking to make possible a generation of peace, which was threatened by the bombing of Hanoi and Haiphong.

We express the belief that the Australian Government will continue its effort to press for a prompt conclusion of a ceasefire agreement.

JUDAH WATEN
Box Hill, Vic
12/1/73

(The above letter was also signed by Alan Marshall, David Williamson, Barry Oakley and John Morrison).

PS

WE wish to apologise to Americans in Australia for the outrageous behavior of certain elements of our community on July 4, American Independence Day. We are sure the most insulting acts of the burning of American flags in Sydney and Melbourne are deplored by the overwhelming majority of Australians.

E. J. BURR
MARYLIN L. BURR
Armidale, NSW
9/7/69

AS we have troops in South Vietnam in support of President Thieu and his gerrymander attempts, should not troops also be sent to Queensland to assist Premier Bjelke-Petersen?

ROBERT WARD
Park Ridge, Qld
18/6/70

I WOULD like to express my admiration and support for the action taken by the trade unions against American genocide in Vietnam by their proposed boycott of American enterprises here.

(Dr) P. PICK
Sydney
12/1/73

ON behalf of the people of Australia, I would like to convey sincere condolences to the DLP and the National Civic Council on the occasion of the ending of the Vietnam war.

MICHAEL JEWELL
Zillmere, Qld
2/2/73

The great debates

Catholic view of birth control

THERE has been of late a great deal of criticism of the attitude of the Catholic Church towards birth control. While not wishing to provoke bitter controversy, I feel it is time you represented in your excellent paper the views of an ordinary Catholic wife and mother.

The authority of the Catholic Church has been compared to the authority of a communist society. I utterly refute this because:

(1) The discipline of the former is the self-discipline and self-sacrifice of each individual member and is based on the supreme loving sacrifice of Christ on the Cross, instead of the brute force of communist discipline — in other words based on love rather than hate.

(2) All Catholics are encouraged to read, talk, think and understand their religion. Any communist who dares to think would soon find himself and his dependants in Siberia.

(3) The Catholic Church does not seek to impose her sanctions on those outside the Church. Communism seeks to impose itself everywhere.

(4) As a Christian I do not feel that I should be as well off in an atheist society as in the Catholic Church.

Communism is tyranny, injustice and cruelty and subordinates everything to the state. The Catholic Church offers me charity, love, tolerance and forgiveness.

I do not wish to change places with anybody, not even with the reader from NSW who so pities me my lack of freedom.

How free, in fact, is this reader herself? Can she make herself rich by walking into and robbing the nearest bank? She is not free to do so because she is bound by the laws of the state.

If it is necessary to have expert statesmen and lawyers to interpret man-made laws, how much more important it should be, surely, to have some expert authority to interpret divine law?

The Catholic mother, by accepting the Church's interpretations of divine law in regard to birth control, is **not** bound to have as many children as possible. On the contrary, the Church permits and encourages family planning by methods which do not interfere with the natural law.

If Mrs A has 12 children then it is either because:

(1) Mr and Mrs A want it that way.

(2) Mrs A has an irregular menstrual cycle which prevents her from planning her family.

(3) Mr and Mrs A could plan, but lack the necessary willpower to do so.

The question is much larger than Mrs A's 12 little problems, e.g. where does birth control end and sterilisation begin? Or illegal abortion become legal?

Perhaps after the contraceptive pill will come the lethal pill — to put all unwanted children (for their own good, of course) out of their misery.

The whole vexed question is at the moment under review by eminent gynaecologists and theologians. As one who will be directly affected by their decisions, I still hope that there will be no radical change to the Church's teaching for the following reason:

If the Church "modernises her thinking" because of public pressure, then she will turn from the logical and consistent protection of divine truth to the illogical and capricious whims of present day society: in short from the solid rock of Peter to nothing but shifting sand.

CATHOLIC MOTHER
Albion, Vic
8/8/64

PS

NOW that various psychiatrists have volunteered their gloomy predictions regarding the use of the pill, I should like to ask one of them for a text-book comment on the mental health of Australia if fewer babies were born but all, or nearly all, of them were wholly loved and wanted.

MAX PRAED
Lismore, NSW
30/11/65

The pill

Promiscuity is in the eye of the beholder

THE pill's removal of the last barrier to "promiscuity," as Dr James Smibert so unscientifically described it in his otherwise sound diagnosis reported in *The Australian* (14/9), ought surely to be regarded as giving us easier access to that much-vaunted freedom on which we expend so much hot air and cold war.

Promiscuity is in the eye of the beholder; those who use the term in a sexual context are wont to apply it promiscuously to any experience, real or imagined, more extensive than their own.

What Dr Smibert seems to forget is that in days of yore, when it was necessary to arrest the spread of disease, to protect the male inheritance of property and to prevent some of the fears of pregnancy, wowser morality was all that could be invented.

Now that hell fire has been quenched by contraceptives, antibiotics and public health departments, the old morality is about as relevant as a suit of armor on St Kilda beach.

But while we try to ignore the vulgar yelps and agonised screams emitted by its passing, we do need to evolve a new morality, tenderly and responsibly; one which extends and enriches our prosperity, our freedom and the ability that medical technology has newly given us to know one another and — perhaps for the first time after all those centuries of exhortation to do the impossible — to truly love one another.

It will not be without its emotional problems, of course, for a society cannot cast off overnight, as it were, centuries of human intercourse based on fear, exploitation and the possession of human property.

But please don't remind me of that old Gibbonesque Victorian myth about the fall of Ancient Rome. It is rather the fall of Contemporary Rome that should be hastened by modern pill-celebrators.

OWEN WEBSTER
Ashburton, Vic
20/9/65

A convenient excuse

WE protest against increasing publicity linking the contraceptive pill and world over-population. Is it seriously suggested that if Australians have fewer children, they will materially assist the many under-privileged people in the world?

We have four children and we hope to have more. If we are financially able to shelter, feed, clothe and educate them, are we more of a threat than those around us with two children?

It would be easy for over-population to become a convenient reason for people in our society to limit the size of their families, while continuing to enjoy what is by some standards a fabulously high standard of living, and doing little to ease in practice the lot of those who have so little.

JOHN and MARIA FARNAN
New Lambton, NSW
17/3/65

O tempora! O mores!

THE Australian is to be congratulated for publishing the following statistics:

That 54 per cent of Australian married women between the ages of 21 and 25 and 44 per cent between the ages of 26 and 30, are taking oral contraceptives (University of NSW report on the pill).

That from 1963-4 to 1964-5, the natural increase in population has dropped from 1.24 per cent to 1.11 per cent (Commonwealth Statistician).

These figures surely indicate the growing irresponsibility, both in the community at large and among the medical profession in particular, to sustain a birth-rate that will give us the necessary strength to resist the inevitable attempts from the north to invade our country and destroy our European culture.

To whom are we to turn in building up our white population?

To Europe? The Minister for Immigration says that the sources of European migrants are drying up.

To the U.S.? Hardly!

To ourselves? We seem to be living only for the pleasures of the moment.

And our medical advisers seem to be intent on finding more avenues for lucrative gain rather than on service that will promote the long-term welfare of the nation.

O tempora! O mores!

PAMELA JERVIS
Lindfield, NSW
9/11/65

The pill

Papal gobbledegook

AS a retired Catholic whose current religious position could best be described as one of amused scepticism, it is none of my business what the Holy Father may or may not decree for the benefit of the faithful.

There will undoubtedly be many letters to comment on this rearguard effort of a tired authoritarianism and its parallels with the problems of Russia in Czechoslovakia.

There may even be unkind remarks about the Galileo faux pas and other little problems, but I feel that the public at large should be urged to a close reading of the papal encyclical on birth control as a most rewarding experience in English expression.

In fact, it could profitably be set as part of the Higher School Certificate English paper.

To quote, "to justify conjugal acts made intentionally infecund, one cannot invoke as valid reasons the lesser evil, or the fact that such acts would constitute a whole together with the fecund acts already performed, or to follow later and hence would share in one and the same moral goodness."

To a simple-minded person this could appear to be at best jargon, or at worst meaningless gobbledegook.

The reasons cited against contraception include loss of respect for women, immorality etc and are all reminiscent of reasons advanced by conservatives against almost every change in the last 100 years.

Votes for women, female equality, even the baby bonus and child endowment have been supposed to lead to degradation of the "true role of women" and inevitably sap our moral fibre.

W. J. O'REILLY
Balmain, NSW
7/8/68

Only wanted children

YOUR articles about the oral contraceptive tablet were very interesting. However, the second article seems to consider "the pill" on purely financial grounds without any consideration of the psychological, sociological and moral issues involved.

If the use of a completely reliable contraceptive becomes widespread, then the only children born will be children sincerely wanted by their parents.

The child who is secure in the knowledge that he is loved and wanted, grows up to be a much happier, better adjusted member of the community than the child who knows he was a "mistake."

If all our future generations were emotionally stable children of emotionally stable parents, then surely we would be on our way to the type of society which many people believe God intended us to have.

The moral issue involved then is not whether use of the oral contraceptive tablets is morally right, but whether anyone has a moral right to ban their use and therefore put yet another obstacle in the way of the attainment of the ideal society.

(Miss) J. VERNON
Paddington, NSW
6/5/65

PS

BY the time our second child was due, we could afford a pram. After much searching we finally managed to buy one from a middle-aged couple who parted with it, firmly believing that the very act of sale would curse them with a resurgence of fertility. Now, some years later, we wish to dispose of the same vehicle; but to date our efforts have been without success. Is the over-supply of second-hand prams a sign of growing affluence in our society — or is it a sure indication of the effectiveness of the pill?
K. G. FLETCHER
Black Forest, SA
6/12/65

NON-CATHOLIC girls could find themselves to be more sought after by Catholic boys, since the Pope's recent encyclical forbidding Catholics to use the pill.
ROBERT J. McCARTHY
Cooma North, NSW
8/8/68

POPULATION growth will not be curtailed by "natural" (rhythm) methods of contraception because of their great unreliability. The Pope should descend from his ivory tower and look upon the "happier, more truly more continually happy" people of India watching their "fruits of love" starve to death.
S. ROBINSON
Northbridge, NSW
26/9/67

The pill

The testing of authority

YOUR coverage of the controversy over the papal decree on birth control and the article by Father Crotty raised some interesting questions.

As with at least one other priest in England, Father Crotty was suspended. No doubt there will be others. They may be suspended, but are their arguments suspended, too? It seems not.

These men felt obliged in conscience to speak out and they considered this necessary despite the fact that the Pope had spoken otherwise.

With Father Crotty, his articles are patently sincere and on his premises, well reasoned; yet when suspension came, no corresponding answer to his arguments has been proposed.

This reflects one of two things: either all Catholics are expected to forgo an intelligent approach to the decree, by having arguments both for it and against it thoroughly reviewed; or else, there is no adequate answer to the objections raised.

The usual answer to the first alternative is that for Catholics, who believe in papal authority, there is no longer any room for debate.

But this is to beg the very question that many are asking: how authoritative is a decree that gave no replies to the reasons of the majority report of the Papal Commission, that ignores the plea of the International Lay Congress and that fails to satisfy the majority of the Church's own theologians?

It is little use appealing to authority when that authority itself, at least in this matter, is being questioned — not in rebellion or unbelief, but, in the vast majority of cases, in a sincere effort to seek the truth.

Even to say that failure to follow the decree is a grave act of disobedience, as the statement of the Australian bishops does, is to fail to meet the questions being asked.

As many people see it, the decree is a sincere attempt to meet the problem, but it is a mistake and it is one's duty to register disapproval.

The only honorable way of replying to such objections, both in this country and overseas, is to give them a fair hearing, then to answer them point for point, with the same depth and sincerity with which they have been proposed.

This raises the second point above, as to whether there are adequate answers to the objections being raised. Suspension without replying to the reasoning as stated (for instance by Father Crotty) will not bring back those Catholics who cannot agree with the decree and will certainly raise doubts in the minds of many more.

In conclusion, the Church should be reminded that in this case it is dealing with the truth and not only with individuals. It cannot ignore the reasons of those who earnestly disagree, then expect to be believed.

It cannot rely on authority without thoroughly tested reasons to justify the ways in which authority is exercised.

Clearly differences exist and it is about time sincere and responsible moves were made to create understanding.

What is happening here and overseas betrays a tragic lack of communication and understanding.

Without doubt, this is the real danger to faith and to the credibility of the Catholic Church.

IAN G. WEEKS
S. VAN HOOFT
University of Melbourne
Parkville, Vic
26/8/68

Sex and self control

MAY we commend Dr Leslie Hemingway for his most pertinent comments in regard to contraception (*The Australian*, 25/9)?

While agreeing that there exists in many parts of the world and within many individual marriages the need for planned families, we share Dr Hemingway's view that people "should look more closely at the alternative (to contraception), self-control."

If mature persons are expected to control their eating and drinking habits, their temper and other feelings — then surely it is both possible and desirable that people should exercise self-control in matters of sex.

We believe that Dr Hemingway goes to the heart of the matter when he talks of "disrespect for authority and human life, selfishness and self-indulgence."

His comments could well be pondered upon by those who glibly talk of issuing young people with contraceptives on the grounds that, for the young, self-control is impossible.

**DES AND MARGARET
TOBIN**
Malvern, Vic
3/10/67

The pill

Call for a new papal vision

FOR the improvement or even maintenance of life on earth man must achieve a maximum reduction of population and a prevention of the progressive destruction of the earth's irreplaceable resources.

These proposals are not original, but have been repeatedly put, in variable format, during the past decade by a countless number of expert study groups — both national and international. Nor has it mattered whether these studies were directed at peace, poverty and/or pollution, a key recommendation universally appears: control population growth.

The last papal encyclical on birth control then is clearly a tragic irresponsibility. It is not only medieval and without scientific valid-ity, but is unethical from a personal or family viewpoint and impossible ecologically.

It misleads the innocent and supports those who place their hopes in purely technological, rather than biologically moral solutions to human ills. These are antagonistic to any religious ethic.

Surely no Catholic or non-Catholic could ever be persuaded by the encyclical that the Church can be a source of light, liberty and love, for the inevitable result of the current population trend is war and famine on a gigantic scale and a decimation of life.

It is simply just a question of time. Sooner or later civil laws will enforce what is now needed in the religious ethic. Then, children will only be by permit only.

The modern church, like many other organisations fulfilling public needs, must redefine its role regarding population counselling, unless it wishes to be guilty of the blindest irresponsibility.

After all, major changes in the Catholic doctrines have been necessary in the past, for example the Church found it needed to align itself with Galileo's findings. Hence can we not reinterpret and rethink the scriptures and our old traditions with new vision? Can we not subdue the earth with responsibility and populate it with reason rather than "be fruitful and increase, fill the earth and subdue it?"

K. HAMMOND
Sydney
16/11/70

Standing room only? Really!

ALLOW me to reply to the letter of Mr Joseph Firth, who mentions that there will be standing room only on the earth by 2000 AD.

Really Mr Firth! Is this how desperate justification for contraception has become? Any schoolboy knows that the area of Australia (the smallest continent) is 2000 million acres — one acre each for every living person.

Pill advocates remind me very much of King Henry VIII. Having adopted immoral means to solve a personal problem, they demand approval from the Catholic Church (to solve uncertain consciences?).

Meeting disapproval, they cannot decapitate the Pope as Henry did to Fisher and More, but they can show a similar hysterical iconoclasm.

Henry was guilty, not of his desire to preserve his posterity, but of the means he took to do so. "Pillists" fall not in their desire to preserve their prosperity, but in the means with which they wish to do it.

Both question the Pope's authority when it is uncomfortable, both drag in the opinions of sundry dissenting bishops, theologians and spokesmen who support them — as if numbers will ever make them right.

The usual catchcry of "world overpopulation" comes forth — as if this has any weight in under-populated Australia.

Our friends will have to look further for justification of their position in affluent Australia and America, lest their present hysteria be too revealing.

K. C. McMANUS
Ashfield, NSW
8/8/68

┌─ **PS** ─────────────

MAY I suggest a slogan behind which all Catholics may unite: "Down with the pill."

PHILIP CROWLEY
Glenhuntly, Vic
9/9/68

The great debates

White
Australia

"There but for the White Australia policy go I"

Asians are just too law-abiding

AUSTRALIA should keep her White Australia policy. I don't think Asians would make good Australians.

I have studied the conduct of those already here and they seem a poor lot at forming rape packs. I haven't read of any good robberies or assault cases being perpetrated by non-Europeans, either.

They also make poor spectators at sports meetings and do not add to the glamor of football games by having punch-ups and fights with knives.

They are too law-abiding and dull for Australia.

(Mrs) J. PADDEN REW
Forestville, NSW
19/8/65

White Australia

Unashamedly, we are superior

THE recent articles on the White Australia Policy have been more than interesting, if only because no valid reasons have emerged to change the policy, nor to change the name, nor to suggest that it means anything other than what it meant when it was first so called.

The argument is advanced in various forms that the White Australia Policy is an insult, an affront, a hurt to Asiatic feelings and so forth; also it indicates that we regard ourselves as a superior people.

As a much-travelled Australian, I confess unashamedly to that belief. The more I contemplate what Asiatics are doing to each other the more confirmed becomes my belief.

I also have not the slightest guilt complex about the high standard of living enjoyed in Australia, by comparison to our Asiatic neighbors and only wish it were higher.

Our contribution to the Colombo Plan should come after we have provided for the needs of the underprivileged in our own country. Hospitals and homes for the aged, schools and child welfare are only a few of the areas to which we have a prior liability.

Intermarriage and integration, we are told, can and should take place in Australia. What a monumental impertinence is this assertion. Where has it already taken place on a nationwide basis? In what country is there peace and harmony between white and colored peoples?

It is fatuously suggested that highly educated Asiatics should be allowed entry to work in Australia, as some kind of reward, apparently. Surely the talents, skills, knowledge inferred by "highly educated" could and should be used in their own countries.

The abolitionists of White

Australia would regard themselves as progressives in the realms of the avant garde. Their motivations — if sincere — are elusive and not founded on fact. The dangers that face Australia are such that their activities can no longer be regarded with indulgence.

The sombre facts facing this fair country are positively appalling. In terms of world politics and world political bargaining, we are, at the best, expendable in the confrontations of the colossi of the northern hemisphere. The real pressure to make Australia Asiatic by population will come not from Asia — but from Europe and America.

The urgency is now for Australians who are Australians to assert without hesitation that Australia is a white man's country and will remain so.

FRANK J. EVERINGHAM
Normanhurst, NSW
6/7/65

What rudeness and absurdity!

YOU are far too pessimistic in your editorial (26/11) on the White Australia Policy. You lament the "weariness" which the issue now provokes among the public.

Frustration there may be, but the many Australians who reject and resent this racialist hangover from less enlightened days will be heartened by your attitude. I certainly applaud it and honor you for your mature view.

Can we not reasonably ask that the 15 years residential requirement for colored persons be reduced to five years — as required for Caucasians? This change would be a

sensible gesture at a time when our actions encourage those who categorise us as "white supremacists."

At present, we receive about 120,000 migrants a year. Yet no London West Indian bus conductor may apply; no Californian doctor whose grandparents were Japanese; no Indian Master of Arts; no carpenter, architect, painter or typist from Paris, Ottawa or Stockholm may live here unless his origin is predominantly white. What gross rudeness and absurdity!

Our immigration policy has never been anything but selfish: it contrasts strik-

ingly with that of the United States where a huge undeveloped continent became a mecca for people who wished to be made welcome somewhere and where a huge stone monument boldly proclaims the fact.

It is notable that even today the United States, embarrassed as it is by a huge minority of Negroes, does not refuse entry to colored migrants on the grounds of their color.

This magnanimity in migration is something we could well emulate.

ROSS GRIEGSON
Kew, Vic
30/11/64

White Australia

The role for students

I FEEL that the letter by S. Shan and D. Lee (*The Australian*, March 17) grossly missed the right spirit of Asian students in Australia.

We are here in Australia to study, not to seek shelter (we are not refugees!): we are here to acquire the technical knowhow so that we may, when we go back to our home countries (not Canada or other similar countries), help those at home live a better material life.

This is why Mr Opperman said: "It would be quite wrong to offer to Asian students in Australia the right to settle here after five years of study."

I feel that the application of the White Australia Policy to Asian students is justified.

It is in Australia's interest to train Asians, then send them back home, not so much because of racial prejudice, but because these trained Asian students will help to develop and hence stabilise their countries. This will then contribute towards the safety of Australia.

Also, people of the present age are not ready to accept a multi-racial society.

Racial injustice can be overcome only by levelling the living standards of all races all over the world, not by protests, or use of violence.

Trained people are a great help towards raising living standards — so go home, all Asian students, when you finish your courses!

T. V. LEE
University of Sydney
Newtown, NSW
12/4/66

What will they think?

MR Hasluck's recent reference to the evil that racism works in the world will undoubtedly be regarded with more than passing interest by Australia's non-white neighbors.

If the statement is published in Manila, one wonders what reception it will receive following intense Filipino denunciations of Australia's racist immigration policy.

Likewise, non-white tourists may pause to ponder the paradoxical behavior of the Government of the "great white land."

Necessarily, this will be a long pause, as these people wait up to six months before they are permitted to touch our shores (the length of time probably being directly proportional to the darkness of the skin).

However, Mr Hasluck is to be congratulated for recognising that racism is evil — this is quite an achievement for an Australian minister.

In fact, in optimistic moments one may hope that with the end (theoretically) of the "Ming Dynasty," Australia may throw off the ultra-conservative gag and officially recognise that skin color and race are not grounds for discrimination against any person.

PAUL BOWKER
Chadstone, Vic
1/2/66

From the racial front line

I MUST have been one of those "thrust into the fighting front line of the racial struggle" in the United States, mentioned in a letter by Professor Francis on September 20 — and I can't agree with his views.

Veterinarian Francis, with a bias towards quarantines, apparently feels that broad cultural development should be as carefully excluded from Australia as hoof and mouth disease.

An influx of newcomers certainly would change some aspects of Australian living, but I think that the benefits would far outweigh the disadvantages. The United States has gained a great deal through the immigration of diverse races and cultures.

Riots in Watts, civil disobedience in Chicago and marches in Mississippi make the headlines.

Norm Sanders, European Anglo-Saxon, attending high school in Los Angeles with Charley White, Negro; Eddie Solis, Mexican-American; Chris Pontrelli, Italian-American and Paul Wisegarver, of German descent, certainly didn't make the papers.

I survived that front-line struggle with very little difficulty, but I didn't emerge unscathed.

I was left with a broader outlook and better appreciation and understanding of other people.

I think that Australia could benefit in the same way.

NORMAN K. SANDERS
Sandy Bay, Tas
29/9/66

White Australia

In defence of Enoch Powell

I HAVE just read the full text of Mr Enoch Powell's recent Birmingham speech which led to his dismissal from the British Shadow Cabinet and his being labelled by many newspapers, including your own, as "racialist."

His wording is very careful, there is no mention of genetic inferiority or inequality.

Mr Powell merely recognises that racialism — on the part of all races — is widespread in Britain today and that this is damaging to the nation.

I recently taught secondary school in the East End of London for a year. There were many Negro and Indian pupils at the school.

I was amazed and horrified by the general, unabashed expression of racial antagonism. Negro children kept apart from the others and were openly called by such names as "boot-black."

I cannot believe that any sort of legislation will mitigate the lasting sense of difference and mutual hatred in children who have such an experience.

Of course, this melancholy phenomena is world-wide.

What is unusual about the British is their overwhelming sense of guilt about their own racialism. As a result, the nation now seems to be masochistically embracing forces which will divide and undermine.

The present legislation before the House of Commons is the very ecstasy of national suicide.

As I understand it, the Race Relations Bill makes provisions which apply to coloreds as coloreds, to whites as whites and gives to colored groups special rights not available to whites. This can only exacerbate fear in the white population.

One senses an increasing impatience with democracy and a resurgent flirting with fascism. One is awestruck and appalled by the long and present precedent of racial incompatability in the United States.

In seeking to prevent those things in his own country, Mr Powell is not a racialist — merely one who is not mad.

JAMES PEARCE
Parkville, Vic
26/4/68

Time running out for whites

THE time is rapidly approaching when many British migrants will be coming to Australia to escape the rising influx of Asian migrants.

Far from being wild conjecture, one has only to consider the large number of South Africans who came to Australia in the early 1960s after the Sharpeville incident, fearing that the country was on the verge of a non-white anarchy.

One has also to consider the growing number of Americans who are migrating to Australia because of the Negro riots, which have become a regular summer occurrence.

The lesson we in Australia can learn before it is too late is that once you begin to allow non-white races into the country, you've got to concede that pretty soon you are going to be saddled with

sociological problems, the enormity of which you had no conception when you first attempted to be "jolly democratic humanists."

It may well be that the time of the white man on earth is limited: that we cannot hope to continue holding the reins of progress and civilisation after the year 2000 A.D.

That chap Alf in the TV series Till Death Us Do Part is playing a role which probably highlights the feelings and emotions of more people than we'd like to know about, through all levels of society from Joe Blow to Lord Haw Haw.

REGINALD BLUNT
North Wollongong, NSW
29/2/68

PS

IN the July issue of American Playboy magazine (a prohibited import), a reader asks the editor about migration to Australia. The reply states that . . . "A migrant must be deemed desirable and this is understood to exclude black people and Asians. According to the latest published figures of 918 blacks and Asians brave enough to file applications since 1966, only 376 have been accepted." No wonder we are getting a reputation as a racist country.

S. PATRICK
Woollahra, NSW
11/11/69

White Australia

Opening the door to Asian migrants

THE Singapore Prime Minister, Mr Lee Kuan Yew, in his criticism of Australia's immigration policy of accepting only the skilled professionals from Asian countries is quite valid.

From 1900 to recently when the so-called White Australia Policy was rigidly implemented, Irish laborers, southern European peasants, British and Dutch farmhands were preferred migrants to Japanese engineers, Chinese professors or entrepreneurs, or skilled Malay craftsmen. The late Arthur Calwell made this quite clear with his "Two Wongs don't make a white."

It was not until the late Liberal Prime Minister, Mr Harold Holt, assumed office that a few Asian professionals and businessmen were allowed in as settlers.

But it is to the present Labor Government's credit that some positive moves are being made to erase the discrimination towards non-Europeans as migrants.

Whether the Government can really practise what it preaches remains to be seen, especially from the eyes of Chinese in Australia who are the most discriminated minority after the Aborigines.

Certainly the Chinese have been discriminated against far more than the Jews, or any other migrant groups since the first Chinese gold diggers arrived in Australia over 120 years ago.

Mr Lee

However, in fairness, the extent of discrimination has lessened in recent years and in comparison with how the overseas Chinese are treated in many South-East Asian countries (as Mr Lee well knows), the Chinese in Australia are much better off.

As for discrimination in migration policy, Mr Lee similarly practices it himself, for does not he only welcome migrants who are engineers and technicians as well as the wealthy Chinese businessmen who can bring much-needed capital and know-how from Hong Kong, Taiwan and other South-East Asian countries? What about the poor penniless Chinese refugees in Hong Kong?

EDMUND YOUNG
Beaumont, SA
(The writer is information officer of the Chinese Association of SA.)
13/8/73

Shameful

AUSTRALIA is filled with hypocrites and selfish wowsers. This includes a number of leading RSL delegates who unanimously carried a motion to put pressure on the Federal Government to return to the White Australia Policy.

In his religious column (*The Australian,* 9/7), James S. Murray has every reason to be ashamed of the RSL. It is ridiculous to think that the RSL would go as far as stating that Australia must remain free, white and basically Christian.

Although many Australians feel that something should be done to wipe out the continued threat of racial riots, street fighting and a violent society flaring up in Britain and America, I feel that bringing back a White Australia Policy would be shameful.

Instead of barking up that tree, the RSL delegates should have moved a motion calling on stricter immigration laws to rid the country of foreign trouble-makers, such as drug dealers and terrorists.

It may take time to control such a flow of criminals, but at least we could gradually wipe out extremists rather than introduce a White Australia policy that Australians have cut out to protect innocent foreigners.

The RSL states that Australia's defence would be at risk if immigration policies did not change. This may be so, but I bet there would be a lot more new Australians ready to fight for this, their adopted free country, than there would be normal lazy and gutless cowards who are on unemployment benefits right now, all fair dinkum Australians.

PAUL BALLANTYNE
Mornington, Vic
18/7/81

White Australia

We must remain homogeneous

THE call by the Victorian RSL to increase the percentage of white immigrants to Australia should be heeded if Australia is to remain a relatively homogeneous society and avoid the racial problems of countries such as the UK and the U.S.

A call for priority for white immigrants would have passed almost without comment in the 1960s, when both major political parties supported the White Australia Policy.

Mr Arthur Calwell, the leader of the A.L.P. for most of the 1960s, put the case against Australia becoming a multi-racial society in his, book, Be Just and Fear not.

He said: "I reject the idea that Australia should or can ever become a multi-racial society and survive.

"If Australians were ever foolish enough to open their gates in a significant way to people other than Europeans, they would soon find themselves desperately fighting to stop the nation being flooded by hordes of non-integratables. Every

Mr Grassby

country has the inalienable right to determine the composition of its own population."

Prominent Australians such as Jack Lang, Henry Lawson, Sir Robert Menzies and Sir Isaac Isaacs agreed with Mr Calwell that Aus-

tralia should remain racially homogeneous.

The right of Australians to discuss whether we should become a multi-racial society and to vote on the issue is a basic civil right. The frantic attempts by Mr Grassby (Commissioner for Community Relations) to prevent any debate by threatening prosecutions under the Racial Discrimination Act are ludicrous and a serious threat to civil liberties. Would he have prosecuted the Australians, such as Arthur Calwell, referred to above?

The belief shared by most Australians that Australia should remain overwhelmingly white is not based on feelings of racial superiority, but on a preference shared by all racial groups for their own kind. This preference is inherent and will not be affected by the activities of Mr Grassby's "thought police" and their attempts to stifle freedom of speech.

JOHN BENNETT
Carlton, Vic
28/7/81

Racial hatred firmly rejected

I REFER to letters by John Bennett and Mr B. W. Simpkins (28/7) in favor of a return to the old discredited White Australia Policy and suggesting that I am trying to stifle their views.

I believe the record should be set straight for both gentlemen. They are free, as you have indicated by publishing their letters, to call for a return to racist policies, but it is equally important from my point of view that those who would be the object of their victimisation should be reassured that the law of

Australia prevents such victimisation on the grounds of race, color, ethnic background, or place of birth.

It is also important to point out that in recent surveys in Australia 80 per cent of Australians of all backgrounds have firmly rejected racial discrimination as a policy for our country today.

I would urge both gentlemen to reconsider their position because by preaching division, denigration and hatred on the grounds of race, they are doing a grave

disservice to Australia and creating tension, fear and uncertainty.

Whenever there are calls for some Australians to be victimised on the grounds of their race, there must be a clear statement that the nation as a whole rejects that and guarantees that the old victimisation will not prevail.

A. J. GRASSBY
Commissioner for
Community Relations
Canberra
7/8/81

The great debates

...AND I'VE A SNEAKY SUSPICION WE WOULDN'T NEED ABORTIONS AT ALL IF IT WEREN'T FOR THAT OTHER NASTY HABIT!!

We should follow the British example

THE British Government is to be congratulated on its new humanitarian move in passing the Abortion Law Reform Bill at its second reading in the House of Lords.

That a girl or woman should be forced to bear a child against her will, when pregnancy results from ignorance or criminal assault, is unethical.

The present Crimes Act specifies "unlawfully uses an instrument" or "unlawfully administers to . . . to procure her miscarriage," but does not give an interpretation of when such acts are lawful or unlawful.

Although this Act follows the British Per-

son Act (1861) and therefore the British interpretation arrived at in the Rex v Bourne case in 1938, there has, I think, been no test of this interpretation in Australia.

Do we have to wait upon some socially conscious surgeon to gamble his reputation and registration as Bourne did, or shall we have an abortion law reform society, as in Great Britain, to draft a reform bill for presentation to our Parliament?

D. G. ELLIS
Hope Valley, SA
10/12/65

Abortion

Unspeakable crime

A REPORT on the front page of *The Australian* (25/2) stated Dr F. Coggan had said in Sydney that abortion was not wicked under circumstances where the health of the mother was affected and that it was not morally wrong in certain other circumstances.

The fact that Dr Coggan is Archbishop of York may give these statements a certain standing, or authority in the minds of many people. This would be most unfortunate.

There are no circumstances in which abortion — the direct killing of an unborn and, therefore, innocent child — can be regarded as "not wicked" or "not morally wrong."

Christian tradition is unanimous on this and the recent Vatican Council decribed abortion as an "unspeakable crime" (The Documents of Vatican II, Geoffrey Chapman, p. 256).

On the level of ethics alone, it must be evident that a human being's right to life is primary and supreme. Consequently, to deprive an innocent human being of life by direct homicidal action is the greatest injury that can be done him.

To suggest that the mother's health can justify abortion is virtually to accept the immoral principle that "the end justifies the means."

Recently there was much agitation against the legal execution of one particular person. Yet each year approximately 100,000 young Australians guilty of no crime of any kind are done to death.

JOHN A. PHILLIPS, SJ
Corpus Christi College
Glen Waverley, Vic
8/3/67

The most barbaric law

FATHER John A. Phillips' letter (8/3) denying the morality of abortion under any circumstances reflects what is perhaps the Catholic Church's most barbaric law.

That law says that if it is a question of choosing between the life of the mother and that of the child, then it is the mother who must die. This is based on the absurd reasoning that one can never be sure the mother will die. Small solace to the distraught Catholic husband who is told that his wife has a 10 per cent chance of surviving the birth.

Lawyers are familiar with the case of R. V. Bourne, where an obstetric surgeon of the highest qualifications deliberately drew the attention of the English authorities to his performance of an abortion on a 15-year-old
girl, who had been raped, in order to provoke proceedings which would clarify the law. He was acquitted.

Father Phillips and his Church would, however, condemn the abortion and say that the girl must have the baby, not knowing which of her rapists was the father and despite the fact that the continuation of the pregnancy would probably make her a mental wreck.

I do not, of course, support abortion in all circumstances, but in extreme cases such as those that I have mentioned, to condemn abortion is not only inhuman, it is repugnant to the concept of the God which the Catholic Church holds out as loving and merciful.

PETER BISCOE
Sandy Bay, Tas
13/3/67

The right of all women

YOUR correspondent, D. G. Ellis (10/12), is to be congratulated for expressing such a compassionate and forward-looking view on the problem of termination of pregnancy.

The NSW Humanist Society believes that it is time our community faced up to the social problem of abortion for, by shutting our eyes to it, we have allowed human suffering, illness and disability to reach huge proportions.

There is no doubt that if a bill such as that at present before the House of Lords were introduced in NSW, it would have the support of a wide section of the community; it would at least give legal sanction to the current medical practice.

Humanists believe that it should be the right of all women to decide whether or not to bear a child — and that it is wrong that the law should prevent the termination of any pregnancy that will result in the birth of an unloved or an unwanted child, or one that is likely to be gravely handicapped.

Regardless of the law, vast numbers of abortions are, in fact, performed; and nothing is achieved by laws which merely result in such abortions being performed under circumstances which are degrading, expensive and (most of all) dangerous to both physical and mental health.

(Mrs) W. G. WEEKS
Secretary
NSW Humanist Society
Beverly Hills, NSW
16/12/65

Abortion

We must find a way to limit births

WHEN Cardinal Gilroy spoke of abortion as murder, as reported in *The Australian,* he was stating a part of Catholic dogma that stems from the dark days of Origen, when mystery surrounded the whole of human life and when science was almost non-existent.

Some may find such dogma unsatisfactory in a biologically better-informed world but, nevertheless, it is Catholic belief and the cardinal is right, if he thinks fit, to enunciate the dogma emphatically.

But Cardinal Gilroy then proceeded into the scientific realm of human population ecology. He said: "Australia needs population and every child conceived in Australia should be welcomed as a citizen of the nation." At this point his stance is vulnerable.

The cardinal is well aware that the most stupendous problem that has ever faced the human race is raised by the numbers of people on the earth at present, by the cataclysmic rate at which those numbers are increasing and by the quantities of natural resources, expecially food, that they are consuming and destroying.

This is acknowledged by all informed men, including Catholics, to be about to reach overwhelming proportions within the next few generations (50-100 years) unless some way is found to limit the numbers of births (increasing the number of deaths is regarded as unacceptable).

Two-thirds of the population is undernourished now and millions starve each year. Famine and starvation will become more frequent before they diminish — if they diminish. Encouraging the birth of more children is condemning more people to death by starvation and that is murder!

If Australia needs more people, as the Cardinal maintains, although others may not agree, it does not follow that it needs more babies born in Australia.

T. O. BROWNING
Adelaide
(Professor Browning is Professor of Entomology at Adelaide University.)
30/1/69

Decision is up to the mother

MANY articles have been written on the subject of abortion reform. Surely the final consideration in this complicated moral, medical and legal matter can only rest with the individual woman who is faced with an unwanted pregnancy.

I view with horror the BMA decision not to co-operate with the British laws to help women achieve an abortion without the otherwise risk of serious complications.

One wonders if the BMA reaction would be the same if the female membership was a majority force.
(Mrs) BARBARA SCOTT
Medindie, SA
13/5/66

Abortion

The DLP viewpoint

I REFER to the article by Dr Moss Cass (2/11) and his claim that the DLP and the A.L.P. have "exactly the same policy on abortion."

The exact opposite is the case. Unlike the A.L.P., which Dr Cass says has no "official" policy on abortion, the following is the DLPs official policy on abortion, adopted by its last federal conference and binding on all its MPs and candidates:

"The DLP strongly opposes any move to widen the existing federal or State laws relating to abortion to embrace so-called 'social grounds,' because this opens the way to 'abortion on demand.' The DLP regards any moves to introduce 'abortion on demand' as (a) a direct attack on a fundamental human right, namely the right to life; (b) an ultimate threat to the fundamental rights of all citizens."

J. T. KANE
Sydney
(Senator Kane is the Federal Secretary of the DLP)
3/11/72

It's a barbaric solution

JAN Harper crowds several bad arguments into her letter (1/2) criticising the Catholic bishops' statement on morals and human values.

The immorality of abortion lies in the killing of another human being. This is the gravest injustice that anyone can do to another.

It is scientifically absurd to refer to an unborn child as only a "potential" human being. The child is a potential adult, but he is just as much a human being as the mother.

Even if a child is "unwanted" he is not therefore worthless and deserving of death. Many people would be delighted to have these "unwanted" children. To kill them is a barbaric solution to problems that should be solved by social and economic means.

Perhaps the bishops have realised better than Jan Harper that abortion strikes at the very heart of womanhood and sacrifices the fundamental values on which good and responsible family life can alone be based.

JOHN A PHILLIPS, SJ
Glen Waverley, Vic
14/2/72

A discredited old sophism

I NOTE that your correspondent, Emmi Snyder, continues to use that tired and discredited old sophism about "unloved and battered children" in her efforts to justify abortion (27/1). I doubt if anybody buys that argument anymore.

And I wonder if all that "supportive counselling" she is so proud of gives the unborn child any hearing or support. When will the Emmi Snyders cease rationalising about abortion and acknowledge that abortion snuffs out human life?

Of course, nature itself ruthlessly cuts through all the rationalisations. Why is it that a woman needs all that "warmth" and "sympathy" to help her cope with the "sadness" and "depression" following an abortion, but not following say, an appendectomy?

(Bishop) E. B. CLANCY
Blacktown, NSW
16/2/77

Misused

MR I. J. CARDIN (15/11), quoting from Mr Bruce Petersen, makes great issue of a Swedish survey which says that 25 per cent of 479 women who had had abortions "regretted the operation bitterly and one third of those who were not sterilised were pregnant again soon after."

What he fails to say is that this sample was taken from a group of women who had all been granted abortions on psychiatric, or social-psychiatric grounds.

He fails to say that Dr Martin Ekblad, who made this survey in 1955, stated that the women who showed regret were often those who had a tendency to regret their actions in other situations as well.

He also fails to correctly state their real attitude. It was that 14 per cent had occasional regret, 11 per cent had serious regret. Mr Petersen's statement is hardly consistent with the facts, but is a good example of how statistics can be misused.

The opponents of reform have no solution to the incidence of abortion and in most cases they are even opposed to contraception, of which a proper knowledge and use is certainly related to the amount of abortions.

They simply refuse to recognise its existence by trying to maintain the present situation with its health risks, its humiliation of decent women and the constant flouting of the present punitive laws.

WILLIAM DYE
President
Abortion Law Reform
Association
Vic
20/11/68

Abortion

The majority favors abortion

A GROUP such as the Right To Life can have no more influence than people allow it to have. It may in the past have been able to intimidate individual politicians, but its beliefs have been clearly shown by opinion polls, such as that conducted by the Australian Women's Weekly in February this year, to differ from majority opinion and that has been validated by the results of the federal election.

Of more than 30,000 respondents to the Women's Weekly Voice of the Australian Woman survey, 62 per cent said abortion should be freely available to all those who wanted it, and a further 32 per cent agreed with the need for abortion for women whose health was in danger from pregnancy. Only 6 per cent were totally opposed to abortion.

In a breakdown of statistics State by State, in Victoria 67 per cent were in favor of abortion being freely available and 27 per cent would limit the operation to dangerous pregnancies. This indicates that for Victoria, also, only 6 per cent were totally opposed to abortion.

A further analysis of this

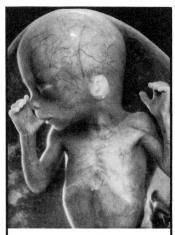

I WONDER how many of the pro-abortion on demand lobbyists have seen a 16-week-old foetus?
PATRICK HAWKES
Kelvin Grove, Qld
6/5/80

shows that for Melbourne, the figures were 70 per cent in favor of free availability and in the country, 62 per cent. In Melbourne 24 per cent and in the country 33 per cent would limit abortions to dangerous pregnancies.

No Victorian member of the Federal Parliament who

voted against the Martyr amendment lost his seat during these elections, with the exception of Barry Simon who lost on preferences.

Those who were defeated had all voted for the Martyr amendment, with the exception of Mr Yates who has no vote recorded on the issue. Those who held their seats by only narrow margins had also voted for the Martyr amendment.

These results show clearly that the Right To Life voice is not speaking for the majority of Australians and there may indeed have been a backlash in Victoria against its manipulations.

Voting on abortion should not be determined on a conscience vote by individual politicians, but a party line which reflects the wishes of the majority of Australians should be adopted. The Women's Weekly survey should indicate that the majority view is that abortion should be freely available to all who want it.
YVONNE CARNAHAN
National Communications Officer
Women's Electoral Lobby
Canberra
19/11/80

What has happened to Australia?

I AM amazed at the variety and the harshness of the charges made against the people who are opposed to abortion on demand. These people are trying to protect the lives of completely innocent unborn human beings.

A large number of members of the medical profession are signatories to a published statement which includes the following: "As doctors, we accept the undeniable scientific fact that human life begins at conception and that every abortion

deprives an innocent human being of his right to continue living.

"Our own practice in medicine makes it very clear that in modern obstetrics we are caring for two individuals, mother and baby."

Why are people seeking to protect unborn babies thought worthy of being treated with contempt?

What has happened to Australia?
J. P. MORRISON
Holland Park, Qld
6/5/80

The great debates

Divorce

'Guilt' provision is an affront

THE appalling state of divorce jurisdiction of today is a mockery of the very word "justice."

As we cannot eliminate divorce, our task is to humanise it. Divorcees are not criminals, yet the law makes little difference, except that no jail sentences are handed down in the decree itself.

The law as it stands, demanding proven "guilt" as a pre-condition for obtaining a decree, is an affront to every man and woman and is uncivilised.

Although it was made with the best of intentions in days gone by, it presently serves foremost those people conducting the cases, to the detriment, or complete ruin of their clients and their children.

The children, so prominently mentioned in the Act, are usually "victim number one."

Court rulings in respect of costs and custody are an open invitation to reckless and often unsubstantiated proceedings. And at this stage, a point of no return has been reached.

There is no law as to who has to pay the costs. Yet, irrespective of her earning capacity, or her actual income, a woman is seldom ordered to pay her own costs, even where she was the main contributor to the break-up.

It is almost impossible to find a court ruling where a woman is ordered to pay costs and alimony to a hus-

band: even where she has wantonly destroyed the home by her own admission, the man is given custody and the wife has no obligations.

If perjury is established, the husband would still be liable for his own defence at least.

Under such conditions, the divorce rate is bound to blossom and 64 per cent of all petitioners are women. Official statistics show that between 1961 and 1967, in NSW alone, divorces on all grounds rose from 3156 to 4555, an increase of 46 per cent.

On the ground of cruelty, decrees rose during the same period from 79 to 334, an increase of 322 per cent; 319 husbands and 15 wives were found "cruel." It is obviously the fastest growing, most effective and best-paying gimmick in the legal field.

Australia is one of the few modern countries where women have not yet achieved the fundamental right of equal pay for equal work. However, in divorce and ancilliary litigations they start miles ahead with little cost or risk to themselves.

Family courts without barristers and lawyers would constitute a healthier forum in which to air differences. They should be given power to dissolve a marriage with no chance of survival in a dignified way.

"Irretrievable breakdown of the marriage" without the compulsory slander would be appreciated by the children and reduce untold misery.

By now, even our judges admit this openly.

E. LOBL
West Ryde, NSW
25/10/68

A complete degradation

AN organisation called the Divorce Law Reform Association has been recently formed in Sydney. The membership is growing steadily.

We have opened a new division in Canberra and are in the process of establishing branches in Melbourne, Brisbane, Orange and Cooma.

The existing grounds for divorce broadly speaking

are: either five years' separation, or evidence of cruelty, adultery or desertion. In all cases, the divorce is granted after a complete degradation and humilation of an individual has been attained. This is what we have set out to change.

The objectives of our association are similar to those presented in Britain by Leo Abse, MP for Pontypool, in **Continued next page**

Divorce

Degradation

From previous page

his Member's Bill on the changes in the Matrimonial Causes Act.

1. The grounds for divorce should not involve a demand for the allegation and proof of adultery, cruelty, or desertion, but the fact should be accepted when a marriage simply is ended. A divorce could be granted on the ground that the marriage had irretrievably broken down. This only means a more rational divorce law, but no easier divorces.

2. After a husband and wife have been living apart for not less than two years after three years of marriage and are unlikely to be reconciled, either party could obtain the divorce if the other did not object. The granting of such a divorce would be subject to certain safeguards.

3. The cost of the litigation could be kept within a reasonable limit if the solicitor investigated the charges with sufficient care before launching them. This should be his responsibility.

I. B. BURNETT
Publicity Secretary
Divorce Law Reform
Association
Darlinghurst, NSW
23/1/68

┌─ **PS** ────────────────

IT is tragic that D. Rogers, a visitor to our shores, must ask (18/11) "Where are the children?" I have felt for some time that babies and tiny children are becoming a comparatively uncommon sight.
B. MARSHALL
Toowoon Bay, NSW
22/11/68

A husband who feels 81.4 per cent guilty

I FEEL I must raise my voice at a national level on the injustices and descrimination against men being dished out in the divorce courts.

Last April, my wife left me and petitioned for divorce on the grounds of cruelty.

At a short hearing in the lower court, at which I was not present but represented, the judge awarded my wife $35 a week under an interim order. The maximum she could exact under the one-third plus rule was $43 a week; thus, by simple mathematics, I am 81.4 per cent guilty.

For those who are unaware, an interim order is an award which generally lasts about six months before a trial, because the courts are so much behind time.

My wife, who was living at her mother's with the children, was now twice better off than before she left — and living rent free.

I could not keep up the payments on the matrimonial home and was eventually evicted. In addition, she hired a pantechnicon while I was at work and removed all the furniture — a practice which I am told is a daily occurrence by women seeking divorce.

Under the Universal Declaration of Human Rights, a man is innocent until proven guilty; so by what means does the judge arrive at my being 81.4 per cent guilty?

Due to emotional stress, I fell behind on the payments and was ordered to appear in court under a "leave wife without support" notice similar to the one under which the $35 a week was awarded.

I appeared without counsel and was not given a chance to say anything until after I was sentenced to 34 days in jail with six weeks to pay the arrears. The judge said: "I will sentence you first then hear what you have to say."

I was so flabbergasted at this departure from the Universal Declaration of Human Rights I ended up saying nothing. The departure from the declaration was bad enough, but under habeas corpus a man cannot be sent to jail without a trial.

Furthermore, my wife would only let me see the children for three hours on a Saturday morning.

I do not wish to disclose personal facts but feel readers must have some background details: 81.4 per cent guilty without a trial is equivalent to being in the condemned cell awaiting the hangman.

Men who go to jail for non-payment of crippling maintenance are being treated like drug addicts, down-and-outs, rogues, vagabonds, or anti-Vietnam supporters.

I call for an Act of Parliament to take divorce out of law courts and set up family courts with social workers to help (and stop solicitors from making fortunes out of the miseries of people).

"HUSBAND"
Newcastle, NSW
(The writer's name and full address were supplied to *The Australian*, but are withheld for personal reasons.)
26/1/70

Divorce

A new kind of 'marriage'

DO Australian women realise the full implications for them of the Family Law Bill, which was read for the first time in the Senate by Senator Murphy on August 1, 1974?

This bill is not one relating merely to divorce and its consequences, but is one which creates a new kind of "marriage," a "marriage" which is more like a temporary trial association of two people, which can be terminated by the wish of one of the parties without the consent of the other.

Under the provisions of this bill, a husband can abandon a faithful wife even if she is pregnant, has small children, or has been at home many years looking after her husband and children and be legally entitled to a divorce provided they have lived separately for twelve months.

During this 12-month separation period, a husband can continue to reside in the matrimonial home, even co-habiting there with another woman and still be entitled to a divorce, leaving the faithful wife to bear her own costs.

This bill imposes upon a wife a positive primary legal duty to maintain herself and a positive legal duty to maintain her husband in certain circumstances, both in marriage and in the divorce situation.

"No fault" divorce, as provided in this bill, removes from the marriage contract the normal legal safeguards to an injured party, which all other classes of contract provide.

On August 16, 1974, this bill, having reached the second reading stage, was referred to the Constitutional and Legal Affairs Committee for consideration and report back to Parliament. The date fixed is October 17 and the bill could become law very quickly after that time.

The committee has reported that it has received only six submissions with regard to the bill. This no doubt is due to the fact that the public, the churches and interested organisations have been unaware that they could make submissions to this committee.

This committee has also reported that it will be recommending substantial amendments. Due to the delay of printing Federal Hansard, the public will be unaware of these amendments for at least four weeks after they are reported to Parliament.

If there is to be genuine "open government" in Australia, this bill must be on the table in Parliament for several months for proper examination by the citizens of the country. The present Matrimonial Causes legislation was given six months airing in Parliament before final debate.

While acknowledging that some changes in the present divorce laws are desirable, we do not feel that this bill records and confirms what is in the minds and hearts of women in Australia. Therefore we look to our resposible parliamentary representatives to delay further debate on the Family Law Bill until all citizens have time to make a responsible assessment of it.

JEAN BENJAMIN
FRIEDA BROWN
MONICA GALLAGHER
MAUREEN GIDDINGS
CLAIRE ISBISTER
MARGARET SLATTERY.
Sydney, NSW
15/10/74

Church welcomes the reform

THE community debate of the proposed Family Law Bill (1974) has indicated the depth of feelings there is about the whole concept of marriage, family life, responsibility regarding children and divorce.

The members of the Social Responsibility Committee of the Congregational Churches in NSW have been concerned at the suggestion, implicit in media reports, that all churches are polarised in opposition to the bill. While acknowledging that there is a strong, vocal anti-bill lobby identified with the churches, e.g. the joint statements of the Anglican and Catholic archbishops of Sydney and by the Festival of Light, there are other opinions held by church people and expressed by some leading representatives who have the right to be heard as well.

This committee commends many features of the bill. For example, the removal of the "fault" clauses, with their punitive and guilt implications, will save the hurt traditionally added to the already emotional situation; the provision for dissolution after 12 months separation, while open to abuse, makes it possible for dangerous si-
Continued next page

Divorce

Divorce by post is condemned

CONGRATULATIONS to the Anglican archbishops for their strong condemnation of the Federal Government's projected changes to the Family Law Act, which would permit "divorce by post."

When the Family Law Act was first introduced, concern was expressed that the Act was preoccupied with termination of marriage rather than its reinforcement.

The results of the first six years of its operation confirm the worst fears, as the number of divorces snowball.

The proposed new clause 98A would permit divorce to be granted in certain circumstances without either of the parties, or their legal representatives being required to be present in court.

Obviously, we are moving rapidly towards provision of divorce without formality by mutual consent and the stability of marriage and family life is under serious threat.

Already marriage breakdown represents a major social disruption to the community.

P. GREEN
Doncaster, Vic
18/11/81

Figures are a calamity

THE latest divorce figures (year 1979) released by the Bureau of Statistics reveal a substantial increase in the number of young people being divorced. Divorces where couples were aged under 20 totalled 3307 in 1979, almost double the number for the previous year.

This is indeed a calamity, but it is not altogether surprising. The Family Law Act, which permits the marriage contract to be broken at the whim of either partner on 12 months' notice, has destroyed the concept of permanency of marriage.

A side effect of the Family Law Act has been the growth in the number of one-parent families. This has given a not inconsiderable boost to our escalating social welfare costs.

Family law should be directed to the good of society and all its members, rather than the convenience of those who want to break the partnership of marriage.

For those who believe in traditional permanent marriage, there should be an option of a written contract involving mutual rights and duties enforceable through the usual remedies of law.

The optional marriage contract would make plain to couples their duties and responsibilities, not only to each other but to their children. It would provide, in the event of marriage breakdown, for a pre-determined division of property, the custody of children and in case of fault, damages.

P. P. LORENZ
Ivanhoe, Vic
8/6/81

Reforms backed

From previous page
tuations to be relieved quickly; the provision for joint discussions for the settlement of custody arrangements, even including consideration of the child's wishes, will remove much of the tension created by the present court decision.

Perhaps the most important feature of the bill is the basic concept that marriages are not held together by laws, but rather by the people involved. The best interests of all concerned are preserved by the law when those people decide to end their relationship.

This committee welcomes the steps being taken to bring about these changes in the marriage and family legislation and encourages the Australian Government in its attempts to place the responsibility for happy marriages and strong family relationships on those who marry and have families, rather than on the laws of the land.

JOHN BROOKFIELD
Sydney
(The writer is secretary of the committee.)
14/10/74

PS

WHAT a sad indictment of family life in Australia that some 1800 parents contacted the police in Melbourne anxiously seeking information on the identity of three female bodies found in dense scrub.

D. PATERSON
Melbourne
15/12/80

The great debates

Fallacious statistics on lung cancer

I AM glad you have published Dr Lovegroves' letter (1/8) about smoking and cancer; his experience is the experience of all practising doctors.

Cancer of the lungs is not common in practice because (says Dr Starr in NSW Cancer Publication 10, 1964) cancer has not increased lately. The incidence of cancer has been the same for 100 years; if lung cancer is being diagnosed more frequently stomach cancer is less common.

In Sydney, Dr Rubinstein (Medical Journal of Australia, 5/9, 1959) reported that undiagnosed lung cancer was found in only one in every 2000 patients X-rayed in a TB survey.

Furthermore, one in seven of Rubinstein's lung cancer patients had never smoked. This indicates finally that smoking is not the cause and can only be an unimportant secondary cause.

Statistics are notoriously deceptive when used for an improper purpose — the discovery of causes. Against the "increase" of lung cancer discovered by fallacious statistics, we must place the solid statistical fact that cancer has not increased.

MICHAEL KELLY MD
East Melbourne, Vic
13/8/64

Self-destroying industry

THE British Broadcasting Corporation has just banned the advertising of cigarettes in all its publications, including the multi-million circulation Radio Times.

It is a pity that only the Reader's Digest has seen fit to do the same in Australia. It is perhaps the only publication with a conscience.

Perhaps in the end it will not be necessary to take steps to combat cigarette advertising as the tobacco industry is the only one in the world which is self-destroying.

Every year 13,000 heavy smokers die from the effects of their folly and a large proportion of these are only in their forties and fifties.

Eventually there will be only non-smokers and light smokers left and the huge tobacco industry will die a "natural" death!

RICHARD S. L. JONES
Manly, NSW
14/1/69

Where is the proof?

ON the question of smoking, the Government should appoint a royal commission. There have been numerous commissions on much less important questions. The commission should find on whether it has been proved that smoking is harmful; and if so, whether warnings on TV etc are required and their likely effect.

Despite what the anti-smoking lobby says, it has not been scientifically proved that smoking is harmful, its standards of proof being much less than scientific. There is evidence, but evidence is not proof.

I concede the lobby's evidence should not be ignored and until the matter is proved it would be wise not to smoke cigarettes. But let us be guided by scientific standards.

I tell my patients that there is evidence that cigarettes may be dangerous and while this is not yet proven, to be on the safe side they should change over to the pipe. I feel this is harmless and conducive to a feeling of wellbeing.

Furthermore, it prevents the obesity with its serious dangers that so often follows giving up smoking, and eating to excess instead. It also prevents people becoming unhappy and neurotic.

'DOCTOR'
Bondi Junction, NSW
24/5/72

Smoking

We are losing all our rights

ONE feels more these days that if the wowsers had their way, smokers would be obliged to comport ourselves as did the lepers of olden days, jangling a hand bell and mournfully intoning, "Unclean! Unclean!"

We are fast becoming second-class citizens with no rights whatsoever. But I feel strongly that smokers should have rights. After all, we pay for them, by our substantial contributions to the national exchequer and the wowsers are no more than vociferous bludgers.

The well-mannered smokers, however, refrain from lighting up in places either where smoking is prohibited, or where a courteous sign, such as Please Do Not Smoke, is exhibited. Non-smokers are not so considerate.

For example, on one recent morning, the usual double-decker bus that I catch was replaced by a single-decker. A mob of schoolchildren scrambled aboard before anybody else and occupied the entire rear section — the smoking section — of the vehicle.

The remaining passengers, some of whom in addition to myself must have been smokers, were obliged to sit in the non-smoking section.

Had any of us lit up I have no doubt that the conductress would have taken prompt action. But she made no move to evict the juvenile non-smokers from the smoking seats.

It boils down to this. I don't mind being confined to a ghetto as long as I can do as I please within its bounds, but I do resent being displaced by those who do not belong there. Unless the non-smokers are kept in their places they have no right to demand that we remain in ours.

A. BERTRAM CHANDLER
Potts Point, NSW
17/4/75

Smokers whistling in the dark

THE letter from "Doctor" (3/9), which describes smoking as a harmless tranquilliser, is so full of nonsense that several points need to be made.

The case against smoking does not rest on statistics alone. There have been many years of scientific research on the subject, involving animals and humans. American scientists spent years on research before the U.S. Surgeon-General made his famous 1964 report, which stated that there is a causal link between smoking and lung cancer, and that smoking is associated with other illnesses also.

Similarly, many years of research preceded the famous report by the Royal College of Physicians of London, first issued in 1962 and published again with fresh evidence in 1971. Neither report has been convincingly refuted and a high proportion of doctors have given up smoking.

Scientific bodies in many countries have independently issued similar reports after independent research. Fresh reports of new evidence of the hazards of smoking appear in scientific journals almost weekly and contrary evidence is paltry.

The mechanism of the link between lung cancer and smoking is not known, but tobacco tars and smoke contain at least 12 proven cancer-producing substances (among other poisons). Nicotine has been shown to have many adverse effects on the heart and blood vessels.

There are solid scientific reasons for linking smoking by pregnant women with harm to unborn children.

Nor, of course, can "Doctor" simply brush aside the exhaustively analysed and criticised, carefully assessed statistical evidence.

Actually, his letter does not ring true. It is like a man whistling in the dark — or a smoker trying to convince himself his comfort is more important than staying fit.

DOUG EVERINGHAM
Minister for Health
Canberra, A.C.T.
15/9/75

PS

APROPOS Susan Peacock's article (23/2) about counter-commercials on smoking: the most effective one I have ever seen was one in France a few months ago. In translation, it would go something like this: "Why quit smoking? No one needs two lungs anyway!" Should we recommend it to the Australian Cancer Society?

(Mrs) A. SELWYN
Toorak, Vic
2/3/73

Smoking

Draconian prohibition

JOHN Hoyle (28/6) pleads for people to use public transport. I used to go by public transport, but since the stupid and draconian prohibition of smoking, I have taken to driving my car like many other smokers.

How dare the petty tyrants deprive me of my after-breakfast smoke. The Government must be very blind if it has not noticed the great hostility this prohibition has caused in all classes of the community and I hope the voters at the next elections will let them know it.

I have polled members of my sporting organisation and have found that a very large number say they will not use public transport again until this restriction is lifted.

The big joke is that it is all the doing of a noisy minority. Yes, minority, since the majority of people smoke and will continue to do so because everybody knows that in spite of medical propaganda, it is a downright lie to say that smoking has been scientifically proved to be harmful.

It's time the Government stopped being Big Brother and interfering with personal liberty — like compelling motor cyclists to wear helmets and motorists to wear seatbelts. By all means warn people of the alleged dangers, but to bludgeon them with fines is something people are not going to stand.

M. PERRY
Bondi Junction, NSW
6/7/77

Don't pollute my air space

A SYDNEY magistrate is, at the time of writing this letter, trying to decide whether or not blowing smoke into someone's face constitutes an assault.

Whichever way this legal issue is decided, it draws attention to a human-rights issue of far deeper significance:

Smoking in public appears to me to be a totally unwarranted interference with human rights and ought to be prohibited by statute.

I believe that every man is entitled to poison himself, if he wishes to do so, be it with the aid of potassium cyanide, calories or tobacco.

On the other hand, no one is entitled to poison others. This appears to be a limit to libertarianism conceded even by John Stuart Mill.

The law does not permit you to force me to eat food I

do not want to eat, or to consume alcohol if I prefer not to do so, or to ingest a drug which I do not wish to ingest.

On what basis, then, is a smoker entitled to pollute my atmosphere, or to force smoke down my throat, which I happen to think is harmful to my health, shorten my life and which in any event (quite apart from all that) I simply find unpleasant?

One observes with horror that in this country people even smoke in restaurants and at formal dinners and in lifts, an uncivilised practice which ought to be forbidden by the laws of elementary courtesy, even if no other laws prevent such barbarism.

PETER CLYNE
Sydney
5/4/78

Breakthrough

I HAVE recently participated in what I consider to be a breakthrough in air travel, with the result that for the first time in my life, I enjoyed it.

The events which prompt me to write this letter, in the hope that the powers that be at Ansett, TAA and Qantas will rush to jump on the bandwagon, took place in the U.S. on practically all the internal flights I made.

On presenting my tickets at the desk, I was asked, "Smoking or non-smoking, sir?" and allocated a seat in the section of my choice — the non-smoking area, which was approximately half (and the most populated half, I might add) of the cabin area.

This procedure applied on all types of aircraft from the jumbo 747 to the 737 including the DC-9 and 727 — the jets which fly the internal routes in Australia.

Not a trace of tobacco fumes or sounds of coughing fits by the diehard smokers. Such a change from my frequent Adelaide-to-Sydney journeys (or rather ordeals) which knock me out for at least 24 hours.

How about it fellas?

D. CLIFE
Hope Valley, SA
7/1/72

PS

IT was encouraging to read that smoking on Adelaide buses will be banned for a three-month trial period. Let's hope Sydney is big enough to take the same step.

P. I. TUCKETT
Woollahra, NSW
25/2/76

Smoking

The hazards facing smokers

BUZZ Kennedy (*The Australian,* 10/6) is, of course, free to choose and enjoy, if he can, his own poison, as most of us do. Hopefully the community should by now know the risks of both tobacco and excessive alcohol consumption. I wonder, however, about the facts behind Buzz's confident statement that alcohol costs the country far more "than tobacco is ever likely to do."

Estimates of health and other community costs from tobacco and alcohol consumption are very difficult to give with any degree of accuracy, so that Buzz's comparison probably represents hope rather than proven fact.

Your readers may be interested to know the following estimates in relation to smoking hazards (taken from a submission to a State health minister): "16,000 deaths would not have occurred if there were no smoking. This represents an average of 44 Australians each day. This figure of 16,000 may be compared with other causes of death in the community:

IT IS over four times the annual Australian road toll.

IT IS over five times the Australian deaths attributable directly to alcohol (including alcohol associated traffic deaths).

IT IS 3½ times the average Australian annual loss during the six years of the 1939-45 World War.

IT represents more Australian smoking deaths in one year than occurred with Australian troops in an average year of the Vietnam war."

R. L. HODGE
Director
National Heart Foundation
of Australia
Woden, A.C.T.
22/6/81

Decent people made criminals

LIKE many other members of the medical profession, I am appalled by the antics of the anti-smoking zealots.

As medical students we were urged strongly never to accept anything without scientific proof. Yet now so-called medical advisers are claiming that the inhaling of smoke by non-smokers is harmful when there is not one iota of evidence for this — let alone proof.

They may have some case for smokers themselves being harmed although even this has not been scientifically proved, but to say there is evidence that non-smokers can be harmed is a most blatant falsehood.

These fanatics are behind the move to have smoking outlawed on public transport — decent people made criminals. The bogy of fire hazard is just wool to be pulled over the eyes of the public.

They have masses of statistical evidence which they claim shows cigarettes cause harm, but they cannot honestly show any evidence that the pipe is harmful.

Does the Government intend to ban pipe smoking, too, when there is no evidence against it?

Apart from transport, the zealots are inducing shopkeepers to put up "no smoking" signs, no doubt in the hope that in due time it will be enforced by law. There are still plenty of shops that have ignored this campaign, where self-respecting smokers can shop without being subjected to this offensiveness. And it is rather comical that the offensive shops haven't stopped selling tobacco, but still have their tobacco counters in full bloom.

The Government has aroused enough hostility already with its ban on transport. Does it want to antagonise potential voters further by continuing the ban — particularly when there is no honest basis for it?

(Dr) W. H. WHITBY
Bondi Junction, NSW
11/8/77

PS

I WAS brought up in a family in which everyone smoked except me. Then my teenage daughters smoked. I joined them. I was over 40. Now I'm hooked to the extent of 30 a day. Regardless of the fears of cancer or heart disease, I go on smoking. I know I feel wretched. I cough and spit and my appetite is deadened. Don't tell me Dr who-ever-you-are that it does no harm. I'm a living example of what it does.
E. GARDINER
Tempe, NSW
22/1/80

The States

Sydney versus Melbourne

THERE is a rumor from overseas, and we can guess who spread it, that the people of Melbourne are jealous of Sydney and especially the Sydney Opera House.

The story I have heard is that the competition we held in Melbourne for a city landmark was to try and match the Sydney Opera House. This is ridiculous, most Melbourne residents have never heard of the Sydney Opera House.

One strange report was that the Sydney Opera House is the only building in Australia of world renown. This is absolutely wrong. The Melbourne Post Office would be far better known. There is no question that it is more useful.

Regarding the city landmark, after a new look at the city and the mentioned post office, also our wonderful five-storeyed police station, we came to the conclusion that perfection was impossible to improve on.

Please visit Melbourne and avoid cities that use large

I REFER to Mr G. Neild's letter (21/10) referring to Sydney-Melbourne comparisons. In Mackay, we have a competition each year and 1st prize is one week in Melbourne, 2nd prize two weeks.
J. W. SMITH
Sarina, Qld
29/10/80

snail shells to attract visitors.
GORDON NEILD
Warrnambool, Vic
21/10/80

I SINCERELY hope Cassandra's prediction that the Commonwealth will back Melbourne's application to host the 1988 Olympics turns out to be wrong (Sunday Telegraph, 21/12).

The Commonwealth should be looking at ways of ridding itself of unnecessary financial burdens, not of adding to them.

One may sympathise with Melbourne's need for a gimmick to attract visitors, given its unpopularity with tourists and its general economic stagnation.

Moreover, now that it has lost to Sydney its title of financial capital of Australia and watched the cultural centre of gravity shift first to Adelaide and now to Sydney, it desperately needs something to boost its morale.

But to expect all Australians to contribute through extra taxation so that Melbourne may once again host a sporting extravaganza of increasingly doubtful value is to expect too much.

Instead, the Commonwealth should throw its weight behind a campaign to find a permanent international Olympic site — which is what it said it supported at the time of the Moscow Olympic boycott fiasco — and refuse to back the Melbourne application.
(Professor) LAUCHLAN CHIPMAN
Wollongong, NSW
29/12/80

In love with the Gold Coast

IF the Gold Coast environment is that bad, why are there more cheerful, helpful people to the square hectare than almost anywhere else in Australia? The 40 km hinterland is quite remarkable; the river estuaries and headlands are great; the mountains are superb; the shops super; the homes are endlessly varied and exciting; the high-rise breathtaking; the waterways are endless and majestic; the canals are more numerous than Venice and maybe twice as scenic; the restaurants a treat; service is seldom bettered anywhere; the streets are clean; the beaches well kept; entertainment is entertaining; rain forest a retreat. I love it all. And you notice I haven't even started raving about the climate. I love it because it is uniquely Australian, a little hard-boiled perhaps (sure some borrowed ideas), a few faults here and there, but I would be proud to show anybody from any place else in this world around and not feel a need to apologise about anything. And I don't even live there!

JACKSON MITCHELL
North Lambton, NSW
12/9/81

The States

The case for WA's secession

I WAS faintly amused to read some "expert's" opinion that war was the sole vehicle for an Australian State to achieve secession.

Obviously, this gentleman knows nothing of the military arts and precious little of the Australian Army's capability so far as numbers are concerned.

Secession in Western Australia will be achieved only if the greater majority of the people indicate democratically that such a step is their wish. No Australian government would under such circumstances refuse by force of arms to grant their freedom. We live in a Western-style democracy, not a "banana republic" dominated by a jumped-up despot.

We agree that there is no "drill" laid down in the Constitution for a State to secede, but really this is of no account, for after all is it the Constitution that we wish to secede from?

The case for Western Australia's bid to secede is based on 75 years of federal mismanagement and 74 years of tariff-inflicted financial disability. Indeed, our Legislative Assembly heard the first motion for secession as early as 1902, shortly after this federal-imposed tariff became effective.

To a primary-producing State such as we live in, this impost is a severe handicap, as our income derived from world markets is not subject to the frequent increases enjoyed by the communities dependent on manufacturing activities.

The case for secession is, of course, a wonderful topic for the academic theorists to pronounce on, but in reality there is nothing to discuss. If we wish to secede, then we do so — providing the greater majority of West Australians are behind us.

In one of the last paragraphs of your article, I read that Mr Gilbert declares that if Queensland seceded, it would be boycotted and outcast from the rest of the Australian society. I doubt it, for both Queensland and Western Australia are valuable "captive customers" for the industrial barons of Sydney and Melbourne. But secession will bring severe competition from overseas manufacturers and surely help to reduce the inflated cost of living in both States.

Basically, Queensland and Western Australia obtain their income in the competitive markets of the world, but have to purchase their requirements in one of the world's most expensive manufacturing areas, the Australian tariff zone.

DON THOMAS
Westralian Secession
Movement
Nedlands, WA
19/11/76

Questions after Darwin's tragedy

THE tragedy of Darwin will not be forgotten for many years to come and it cannot yet be gauged how much human suffering has been involved in the many deaths and dislocation of nearly a whole city.

However, I believe that now the following questions will have to be asked:

While we have not yet found technical means to divert a cyclone, the warning was made three days prior to its striking Darwin. Why were there no steps taken to at least secure the lives of the inhabitants of Darwin?

Why is it that the Department of Defence or Mr Barnard has taken no action on

receiving advice of the imminent cyclone and if they have not been advised, why was no action taken in preparation for a possible tragedy?

Why is it that small planes remained at the airport of Darwin in spite of the warning that a cyclone might strike?

Why is it that the navy did not move its ships out of the harbor of Darwin into safer waters, knowing full well that a cyclone might in all probability endanger its vessels?

Why were no precautions taken in the city itself and why did the Natural Disas-

ter Organisation not take any preparatory action?

In a time of unemployment, when many builders do not have jobs, why is it that no arrangements are being made for people in those circumstances to be transferred to Darwin to assist in cleaning up and rebuilding the city?

It is no use making an investigation once the impact of the loss of life and the destruction has faded. The questions should be asked now . . . Why was nothing done? Who is responsible for nothing being done?

PETER FRANKEL
South Yarra, Vic
7/1/75

The States

See Alice now . .

A WORD of advice for those people who wish to see the little that remains of the Alice Springs of history and legend: get here fast before the '60s-style development-at-all-costs boys COMPLETELY destroy it!

Right now, plans are afoot to erect a chair-lift on the ancient MacDonnell Range. (Deep down I suspect this is part of a larger plan that won't be complete until a giant Luna Park mouth surmounts the Heavitree Gap entrance to the town.)

In addition, the local powers-that-be seem very keen on the Northern Territory Government's fake-lake scheme.

It looks as if a recreational lake will be constructed close enough to the Old Telegraph Station as to mar the history of that site. Even if it is not visible from the Telegraph Station, it will make its mark in the same way that a shoppping centre located close to an area of untouched bush would destroy that place's aura of wilderness.

Is it possible that there can be local support for these projects? Can a landscape be so deeply disliked by the people who choose to live in it?

If a fake-lake is felt to be needed by sea-starved Centralians, how long before the glorious Mt Gillen is refrigerated to provide an Alpine wonderland for residents who miss the snow?

Take my advice, see Alice Springs now.

GORDON WILLIAMS
Alice Springs, NT
28/10/81

Civilised Tasmania

AS an Englishman retired a year ago to settle in Tasmania, I must take issue with Max Harris' patronising article, Stately Homes and Cerebral Gnomes (19/8).

In it, he infers that Tasmania should concentrate on becoming a touristic mecca and forget all about hydro-electric development.

This is ludicrous. At the last count, tourism brought $16 million income to the island. Other trade, mainly based on his despised hydro-electric power brought $337 million.

Does Max Harris seriously expect Tasmanians to throw away all the benefits of the cheapest hydro-electric power in Australia (probably in the world) and devote themselves to arty-crafty peepshows for goggling tourists?

The development of the tourist industry is a legitimate objective, but it should never, ever, take precedence over the natural healthy development of the local community. And (dare I say it?) some forms of tourism constitute pollution in themselves.

There are many Tasmanians who consider the Wrest Point casino tower a much greater offence against the community than the Lake Pedder business.

Tasmanians are rightly proud of their hydro-electric schemes and the pollution-free influence of widespread power is one of the main factors in Tasmania's civilised and serene atmosphere.

T. W. STANIER
Hobart
7/9/72

City of flies

HOTEL proprietors have blamed the hot weather for the failure of Canberra to attract many tourists.

Although the weather may have been a factor, the menace of the flies has been entirely overlooked.

Every visitor to Canberra whom I have met has complained about the flies. It is about time something positive was done about it.

Peking used to be a city of flies. The problem was recognised and the authority gave each citizen of Peking a quota to kill flies.

Very soon the city was rid of flies.

ONG SENG-KOK
Australian National University
Canberra
19/1/67

In despair

YOUR front-page article on weather (24/11) has another of those eternal, infernal pinpricks that are the despair of every Tasmanian.

If Sydney, Melbourne, Brisbane, Adelaide and Perth need brollies or bikinis for Christmas, what about Hobart?

You forget that there is a sixth State capital too often.

(Mrs) MARCIA SOLOMON
Eaglehawk Neck, Tas
3/12/71

Go West . .

AS a West Australian, living in Canberra, who wishes to maintain a regular link with kith and kin in Perth, I hope the Federal Government's inquiry into Australia's tourist industry will find a way to make Perth competitive with Fiji and other "goodies" offered by Qantas.

ELSIE SOLLY
Deakin, A.C.T.
13/9/76

Waltzing Matilda

A patriotic lump in the throat

NOW that the shouting has died down from the Commonwealth Games, I would like to publicise a feeling that I experienced in my position as ABC Television front-man at the Games. (And I hasten to add that this was a purely personal reaction, not an ABC one.)

The Australian national song, Advance Australia Fair, was played at every medal presentation involving Australian athletes and not once did I feel an ounce of patriotic fervor or pride. On the other hand, whenever Waltzing Matilda was played (as it was, for example, when Australia's swimmers marched into the Kinsmen Aquatic Centre), I felt the familiar lump in the throat. What's more, even the Canadians knew the tune and would start singing along with us Australians. Let's face it, the whole world identifies us with Waltzing Matilda and most Australians can at least sing part of it.

On the other hand, very few of us know the words of Advance Australia Fair, as was shown at the flag-raising ceremony at the Games Village, when a few officials tried to sing, but faltered after a couple of lines, in what was just an embarrassment.

Perhaps it is too late to change now and you may argue that the referendum expressed the will of the majority, but I wonder how many Australians have felt

It's stupid!

SO Mr Whitlam thinks that the Australian national anthem will probably be Waltzing Matilda.

If this is the best we can do why not give serious thought to such songs as Tie Me Kangaroo Down Sport, Me Boomerang Won't Come Back, The Dog Sat On The Tucker Box or let's even pinch the old English ditty Roll Out The Barrel.

The above songs are all just as stupid; so if we are going to have a national anthem let it be something worthwhile which we can be proud of and not something which, after all, is only a historical ballad.

K. N. BROWN
Prospect, SA
18/6/73

the same, say, when overseas?

PETER MEARES
ABC Sport, Qld
31/8/78

I WAS delighted to read your editorial (29/1) on the subject of the tune Waltzing Matilda and agree that it is so Australian and so identified with this country in the minds of the rest of the world that it should be the one for our national anthem. A magnificent arrangement of it by my colleague Peter Rorke is used to open ABC station 3AR, Mel-

bourne every morning and I commend it to your attention as an example of just what can be done with the basic melody.

ARTHUR BURRAGE
Sydney
12/2/73

WHY all the fuss about a new national anthem? Although Waltzing Matilda is bushy in origin, it is obviously heavy with symbolism revealing the attitudes and aspirations of today's contemporary Australian society and thus it is a song for all seasons.

The swagman is obviously the itinerant free-wheeling generation of old Aussies, migrants and their children grabbing the good life (jumbuck) and stuffing it in their tucker bags before anyone else can get their cotton-picking hands on it, revealing the "I'm all right, Jack," urban society.

Once captured, the good life contains the seeds of its own discontent. And the troopers, representing the guilt of the Australian puritan alter ego, descend like a load of proverbial bricks on the luckless swagman who leaps into the billabong ending it all.

JOHN HAY
Wollongong, NSW
29/6/73

MY suggestion is God Save the Queen to the tune of Waltzing Matilda.

MARY ZIEGLER
Double Bay, NSW
15/6/73

Strikes

Work while you strike idea

IN view of the recent spate of industrial disputes, it would be worth while to study a unique "work while you strike" plan, which may change the face of future labor-management relations in the United States.

It penalises both strikers and employer, while benefiting the local community.

Written in as a separate trial clause in a three-year contract between an AFL-CIO union and the Dunbar Furniture Corporation, Berne, Indiana, it will be in force for the first 12 weeks of the next strike.

Under the clause, strikers show up for work as usual and maintain productivity without slowdowns. But they draw only half pay, the other half being deposited in a local bank. The company matches this deposit from its funds.

If the strike is settled within six weeks, workers and company get all the money back. If it goes to nine weeks, 75 per cent of the money is returned; to 11 weeks, 50 per cent; settlement in 12th week means a 25 per cent refund.

Should the dispute continue, the union can start an actual strike, or the company can initiate a real lockout.

The contract is automatically renewed for a year if no action is taken by the end of the 13th week. In any case, strikers and company have forfeited their deposits to the community and both can suggest a project on which to spend the money.

What good is this plan? Firstly, it limits the dispute to workers and management. Company's customers and the public are not affected.

Secondly, the financial drain on both puts pressure on union and company to settle differences quickly.

With suitable modifications to meet local conditions, this idea might be given a trial in Australia.

A. ABOLINS
South Yarra, Vic
28/10/64

Green bans applauded

IT may be of interest to readers to know that following a one-hour program on BBC television, dealing with the Sydney Opera House, the most favorable response from my English friends concerned the builders' laborers and their imposition of a green ban on the proposed car park.

What amazed my friends was not so much the proposal to replace those splendid Moreton Bay figs with a cement monstrosity (equally stupid planning decisions are made in this country), but the action taken by Jack Mundey and his union in effectively blocking the car park's construction.

Perhaps with strikes over pay and working conditions being so common over here, the locals regard a dispute over a piece of parkland as being a refreshing change and, in turn, were heartened by the interest shown by these workers in the environment.

Like many Australians, I was rather annoyed by this ban at the time (strikes were certainly becoming much more numerous then), but I cannot help thinking that history will regard the builders' ban in a far more favorable light.

R. H. CLARKE
Cheltenham, UK
23/11/74

Strikes

Philosophy behind the green bans

YOUR editorial, Developing New Thoughts On An Old Battleground (25/5), was quite positive and a welcome change from the days when resident action groups and unions with a social conscience in imposing green bans were soundly condemned.

The widespread public support of diverse socio-economic groups for the green ban philosphy is acknowledged.

Green bans fall into two categories. One is the type of ban exisiting on Centennial Park and the Botanic Gardens, Kellys Bush, historical buildings and inner-city freeways; this type will last forever and they are not negotiable.

Those green bans which are negotiable and will eventually be resolved are those in which the people concerned have participated in the planning process and are satisfied with a new scheme.

The initiative of Tom Uren and the response of the NSW State Government and Sydney City Council are encouraging sights, as evidenced by the co-operation in preparing an alternate plan for Woolloomooloo.

People having a greater say in their own community is imperative; and the time when politicians and bureaucrats could decree from their lofty heights how ordinary mortals should live in their community is gone. The people concerned must be consulted.

When one considers the incredible folly of half-empty office buildings standing

Jack Mundey

idle while at the same time homes, flats, schools and hospitals are required, it is easy to see that a completely new approach to planning the building industry is required.

Therefore, I believe the time is ripe for an all-in conference involving the Ministers for Labor, Department of Urban and Regional Development, Housing and Conservation, the Urban Development Institute of Australia and the national building unions to plan a more stable building industry in which community needs are placed before the selfish attitude of a handful of large property developers.

So as to take advantage of new possibilities, I believe such a conference should take place now in the interest of all connected with this important area.

JACK MUNDEY
Croydon Park, NSW
29/5/74

PS

MR Hawke claims that the Medibank national strike was a success because it had initiated a public debate. I am not an economist like Mr Hawke, but at a cost to the national economy of about $100 million in lost wages and $500 million in lost production, it seems a rather expensive way to initiate a public debate.

P. LONG
Ivanhoe, Vic
19/7/76

SINCE the strike situation seems a permanent fixture, the Australian Post Office could perform a valuable public service (as well as earning itself extra revenue) by providing a new recorded service. This would be called "Dial-a-strike" and would state who is on strike, for how long and what is thereby affected.

K. KENNEDY
Waverton, NSW
27/7/71

WE, the undersigned passengers of flight QF94 from Nadi (22/2), wish to register the strongest possible protest against the union and all others connected with this senseless Qantas strike. We especially pay tribute to the crew and hostesses who have defied the ban to look after us and put the travelling public's welfare first. We deplore the methods unions use, harassing the flight crew and hostesses while on and off duty.

FLIGHT QF94
(231 signatures)
27/2/81

Strikes

Has the Govt the fibre to act?

SIR James McNeill (the chairman of BHP), in warning that militant union action was threatening the imminent resources boom, left much unsaid in regard to the future of Australia.

While the Melbourne Chamber of Commerce applauds and supports his comments, press reports did not refer to the deleterious effect militant union action is having on other sectors of trade and industry, and the economy in general.

An examination of the building industry in Melbourne alone indicates that militancy has crippled an industry that was already in some difficulty.

Union heavy-handedness has all but destroyed any chance Victoria ever had of achieving a modern and, more importantly, a reliable system of public transport.

Victoria and NSW have been beset by so much militant union activity that overseas countries and foreign investors are loath to consider Australia.

During a recent mission to EEC countries, organised by the Melbourne Chamber of Commerce and led by the Victorian Premier, Mr Hamer, it mattered not where one went, the question was always the same: "Why do you have so many strikes and industrial unrest in Australia?"

Laissez-faire has become a policy very much to the national detriment.

While Australia's reputation overseas is already sorely tarnished, there is still some little time left to take the strong action recommended by Sir James. However, the question is: Does the Government or the Arbitration Commission and other tribunals have the stamina and fibre to resist militancy?

JOHN N. VIAL
Executive Director
Melbourne Chamber of
Commerce
17/11/80

Don't strike us off the map!

OVER the past 15 years, I, like most other Australians, have accepted all the industrial disputes and problems and have only become upset when petrol was not available.

I have now been one of the many victims of the strike by air hostesses and feel I must voice my opinion.

I attended a conference in Adelaide, made up of approximately 90 delegates from all States of Australia and a group of 36 international delegates (U.S., Canada, Mexico) — all stranded because no airlines were flying.

Our conference was cut short and a lot of our time was spent trying to organise trips home; eventually, I think all were able to make some alternative arrangements.

One chap had to be back early, so arranged an overseas flight to New Zealand, then return to Sydney.

Some returned to Western Australia without all of their luggage and our international contingent and NSW delegates spent two hours standing at the coach pick-up point in very cold temperatures as the coaches were late arriving.

This is just one of thousands of such instances that must have taken place throughout our "lucky country" during the last week.

Girls of Ansett and TAA, I hope you are proud of your actions. Even if you don't care about your fellow Australians — please, next time, give some consideration to the overseas visitors who have chosen our country as a nice place to visit.

Don't strike Australia off the map!

TREVOR CUNNINGHAM
Killarney Heights, NSW
1/5/81

┌─ PS ─────────────

GLOSSARY of trade union terms:
Meaningful negotiations: Give us everything we demand.
Free speech: We'll be heard, but you won't.
Employers' reply: Confrontation.
Basic democratic rights: We shall do as we please, lawful or not.
Free thinker: Scab.

Peaceful demonstrations: The streets are ours and you can be inconvenienced.
Opposing view: Union bashing.
Solution to disputes: Bring the country to its knees.

R. W. WALKER
Cottesloe, WA
15/8/81

Aborigines

...ONE DAY, SON, ALL THIS WILL BE THEIRS

RICH FELLA MY COUNTRY

THE Commonwealth Arbitration Commission is hearing a union application to give Aborigines on Northern Territory cattle stations equal pay with white workers.

If the commission makes a decision in favor of equal pay, it will have the support of the majority of Australians.

Most notable of the recent pronouncements for equal pay for Aborigines is the Victorian Council of Churches. Churchmen from seven different denominations have urged that all discriminatory legislation in our land be removed and have said there is an urgent need for full education and training of the illiterate and unskilled to eradicate poverty and sub-standard living among Aborigines.

Dr Colin Tatz, newly-elected member of the Victorian Aborigines Welfare Board, after a tour of 30

Growing unrest

Northern Territory cattle stations investigating wage conditions of Aborigines, speaks of growing unrest among Aborigines and their deep-seated, bitter contempt and hatred for their white mentors.

We often read these words in connection with South Africa and other nations, but let the average citizen be aware — the Aborigines mean us, right here in Australia.

What will happen if the Aborigines take a leaf out of the book of other indigenous people and try to take their land back by force? Will we throw up our hands in horror, or will we realise their patience is at an end?

Why not give the Aborigines the right to manage their own affairs and decide what they want to do? They will make many mistakes, but haven't we made mistakes also?

The present arbitration hearing will listen to submissions from the Government, trade unions and graziers — but will it hear submissions from Baron Vestey?

A recent newspaper article reported that Baron Vestey has so many millions he can't count them. His fortune is estimated at £300 million; he controls 20 million acres of grazing land in Australia; controls half a dozen meat processing works and owns 60 ships besides his other interests in fishing, wool, prawns and crayfish.

How did a company amass such a fortune? Was not a contributing factor £2/8/3 weekly wages paid to Aboriginal station workers?

MARJORIE BROADBENT
Alice Springs
23/7/65

Aborigines

Challenge for white Australians

ALTHOUGH I've only seen the fourth of Graham Williams' articles on the Aboriginal problem, I do appreciate the interest of *The Australian* in this great human issue.

From a knowledge of some Victorian Aborigines, I would like to offer a list of actions and attitudes required if an answer is to be found. They are:

1. We need to recognise "color" as one of the world issues of today surpassing "class" as a determining factor in current history. We face this world issue in our dealings with the Aborigine.

2. The white man carries major responsiblity for the plight of the Aborigine today.

3. The Aborigine has many good characteristics as well as certain weaknesses, in the same way that white men have "Dr Jekyll and Mr Hyde" qualities.

4. The white man cannot answer this situation by leaving it to a department. Australians of white background must show a sincere acceptance of their responsibilities and see that Aborigines as they move into white society receive patient care, attention and advice in facing up to their problems.

5. In these activities, the white Australian should focus for the Aborigine his responsibility to his children and to other Aborigines in overcoming the very real difficulties involved in moving from one way of life to another.

6. The white Australian also needs to set an example of the way of life we want for the Aborigine. If we want the Aborigine to avoid liquor and gambling, our example will be the best way of persuading him to do likewise.

This is one of several crucial moral challenges facing white Australians today that we avoid at our peril. However, I'm convinced the white Australian has the latent generosity and capacity to bring an answer and make assimilation successful.

He needs, however, the continual challenge accompanied by an indication of his own responsibility. *The Australian* can make a real contribution in this direction.

T. H. UREN
North Balwyn, Vic
18/7/65

Aborigines used as tourist bait

IT was with something akin to astonishment and horror that I, as a former superintendent of Milinjimki and Yirrhola mission stations, saw displayed the TAA announcement that one could now travel on Safaritour to Maningrida, in the Arnhem Land Reserve.

In true two-airline competitive operations, one can envisage the forthcoming advertisement of ANA that the Aborigines' Mission Run now operating out of Perth and Darwin will carry Safaritour trippers through the mission stations.

The idea that our Aborigines can be viewed as zoological specimens, thus confirming the general attitude of certain Australians to the Aborigines as a people, is disappointing.

The known deterioration of mutual regard that has resulted from a similar tourist use of Hermansberg should have been enough deterrent for a permit to have been refused for the extension into Arnhem Land.

In the present state of unsettled standards, when both the Aborigines and the white community are manoeuvring towards more stable and permanent relationships, this cynical disregard of the finer feelings of the Aborigines can only encourage the bodies being stared at, openly discussed, photographed and generally made into objects of either scorn or pity to react in behavior patterns to match the circumstances.

The lamentable Saturday night at Alice Springs is partly a reflex action to similar treatment.

One would hope that the principle of using the Aboriginal people as tourist bait by exposure would give way to a more positive program of preserving those aspects of Aboriginal culture which would be valuable to us by a careful cultivation of theatrical skills for use at intervals of national importance when groups of selected Aborigines could perform under paid and disciplined conditions.

By the method of exposure now proposed, we shall retard the chances of mutual regard coalescing into a unity of purpose and create antithetical groups — the starers — and the ones who look back.

(Rev) E. A. WELLS
Bulimba, Qld
27/3/67

Aborigines

The key is a deeper spiritual awareness

ARTICLES on black power and letters by white do-gooders on this issue in recent months have had a mild interest to me; however I do get a little disturbed when these articles and letters confuse the Aboriginal Australians with the black Australian cult.

I am an Aboriginal Australian and do not acknowledge the need to wear a badge that proclaims my identity as such; I have a much more substantial inner awareness of my identity as a person.

We Aborigines do not identify with the color black. Our identity is based on a much deeper spiritual awareness of ourselves as people. We were not endowed with a permanent skin pigmentation so that the color of our skin has never been acknowledged as part of our culture.

Biologically, I am not so very different from most European Australians, yet I identify as an Aborigine as strongly as any full-blooded Aborigine and am able to do so without the aid of a black uniform and badge.

Individuality has always been a unique aspect of Aboriginal culture and religion. Recognition and appreciation of individual differences in intra as well as inter-tribal situations has always been very much a part of the Aboriginal way of life.

I, personally, am not hung-up on tradition, but I cannot appreciate the connection between those people whose basis for identity is nothing more substantial than the mere color of their skin and the claim for Aboriginal land

Here, here!

I REFER to the letter of Mr Ted Fields (14/1), in which he proudly identifies himself as an Aboriginal Australian.

For this and the common sense meat of his letter, I convey my sincere congratulations: I heartily endorse every word.

Congratulations are also in order to your newspaper for printing such sanity.

NEVILLE T. BONNER
Brisbane
(The writer is Liberal Senator for Queensland.)
26/1/72

rights; nor can I acknowledge their right to suggest that Evonne Goolagong should be their spokesman, or that she should not accept the MBE awarded her.

Evonne, of whom her people are justly proud, does not identify as black. She identifies as Aborigine, which is more national and specific.

I do, however, acknowledge the right of the black Australians to form their own club and wear a uniform and badge that declares that the wearer is black and I wish them well in their struggle for recognition as such and trust that they, in turn, will afford us Aborigines the same courtesy.

TED FIELDS
Armidale, NSW
14/1/72

Bloodbath

AS an American living in Australia who has watched the racial turmoil in her own country with ever increasing horror, I can only deplore this Government's policies regarding Aborigines. At no time in history has racial separation and a rigid control of human life produced anything but hatred, mistrust and fear.

The assumption that time will bring the Aborigines to a point where they can easily be assimilated into a white Australian society is simplistic and foolish. It has also been painfully disproven elsewhere. If assimilation is difficult now, it will be much more so in 10 or 15 years. Racial prejudice will not die by keeping the whites and Aborigines apart. It will only grow — out of fear of the unknown.

Once the Aborigines unite and become politically conscious, as inevitably they will, the bloodbath which could occur here will be far more intense and violent than anything yet seen in the United States.

NANCY BLACK
Balmain, NSW
3/11/70

PS

AS part of our National Aborigines' Day celebrations, a corroboree was to be performed. The local radio station broadcast promotional copy to the effect that on the Saturday morning there would be a 10-minute corroboree in the carpark behind Woolworths. Assimilation or degradation?

ROD HURLEY
Armidale, NSW
24/7/70

Aborigines

Shamed

MY wife and I have returned from a holiday tour through central Australia.

Our greatest and worst impression of the entire tour is horror and disgust at the treatment of our Aborigines by the Federal Government.

We saw Aborigines at close quarters on several station properties. One of the worst of all in treatment of natives is not far from Alice Springs.

These people lived in the shade of an old decrepit wagon in the dirt. Their clothing was filthy, ragged and rotten. They were underfed.

Several children, eight to be exact, were pitiful. My wife and I experienced a feeling of deep shame. They will haunt me. Mr Howson, Minister for Aborigines, should be utterly ashamed to head a department which is charged with the care of these poor people and neglects it.

All of these youngsters were ill fed, diseased and filthy, some of them naked. The common disease was trachoma; they all had it. One boy's right eye was almost eaten out.

Nothing is done for these children.

GEORGE STACK
Northgate, Qld
17/11/72

Symbol of belief

NAMATJIRA'S last years and untimely death were seen by many here and overseas as evidence that Australians in general were both philistine and racist in their attitudes.

One would have hoped that the image was beginning to change, yet the issue of the Yirawala head throws grave doubts upon the validity of assumptions about improvement in either area.

Yirawala, beyond question our greatest painter in the traditional Aboriginal manner, claims that his powers have been taken away as a result of a bust being made.

He asserts that the only way for him to recover his powers, and indeed his health, is for the bust to be returned to him for burial in his sacred country.

As the bust is in the possession of the Art Gallery of South Australia, it would be quite practicable to present it to Yirawala as a significant symbol of respect by a white government for Aboriginal beliefs.

Yet old contempts die hard. Despite Mr Dunstan's reputation as the most

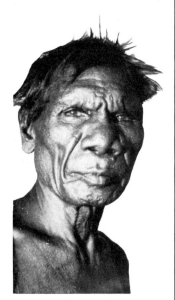
Yirawala

progressive of the premiers, a hard-line attitude towards the return of the Yirawala head seems to prevail. Surely someone can show a little bit of imagination and seek to look at this issue in historical perspective.

JAMES THOMSON
Toongabbie, NSW
22/8/75

One man's idealistic view of his brother

IN 1951, when Sir Thomas Playford was Premier of South Australia, the present Premier, Mr Dunstan, began practice as a barrister in Adelaide.

The South Australian statutes were then burdened with repressive laws restricting the lives of the Aboriginal people.

As secretary to Mr Dunstan at that time, the writer became acquainted with his attitudes to those laws and witnessed his defence of the Aborigines whose cases were referred to him by the Law Society Legal Aid scheme.

Mr Dunstan resolved then that, should the opportunity ever present itself, he would endeavor to rid the statute books of those laws. History relates that he kept that resolve.

Could a cynical world possibly accept the view that the appointment of Sir Douglas Nicholls to the highest position in the State is but a logical expression of one man's idealistic view of his brother?

PATRICIA RATCLIFF
Launceston, Tas
24/8/76

Aborigines

Our reputation is sullied

THE report of the World Council of Churches' delegation on the condition and status of Aboriginal Australians is a salutary reminder to Australians generally that their international reputation continues to be sullied by their neglect and inhumanity towards these Australian citizens.

There is nothing new in this report: its judgments can be validated in the work of independent academic research workers and in the reports of parliamentary and other committees, and commissions of inquiry.

The report perhaps gives insufficient acknowledgment to the improvements which have been won over the past decade in the face of strong resistance to the increasing support among the general community for the Aboriginal cause and above all to the widespread evidence of growing Aboriginal capacity to manage their own affairs. Nevertheless, in substance it remains a just assessment and a damning indictment of Australian governments and parlia-

ments, and of many powerful interests.

Attempts to attribute bias and political motivation to the delegation reflect simply the refusal of Mr Bjelke-Petersen, Sir Charles Court and others to accept the truth. Their response demonstrates that until the Commonwealth Parliament accepts the responsibility clearly given it in the referendum of 1967 to legislate in relation to Aborigines, there is little prospect of justice and fair dealing for Aboriginal Australians.

It is a pity that the Commonwealth Minister for Aboriginal Affairs has followed his predecessors in making sympathetic noises, but in fact passing the issue back to the States where **he knows** that in most States and Territories the report will be ignored. This response is in essence a cowardly rejection of a clear obligation which he and his Cabinet colleagues share.

The Aboriginal Treaty Committee calls upon the Commonwealth Parliament to act. The Committee sugg-

ests that either or both Houses resolve:

1. To accept in principle the need for a freely negotiated agreement with the binding force of a treaty between the Commonwealth and Aboriginal Australians.

2. To establish a committee to confer with the NAC and Aboriginal organisations and committees, and report on:

(a) Action necessary to enable Aborigines effectively to prepare for negotiations;

(b) Procedures by which negotiations could fairly be conducted;

(c) Issues which should be covered in such an agreement;

(d) The legal and constitutional form and status of such an agreement.

The committee invites all Australians to support this proposal by writing to their parliamentary member and senators.

H. C. COOMBS
Chairman
Aboriginal Treaty
Committee
Canberra
20/8/81

Condemned for racial hypocrisy

THE majority of you Australians must be the biggest bloody hypocrites in the world! Here you are condemning South Africa and Rhodesia for our race policies when some of the laws on Aborigines, passed as recently as 1971 in some States, are far more odious and restrictive than any of ours.

In fact, the report released by your Community Relations Commissioner, Mr A. J. Grassby, last year accused at least two of your States, NSW and Queensland, of

discriminating against Aborigines "in practically every aspect of their lives."

Please also bear in mind that the black population in Rhodesia has increased from around 600,000 at the turn of the century to six million today. Can the same be said of your Aborigines?

Our black schools and medical facilities are second to none on the African continent. Do you provide the same service for yours, even though they are only a small minority?

May I suggest that you

carefully examine your own legislation, to say nothing of your conscience, regarding the way you treat your own blacks before telling us how to treat ours, or is it perhaps true, as I have heard, that you do not regard your Aborigines as human beings and therefore do not treat them as such?

Come off it, you sanctimonious lot, and show us a bit of the fair play that you are supposed to be so proud of.

N. V. DACOMB
Bulawayo, Rhodesia
16/8/77

The dole

Curbs will promote the cheat syndrome

WE wish to seriously question the Federal Government's latest decisions to make it more difficult for jobless people to obtain unemployment benefits.

These decisions (report, 24/3) will only promote the "dole-cheat" syndrome in our community.

We don't deny that a minimal minority may abuse the present system. But we do believe that the majority of unemployed workers do want a job. For many young people we know, the soul-destroying effect of being unemployed has only been increased by the growing public feeling that the jobless are dole cheats and bludgers.

And yet last September, a survey by the Department of Social Security revealed that no more than 6 per cent of registered unemployed people were found to be unwilling to work. What then, are the objectives behind these latest restrictions, when they will affect all unemployed people and not just those abusing the system?

In fact, these restrictions will also affect those with jobs. For example, the regulation that benefits will not be granted to workers for the first six weeks after voluntarily leaving their employment, denies the basic right of a worker to freely change jobs and receive benefits during possible intervening unemployment.

This regulation — together with the possible postponement of benefits for up to six weeks if sacked for "misconduct" — is open to abuse by employers. Employers can pressure workers through fear of not receiving benefits for six weeks if they leave their job. Added to this is the fear that a worker has only six weeks to find a suitable job before being forced to accept any job, or lose the benefits.

We find it difficult to understand why these restrictions were introduced when the Minister for Employment and Industrial Relations, Mr Street, is quoted as saying that the Government did not know how many abused the benefits, how many would be affected by the clampdown, or how much it would save.

It all seems to point to a saving of money behind the "dole-cheat" syndrome at the sacrifice of workers' rights and dignity.

JOHN BONNICE
President
(Fr) M. CASEY
Chaplain
Young Christian Workers
Melbourne
30/3/76

┌ PS ─────────

THE time has come to rename the Gold Coast: the Dole Coast would be more apt.

W. R. SCOTT
Surfers Paradise
23/11/74

Irrelevant degrees

MR V. E. Jennings touched on a particularly topical subject when he mentioned the lack of reality in present day approaches to education and vocational training in Australia, in his article in Australia in Action (28/5).

We can all see the effect of this in the existence of a large body of unemployed young people side by side with a large number of jobs that cannot be filled because adequately skilled applicants are not available.

My own management-consulting organisation is constantly approached by young people with high academic qualifications that are quite irrelevant to any potential employer's economic needs. These people have little prospect of ever getting an economic return on the years of effort they have put into earning such qualifications.

Likewise, the community has little prospect of getting an economic return on its investment in those individuals.

I know of one young man, who has an honors degree, who can find no use for his knowledge except to teach it to other people. As he himself observed, there is not a lot of future for anybody in that.

There was a time when our education system took pride in turning out people who could "get a good job and earn a good living." I suspect this has become unfashionable.

Our education system has
Continued next page

The dole

Non people

YOUR article (30/7) stating that there is to be a study on why the dole queue is turning violent hit a sensitive spot with me. I "signed on" at an inner-city employment exchange and was told to report at 8 am the next week, which I did, only to find that about 150 other people had been issued with the same time.

When the doors opened, 150 people stampeded into the building. It reminded me of a cattle round-up, but there the cattle were at least shown where to go. Confusion reigned for about 10 minutes, until a queue haphazardly formed itself.

Two incidents of that morning stick in my memory.

The first was a middle-aged man being told in the most offensive manner to get to the back of the queue or "he would be found a job." The other was of a young man who was told to get his hair cut and not to wear "thongs" to the exchange.

Both recipients of this abuse were completely deflated and retired to their respective places with an air of being a "non person."

This was a few months ago, when unemployment on a large scale was relatively new, but if this kind of treatment is still being handed out, then I'm not at all surprised there is violence. Even "non people" have breaking points and when it's reached it is bound to be violent.

Long periods of unemployment breed their own code of social behavior and nobody seems to realise that it is inevitably going to be a violent code.

ROBIN BOWERING
Alexandria, NSW
4/8/77

Crackdown attacked

COMING at a time of record post-depression unemployment levels, the new crackdown on "dole cheats" smacks of a fresh attempt to scapegoat the unemployed while ignoring the plight and injustices to which they remain subjected.

If the Department of Social Security is now privy to information about the presence of dole-cheats that has not been discovered by the Poverty Inquiry, the Myers Inquiry into the Administration of Unemployment Benefits, or any social survey, then it should declare its source and details.

The department's own published figures for 1976-77 show that the number of prosecutions for dole offences involved less than a half of 1 per cent of unemployment beneficiaries.

The evidence from social surveys is that the greater problem is that of people not taking up their entitlement to benefit, often because of the stigma they feel about being unemployed. The proposed blitz on the unemployed means that numerous people out of work through no fault of their own will now be further victimised by arbitrary investigations and deterred from making their rightful claim to benefit.

A research report called Rough Justice, recently released by this agency, documents the prevalence already of unfair withdrawal of unemployment benefit, a lack of independence of the Social Security Appeals Tribunals, the inadequacy of rights information among claimants and their economic plight.

Since the inception of the tribunals, approximately 60 per cent of all appeals against termination of unemployment benefit have been upheld. That is, even the department's routine investigations — in the absence of the current forays — have resulted in hundreds of unemployed workers being unjustly denied their only source of income.

At a time of record-breaking unemployment figures the chief victims in the community are surely more deserving of initiatives that will ease their situation rather than aggravate it.

GRAEME BREWER
Research Officer
Brotherhood of
St Laurence,
Melbourne
20/2/78

Irrelevant

From previous page
never taken so much out of the economy, but there is not much evidence that it appreciates its responsibility to the community to develop young people who can make a commensurate return to the economy.

I know that in some minds such a view will identify me as a philistine. But the education industry (for that is what it is) will find, sooner or later, that it is subject to all the same economic forces as any other industry.

When those who are providing the resources begin to feel they are not getting the satisfaction they want in return, they begin to clamp down on the flow of these resources.

JOHN P. YOUNG
Chairman
John P. Young and
Associates Pty. Ltd.
Melbourne
31/5/76

The dole

It's a violation of our human rights

WE are a concerned group of unemployed people very actively involved in community work.

We are appalled at Mr Viner's suggestion to cut the dole to under 19-year-olds. This must be a step backwards and one which will be more costly than the present dole system.

The whole idea is ludicrous to order under 19-year-olds to live at home and be supported by their parents. This encroaches on the Universal Declaration of Human Rights.

Article 23, Section 1 of the Bill states: "Everyone has the right to work, to free choice of employment, to job and favorable conditions of work and to protection against unemployment."

Many young people have come from broken homes, or live interstate — away from their parents. Does Mr Viner suggest everyone pack their bag and travel home again? This situation must force more people to be supported by the Welfare Department.

Official CES figures say there are 17,476 unemployed under 21 in South Australia. This means that for every job vacancy for this group there are 29 applicants.

The scheme will mean that teenagers will stay at school longer.

What is the use of forcing further education upon school leavers who will not be able to get a job anyway? Why don't we be realistic and concentrate on teaching "low income living" as part of the school curriculum.

Mr Viner is advocating a system of steeper costs in welfare, high school education and certainly job skills education. All this for jobs that don't exist!

People like us feel proud of our worth in the community.

We get a great feeling of satisfaction from our work and are received with much gratitude from groups that are even more underprivileged than ourselves.

21 UNEMPLOYED YOUTHS
Kurralta Park, SA
30/10/79

Demoralising

YOUR report (14/4) on unemployment among teenagers, Gloomy Jobs Future, notes Mr Fraser's comment that many people in the work-force had virtually priced themselves out of a job.

This does not apply to school-leavers, or many other young people. We have priced them out of a job — society, that is with a helping hand from the Arbitration Commission, in setting impossible wages for them.

It is time a move was made on behalf of young people to correct this most demoralising situation. My sympathies are wholly with the young people who have been conditioned to expect the impossible. A move must be made now to restore to them the dignity of having a job at $75 per week rather than no job at $150 and the dole.

DON McCOLL
Chapman, A.C.T.
19/4/77

ID solution

HUNDREDS of jobs are advertised daily throughout Australia in various newspapers, which creates a lot of interest among employers and those intending to join Australia's work-force.

To reduce unemployment and end the term "dole bludger," we must stop unemployment benefits immediately and re-register those concerned with an identification card bearing a photo of the individual, date of birth, place of birth, previous employment, or schooling and address.

This will certainly reduce unemployment, thus reduce rising taxes of those already employed in Australia's work-force.

Many young people will not work because of the amount paid in unemployment benefits.

Why should Australia's work-force pay for those not honest enough to admit they do not want to work?

How often do you hear the old saying when taxes rise: "It doesn't worry me, I'm on the dole!"

PAUL BALLANTYNE
Mornington, Vic
9/1/79

PS

THE decision to allow people on the dole free travel on public transport will surely help some unemployed to seek jobs. For many, however, there is a big problem — where will they put their surfboards?

VIV FORBES
Indooroopilly, Qld
12/8/80

The Opera House

GOVERNMENT NOTICES

—it will be a concert hall.

ELIZABETHAN THEATRE TRUST

WE have all heard by now of Mr Askin — the leader of the NSW Opposition — and a great exposer of Terrible Government Contracts and the Alarming Opera House Scandal.

We have also heard of his schemes for cluttering up the city of Sydney with more cars by building a tunnel, or a bridge to bring them into the city — as well as, we hope, to take them out again.

So it's all nice and dandy and we can be sure he will be digging up more "scandals?" before the next elections.

But anyone who is capable

One big lottery

of thinking knows that the working class doesn't give two hoots about the Opera House, how much it costs, how long it takes to build, or who builds it.

They are interested in winning an Opera House Lottery and the longer it takes to pay for, the longer the lottery will go on and the more chances they will have of winning one.

These are the people who are paying for the Opera House and if they do not want it, or think it is a "scandal" the way the costs keep rising, they have the remedy in their own hands — stop buying Opera House lottery tickets.

Ask any person buying tickets at the lottery office what they think of the "Opera House Scandal," and they will laugh at you and say: "The only scandal I can think of is that I did not win — last time."

(Mrs) E. L. JONES
Potts Point, NSW
25/7/64

The Opera House

An igloo with air ducts

ONE day a psychiatrist will, no doubt, be able to say why the Sydney Opera House is being built.

This monstrosity, which appears to me as a cross between an igloo with air ducts and an air terminal, is an insult to the mentality of the people of NSW — and no medals can be handed out to the person or persons responsible for the idea.

I am all in favor of Sydney having an opera house, but not at a cost of £25 million and am wondering where this fantastic sum of money is going.

Common sense would prevent any experienced theatre man from building an opera house looking into what must rate as one of the world's finest harbors, where wind could have a devastating effect on the acoustics of the structure.

Full marks must also go to the thought behind the planning of parking space for the patrons' cars — or is it assumed that we here in Australia will adopt the same trend as overseas opera lovers and have the chauffeur or taxi driver unload his passengers, and return to pick them up at the finish of the show?

What does this selected spot offer to the patron who travels by rail or bus, particularly on a wet night? Only the most ardent opera lover would enjoy watching an opera in wet clothes.

The idea of stage props going up and down in a lift is a very excellent one, providing a fuse doesn't blow. This idea is good for a quick change: in and out of the lift and away the scene goes. I do trust the idea proves a success.

Has thought been given to what it costs to bring an opera company to Australia, in fares and production costs? Have we enough opera lovers in Sydney or NSW to meet the costs of producing opera here?

No opera company that is world class could show a profit by playing Sydney alone, or has thought been given to finding other uses of the building to help pay the expenses opera would incur?

Is it going to be an accepted fact that funds from the coffers of the State Government will meet any losses?

It is to be hoped that the selection committee, which is appointing a manager for the opera house, is well versed on this matter — and that no retired army colonels or ex-admirals will be appointed who haven't a clue as to what constitutes the running of a house of entertainment.

I would not like to think that this concrete igloo cum air terminal could turn out to be another Kings Bridge; or just a monument to Joe Cahill and a Danish architect.

A number one cultural centre or hall of the arts could have been built for approximately £10 million, with the £15 million balance going to medicine, housing and education.

THORNTON HEATH
Northcote, Vic
13/9/65

A credit or an abortion?

LET us put the Sydney Opera House controversy into proper historical perspective.

Twenty years from now the Opera House will, if completed by its designer, be a major work of international standing and a credit to Sydney. If completed by a committee of architects, whatever their individual abilities, the result can only be a multi-million dollar abortion of the original concept.

To assume that it is possible for a committee to take over at this late stage and bring the project to an architecturally satisfactory conclusion is to display a naive misundertanding of the function of an architect of Mr Utzon's undisputed ability. Imagination has never notably been an attribute of committees, regardless of the personnel of which they are composed.

One need only refer back to the dismissal of the architect Walter Burley Griffin from his position as designer and supervisor of the town plan of Canberra by William Morris Hughes — a man noted more for his sensitivity to political noises than for any vision — for a similar shameful instance of failure to pursue a large undertaking to its conclusion.

The conditions of the international competition held to select an architect for the building provide that "in the event of any dispute arising other than in connection with the assessors' awards, then the promoters (the Government of the State of NSW) will seek the advice and assistance of the Union Internationale des Architectes in the settling of such dispute." This course would remove the dispute from the political arena.

DAVID CALDWELL
Architect
Melbourne
16/3/66

The Opera House

Utzon's vision like an unfinished symphony

WHEN I first saw the model of our Opera House in the Sydney Town Hall, it took my breath away by its simplicity and beauty of line.

I found my mind crowding with imagery such as the lines of a flying seagull and the white sails on our beautiful harbor.

Is there a realistic question of lack of financial backing for the project? All this talk of the better use of money for hospitals appears to be sheer hypocrisy on the part of a people who regretfully, but willingly, spend millions in the waging of destructive war. One would think that Utzon's vision is a symbol of the eternal value of creativeness in the gathered gloom of a civilisation so much dedicated to destructiveness.

Utzon's vision reminds us of Schubert's Unfinished Symphony and surely no one can agree that a panel of experts, however expert, could finish that masterpiece and remain true to the intimate vision of the artist. How fortunate for the sister arts of music and painting that pen, manuscript and tubes of paint are cheap enough and do not offend the financial instincts of any government. How sad that people can hit back at the artist by either ignoring his product or keeping its market value low — at least until he is dead.

One can be forgiven for the natural pride of an Australian citizen hoping that Utzon's dream could become one of the world wonders of beauty in this utilitarian age.

It appears that there are brothers around who regard

Joern Utzon

Utzon as a kind of Prodigal Son who is wasting substance in riotous architectural planning and, therefore, must be curbed and shown the error of his ways.

Can a government have the insight to understand that a creative artist must have true freedom to materialise his vision?

A Michelangelo must have the finest marble.

As someone quaintly said, "Architecture is frozen music." It is due to the condition of architecture as a craft that it needs more than pen and manuscript for its execution.

Is the agony and ecstasy to end in a note of agony? Or must we enthusiastically give Utzon the power to release the image from the obdurate stone of governmental complacency?

(Rev) G. R. GARNER
Bexley, NSW
21/3/66

Bourgeois values victorious

IN anguish, I thank you for putting beyond all doubt the nature of the Sydney Opera House tragedy: the clash of the sacred and the profane.

It is not a case of irresponsibility censured by disinterested authority, but rather of creative art defeated by bourgeois values.

This has been made abundantly clear by the statements of Mr Davis Hughes (*The Australian*, 23/4), which runs: ". . . Mr Utzon's natural interest in having the project completed as closely as possible to his concept . . ." Poor Mr Hughes and his spiritually bankrupt concern.

It's well for his peace of mind that he is unaware of the damning by faint praise which has been the lot of those who, over the centuries, have essayed to finish an artist's work even when the artist has died!

What terrible monument posterity will raise to Mr Hughes and his culpable generosity is better not dwelled upon.

If the worst comes to the worst and international pressure fails to reinstate Joern Utzon, better to dynamite the Opera House now and have at least an honest wreck than imagine that a few million dollars can be made to balance an artist's desecrated soul.

ARTHUR BURRAGE
East St Kilda, Vic
28/4/66

The Opera House

A swan or a cupboard?

ANNIVERSARIES are popular.

I understand that the 164th anniversary of the tunnel project connecting England with France was celebrated the other day.

We have, in Sydney, periodic celebrations of the starting and stopping of the Eastern Suburbs Railway.

We also have various silver, golden and diamond anniversaries of buildings erected as temporary buildings.

I think it fitting that the first anniversary of Utzon's departure as the architect of the Opera House should not go unheralded.

One year and a day ago, on February 28, 1966, Utzon told his client that if he did not pay him, he would leave him and his Opera House.

The client, on the other hand, said in no uncertain terms that Utzon's staying would only mean that the building would never be finished anyhow!

After this exchange of mutual courtesies, Utzon left.

The issues between Utzon and the client turned out to be subcutanous; the real issues, as we now see, were deep-seated.

A seating specialist had to be consulted.

The noise created by these activities involved the consultation of an acoustics expert all the way from Denmark, so what we lost in a Danish architect we regained in a Danish noise doctor.

There was a great song, that the large hall won't be big enough to face the music; and there was a great dance, that the small hall won't be big enough for ballet.

A cross between a swan and a cupboard is an interesting prospect.

Curiously enough, one specialist, who could be of great help, has not yet been consulted — a psychiatrist.

Now is the time.

Happy anniversary and many happy returns.

(Dr) HENRY EPSTEIN
Architect
Sydney
1/3/67

Restaurant will be sandwiched

THE proposal to exclude opera from the main hall and the resultant controversy over acoustics has diverted attention from another disturbing proposal made at the same time by the new Opera House architects.

They propose to change the position of the restaurant from the separate building designed for the purpose and to squash it instead into the space behind the main auditorium.

This space was designed to cater for the thousands of people who would emerge from the auditorium at interval times — for refreshments and also to take advantage of the harbor views.

There is a need for spaciousness in such places that few theatres have to an adequate degree.

It was to be one of the functional and aesthetic delights of the building.

I shudder to think what other bright ideas Utzon's successors may have if this is the way they are performing nearly one year after his resignation.

ELIAS DUEK-COHEN
Architect-town planner
Potts Point, NSW
8/2/67

Swallow your pride — invite Utzon

OCTOBER 20, 1973, was undoubtedly Joern Utzon day.

We saw The Queen, Prince Philip, Sir Robert Askin, Sir Asher Joel and many others featured in the televised coverage of this important event, but where was Joern Utzon?

Too often the concept of a technologist, whether an architect, engineer or fundamental scientist, is lost in the publicity associated with government or business.

Whether you like the aesthetic or practical aspects of the Sydney Opera House or not, you must admit that some significant recognition rests at the feet of Joern Utzon.

Can those in authority smooth over old wounds or, if necessary, swallow pride and make further efforts to encourage Utzon to visit the material manifestation of his concept?

C. G. BENNETT
George Town, Tas
30/10/73

The Opera House

PS . . .

SHOULDN'T Mr Hughes' glass in the Opera House be rose tinted?
BRIAN DAY
Ipswich, Qld
3/4/71

THEY call it the Sydney Opera House? No, sir! Let it be "Australian" — if the Queen can compare it with the Pyramids, then let it be known with an Australian title — Bennelong's Corroboree Gunyahs.
JOHN MILES
Clermont, Qld
1/11/73

THE Opera House is a rip-off. Recently I went to see the Stuttgart Ballet and paid $1.50 to park the car, $1.50 for a program, 80c for a beer at interval and $5.30 for a seat which allowed me to see only one-half of the show. It would seem only fair that I am entitled to either a $2.65 refund or a seat on the opposite side of the theatre, so I can fill in the gaps.
ELISABETH KNIGHT
Bondi Junction, NSW
5/11/74

HAVING been a regular opera-goer for six years, I find Dame Joan Sutherland's attacks on Australian audiences (4/8) misguided at best. Rather than applause being sparse, I find the audience at the Sydney Opera House opera performances ready to clap at almost any moment, often interrupting the natural flow of the music or shattering the atmosphere the cast and orchestra are trying so hard to create.
PHILIP LAURETZ
Bondi, NSW
7/8/81

How we can save our Opera House

SO our magnificent Opera House has lost $5 million, attendances are down and Mr Barnes feels that it is the economic conditions and a drop-off in "euphoria."

We must face facts. The Opera House is hard to get to. I love going to the opera, I enjoy the Drama Theatre, but I also experience a feeling of relief when I see that a particular Old Tote performance is scheduled for the good old Parade Theatre at Kensington, where I can park my car with ease and sit in a comfortable seat.

Until we get a carpark at the Opera House, it will never be the success it deserves to be. We are a "car" nation and much prefer to drive to the theatre than go by bus or ferry. The disgrace of the Builders Laborers Federation holding a magnificent edifice and those who visit it, to ransom for the sake of saving a few messy fig-dropping Moreton Bays, is a situation which causes amusement and derision from the visitors of the world.

At the end of each performance, quite often on a blustery and freezing night, one is pushed and shoved by an extremely well-dressed pushing and shoving crowd on to a bus for a leaping, twisting ride of fairly thankful short duration, to make one's way to the comfort of one's car. It is hard to keep the magic moments of opera, ballet, drama or music in one's mind and heart while strap-hanging in this lurching vehicle.

I suggested some time ago that one of the graceful old ships, ready for scrap, should be donated to Sydney and refitted as a floating carpark. Painted and gleaming, bedecked with flags, it could be an attraction and would at least blend with the foreshores . . . but I don't know enough about tides and engineering to do a feasibility study on it. Perhaps it could be an interesting project for this year's final year engineering and architectural students.

I have no doubt that $250,000 needs to be spent to make the orchestra pit larger, but more importantly, the audience should be there to hear the music . . . and a foam-filled overlay studded to each of those hard, hard seats may be money more wisely spent.

The answer? Perhaps the continuation of the Opera House Lottery for many years in order to provide those softer seats, a carpark SOON and to reduce the enormous cleaning bills, how about an immediate $10 on-the-spot fine for anybody dropping as much as a cigarette butt or ice cream wrapper ANYWHERE in the vicinity of our one really great new building.
LORRAINE HAVIN
Point Piper, NSW
10/1/78

The RSL

The equivalent of the Ku Klux Klan?

A LARGE number, possibly the bulk, of the post-war generation sees the RSL as, at best, the Australian equivalent of the John Birch Society and, at worst, the equivalent of the Ku Klux Klan.

This may or may not be desirable, but it does show that the league is not regarded as being the watchdog of the ex-serviceman's interests.

Presumably this has come about due to the league's attitude to communism and to the exclusion of Aborigines from some RSL clubs.

Possibly the league wishes to retain its present image and let the ex-serviceman's welfare be forgotten. If so, it is going the right way about it.

What does the league feel about rejection of the Senate's amendment to the recent repatriation legislation?

This amendment sought to give benefits to Boer War veterans and to 1914-18 Diggers.

Its rejection was shocking, but the league has raised no protest at all.

It has not fought for these old soldiers and apparently could not care less.

L. E. RADCLYFFE
Braddon, A.C.T.
12/10/65

The Menzies Wait

W. R. HEMMING (15/8) suggests that the RSL should be portrayed as an organisation continuously working for the welfare of ex-servicemen.

For over a decade, while this league has more than once boasted of its access to the Federal Cabinet, a policy known by returned men as the Menzies Wait has cost ex-servicemen, including pensioners, sick and aged Diggers,up to £300 extra on the purchase of a home, under the War Service Homes Division.

As an Anzac and the father of one, I am amazed that ex-servicemen are not ashamed to wear an RSL badge, while the league wastes its time and energy on matters that are the concern of elected governments, instead of fulfilling the duty for which it was formed.

The apathy of the league and its rank and file towards Diggers who have to wait 20 months for an approved WSH loan to be paid is a disgrace to a body that today is merely a political pressure group seeking publicity on issues it was never intended it should deal with — a body that considers itself above criticism.

J. HOWES
Caulfield, Vic
28/8/64

Viet traitors

THE NSW president of the RSL, Sir William Yeo, has stated that there are "traitors in our midst" and that the issues in Vietnam are the same as in other wars in which Australians have fought and died.

He accuses "an element in the community who oppose the war in Vietnam" of being traitors and anti-Australian.

Permit me to point out to Sir William that over 43 per cent voted for the Australian Labor Party in the last federal election and it would be safe to assume that these voters opposed Australia's involvement in this unjust and immoral war, and that the great majority of Americans are now opposed to the war in Vietnam.

I think it is time that the members of the RSL shed themselves of some of their old guard leaders, as statements such as Sir William's damage the public image of the RSL.

A. D. LANG
Williamstown, Vic
26/4/68

Irreverence

SIR William Yeo, vehemently supporting the status quo, seems an odd spokesman for the Australian Digger. Surely the Digger image is one of irreverence and a sardonic approach to authority.

It seems a pity that all ex-servicemen, many quite deliberately not members of the RSL, should seem to be represented by a bunch of ageing knights.

J. D. O'SULLIVAN
Ex-RANR
Brisbane
5/11/68

The RSL

An ex-Panzer's request

I READ with great interest your interesting recent article and letters about the RSL.

I comprehend that old soldiers will always be unavoidably the targets of charges of militarism: what I take issue with is the eligibility requirements for joining this returned warriors' association.

I occupied a responsible position in a unit similar to your Australian tank corps (Panzer we call it) in North Africa and have several immigrant friends who fought in that war in the British, German and Italian armies owing to accident of birth and location.

It is sad to find that although our skills, such as they are, are needed by Australia, we are not welcome as members of the RSL, though it does not mind us as guests — probably to swell bar profits.

After all, when it comes to the crunch, we are all returned (unkilled) soldiers. Through no fault of our own, some of us served in other military formations and I feel that all members of whatever armies should be "comrades in arms" now that the dust has settled and we are all friends again.

WILLY HERZOG
Geebung, Qld
3/10/74

And a true-blue reply

WHILE ex-Panzer Grenadier Herzog made an appealing case (Letters, 31/10) for allowing him and his fellow immigrants into our RSL, I would remind him that the main object of this body is to perpetuate the memory of the hardships shared by Imperial troops who went to considerable personal inconvenience and danger to ensure that the wishes of Mr Herzog's superiors came to naught.

While he admits he is welcome as a guest at our clubs, I feel relatively confident that members would not altogether feel at ease if they knew they were entertaining someone who perhaps was instrumental in terminating the lives of fellow Australians, for whatever reason.

It is, however, certain that members of the RSL throughout our country will stand firm together to ensure that only true-blue Australians are eligible for admission to this elite of organisations.

ROBERT HARPER
Goodna, Qld
11/10/74

Disenchanted with the league

SIR William Yeo is anxious to discover the reasons for the disenchantment of people under 35 with the RSL.

His own recent statement demonstrates several of these quite adequately.

He labels those individuals and organisations who criticise the league's policy on defence as "subversive minded" and "communistically inspired," obviously not considering that there could be an opinion differing from his own that was not communist.

Sir William and his organisation continually assure us that we are threatened by imminent invasion, but apart from these emotional outbursts, he offers no concrete means by which he supposes the "red hordes" will accomplish this feat.

He finds that unfortunately the "daily press does not in the main present the RSL to the public as the sincere, hard-working, charitable organisation which you and I truly know it to be."

Is the image of the league suffering because of adverse publicity, or is it that the actions of the league speak louder than any press reports and most of the action seen is in the bars and at the poker machines of the league's clubhouses?

Many young people object to the nationalistic-militaristic basis on which the league is founded.

They see, or would like to see, the future more in terms of international cooperation and the settling of disputes by discussion, not by force.

J. GOODWIN
Concord West, NSW
30/8/68

The RSL

In defence of the league

YOUR correspondent, A. M. Wilson of Perth, in his letter (17/11) makes an attack on the RSL and especially those who are at present holding prominent positions in the organisation.

While all those who have any real knowledge of the RSL, its policies and the way it operates would not regard the letter seriously, I would like to reply on one or two points.

Since its inception in 1916 as a national organisation, the RSL has taken an active interest in national affairs, including defence and security. Its first warning on communism was issued in 1918 shortly after the Russian revolution.

It has been repeated at regular intervals since that time. The concern expressed by the league today on communist influence within Australia is not a new policy — it is the expression of an attitude that has been consistent through the years.

Prior to World War II and over the past decade, the RSL has expressed the same concern about Nazism. In the 1930s its warnings fell on deaf ears. Today it believes the Australian Nazi Party should be kept under observation but, at the same time, sees it as essentially an organisation of the "lunatic fringe" type and one that few Australians will take seriously.

It cannot be compared with the Australian Communist Party in terms of political and industrial influence within the Australian community.

The (RSL) national executive, for all practical purposes, consists of 11 members. All have served in the front-line. Five of the 11 possess gallantry awards.

Two of the remainder spent three years confined as prisoners-of-war of the Japanese. All of them worked their way through the ranks to gain any wartime rank they might have held. Certainly none of them answers the description set out in such colorful language by your correspodent.

I can assure Mr Wilson that the league today is involved in a whole range of new and progressive ideas

A. G. W. KEYS
Canberra
(The writer is national secretary of the RSL.)
23/11/70

11th hour, 11th day, 11th month

IT was Shakespeare who adjured us to "summon up remembrance of things past." In recent years, there has been a tendency to go along with the Henry Ford dictum that history is bunk and accordingly has no lessons for us. Nothing could be further from the truth.

On November 11 thousands of Australians, more particularly those who have suffered directly or indirectly from the effects of the four wars with which Australia has been concerned since 1914, will indeed remember things past and indeed recall the lessons that the past has taught them, and that "the price of liberty is eternal vigilance."

It was an Australian journalist who suggested that citizens of the countries of the old British Empire should pause a moment at the 11th hour of the 11th day of the 11th month, at which time the Armistice signed in that forest in France became effective. King George V requested a silence of two minutes so that all might think in quiet respect and gratefulness of those who had laid down their lives in the cause of freedom and might think, too, of the future.

The future has brought us widows and veterans, aged and ill, mentally and physically, from the effects of war. Some 800 of such persons are looked after by the RSL through two trusts in hostels, flats and Darby and Joan cottages. Remaining also to be cared for are many veterans, widows and children in suburbs and towns throughout Victoria who are looked after in their homes by the local RSL.

May I through your columns appeal to all Victorians who will have the opportunity to buy a Flanders Poppy of Remembrance on Friday next, November 5, to do so, each in his own way to assist us discharge a debt of gratitude to those widows and veterans who have suffered for Australia. May I ask all citizens to stand with us silent in deeply respectful remembrance of things past and realisation of things present, at the 11th hour on Thursday, November 11.

COLIN KEON-COHEN
State President, RSL
Melbourne
3/11/76

Christians

The move towards unity

YOUR editorial (4/4) on the historic meeting between the Archbishop of Canterbury and Pope Paul was a welcome addition to the continuing discussion of Christian unity.

However, without doubting the importance of this recent meeting, it is hardly fair to describe it as "the first ray of real hope" since the Reformation.

The modern ecumenical movement traces its history into the last century and made its first step of lasting significance as long ago as 1910 when 1054 representatives of different denominations met together for the first World Missionary Conference in Edinburgh.

From that time onwards, there have existed three ecumenical avenues through which the churches of the world have increasingly met with each other, seriously studied the theological factors hindering union and cooperated on enterprises of both mission and service.

This led, in 1948, to the formation of the World Council of Churches — which today has a membership of 220 churches of the Protestant, Anglican, Orthodox and Old Catholic confessions.

Dr Ramsey, himself one of the six presidents of the World Council of Churches, has contributed to the ecumenical spirit, which is such a distinguishing feature of the Church in this century.

However, his visit to Pope Paul cannot be counted as significant as two previous developments in relations between the Catholic Church and other historic

THE EYE OF A NEEDLE

churches.

The first of these was the withdrawal in December of the mutual anathemas pronounced by the Sees of Rome and Constantinople in 1054.

This act, which may seem quite remote and inconsequential in Australia, removed one of the greatest barriers to union between the two largest Christian churches in the world — the Catholic, with some 500 million members, and the Orthodox, with some 100 million members.

The second recent significant development was the appointment in February last year of a permanent joint working group of the WCC and the Catholic Church, comprising eight WCC representatives and six Catholics.

This has already resulted in the appointment of a joint theological commission and specific acts of practical collaboration, ranging from consideration of common versions of the Bible to the recent co-ordinated appeal by Pope Paul and the WCC for Indian famine relief.

In addition to such developments of significance in relations between Catholic and other churches, there are the positive union steps being taken by chuches in all parts of the world — evidenced in Australia by the current consideration in Methodist, Presbyterian and Congregational churches of a plan for union, and the recent addition of Anglican observers to the commission working on the proposal.

Like you, I welcome the reconciliation now taking place within all branches of the Christian Church and hope for the day when the world can say, as they did of the early Christians, "Look how these Christians love one another" — and say it without a sneer.

VAUGHAN HINTON
Secretary
Australian Council
of Churches
West Ryde, NSW
14/4/66

PS

THE World Council of Churches conference in Sydney has decided against opposition to the conscription of young men for overseas service in peacetime. Once again the Princes of Peace have made their obeisances to the God of War.

H. G. CLEMENTS
Bassendean, WA
24/2/65

Christians

Opportunity missed

I WATCHED the telecast of the national memorial service for our late Prime Minister, Mr Harold Holt, and was deeply moved by the beauty and dignity of the service.

One matter that concerned me, however, was the absence of any attempt to share the conduct of the service between the denominations. I realise the difficulties facing the host denomination, but on this national and indeed international occasion, it surely would have been appropriate if an invitation had been extended to a non-Anglican to take part.

It is time we realised in Australia that there is no one denomination of the Christian church that represents the nation.

We who believe in and work for the unity of the churches in Australia often face the criticism that the ecumenical movement seldom gets past words to action. This I believe is a short-sighted judgment, but I regret that this opportunity for united action was missed.

BERTRAM R. WYLLIE
Past President
Australian Council
of Churches
Greenwich, NSW
4/1/68

A church that cares

I WISH to commen: on recent adverse publicity given to the Wayside Chapel in Sydney. It seems forces are at work to curtail, or even eliminate the chapel's activities.

The Wayside Chapel is perhaps one of the most outstanding developments in Australian social history. The concept is unique and community-oriented in a most practical manner.

The work carried out by the team associated with the chapel is at the best of times difficult.

The team at the chapel has assisted thousands of people and has thus made a signi-

ficant Christian and humanitarian contribution to Australian society.

That drugs can be located at times on the chapel's premises is only to be expected. They deal with human beings who have a difficult problem.

It is the only church I have known in my short lifetime which really cares about people and their problems. It seems because of one small incident such vital community involvement is subject to severe criticism.

CHARLES PERKINS
Rose Bay, NSW
30/1/69

The answer is indisputable

E. P. WIXTED (Letters, 26/3) asks, "Who is behind the moves for church unity — and who stands to gain?" God.

JANET GADEN
Mudgee, NSW
31/3/65

PS

IN The Australian (20/12) you refer to St Paul's Anglican Cathedral in Melbourne as "a mecca for lunchtime worshippers." Ecumenism is all very well, but this is ridiculous.
DENNIS PRYOR
North Carlton, Vic
26/12/67

SO the Victorian Liberals suggest inserting a belief in God into the federal party platform (28/7). Excellent. I assume that they accept the corollary of a rejection of any service to Mammon.
JOHN ROOKE
Toowoomba, Qld
13/8/75

MR Bjelke-Petersen should be congratulated on his timing of the prayers for rain. If it had not rained in Queensland during the wet season, it would be a miracle.
(Miss) MERLE JAMES
Lane Cove, NSW
8/2/78

YOU made an error in describing our Pope, John Paul, as John Paul I. As there may never be another Pope of that name, it is incorrect to designate him "the first." After all, who has ever heard of Queen Victoria I?
ROBERT THOMSON
Wahroonga, NSW
20/9/78

Christians

Celibacy — the female view

ALTHOUGH I appreciate Mr Parer's desire for more open discussion regarding the virtue or non-virtue of clerical celibacy, I find some of his statements quite extraordinary and very much resent the implications contained therein.

Mr Parer states that many priests and presumably brothers and nuns also, are prone to sexual hang-ups and thus tend to be repressed, inhibited and neurotic. It is likely that in a very small number of instances this would be the case.

However, the problem lies not so much in the acceptance or rejection of a celibate life, but in the failure to accept oneself as a sexual being.

Each individual, male or female, single or married, must at some stage of his or her development freely and intelligently recognise his or her own sexuality. A failure to do so negates one's potential and reveals a condition of fundamental immaturity.

Celibacy is not forced on anyone. It is freely and thoughtfully lived. Any person contemplating a dedicated chaste life is well instructed in the value of both the married and single state.

Celibacy does not, cannot and must not imply impotence and/or sterility. Neither is it a denigration of sexuality. A chaste life, lived for love of God, is both fulfilling and liberating. By my life of chastity I am free to love all mankind in and for Christ and this is not only a privilege but an honor.

In effect, what we do is not to eliminate, or divorce our sexual capacities from our lives; to do this is to create a dichotomy which is inconsistent with our humanity. It seems to me that Mr Parer's reference to a failure to integrate "sex" in a clerical way of life is a remark which is spectacularly immature.

(Sister) JANICE CONNELLY
Bundoora, Vic
1/9/71

Celibacy — the male view

THERE is a tendency today to cast priests in two moulds. They are considered either clerical, legalistic and aloof, so cold as to be inhuman; or else so preoccupied with sex as to be positively dangerous!

After the recent emphasis in mass media on the image of the priest as absorbed in sex and burdened with celibacy, has it ever occurred to your readers that there may exist priests who actually want to be celibate? They see value in this style of life. They consider themselves, at the same time, fairly well adjusted. And they are able to love their fellow man without oppressive guilt complexes!

I am a Catholic priest. I am also celibate — not primarily because it is a law of the Catholic Church, but because I believe that through celibacy I can better express my personal love for a personal loving God and share this love with all men.

The fact that a discipline is obligatory makes it no less a matter for free choice and acceptance, be it rules of road or home. Freedom is the ability to choose some good for itself, without inner or external coercion.

Celibacy IS an obligation for the priest. But just as the pledge of fidelity is not an awkward pre-condition for marriage, but a freely embraced expression of love, so through my celibacy I freely express my response to live in love with God and my fellow man.

As one who in his priestly life is just approaching the period when married couples can experience a "seven-year itch," I am not saying I do not experience loneliness, or difficult moments. But this loneliness and longing are the fruit of being human and remind me that, along with all men, I was made for God and ultimately can find complete satisfaction only in Him.

(Fr) L. BISSETT
Dickson, A.C.T.
13/9/71

PS

THE Reverend Fred Nile says his winning of a seat in the NSW Legislative Council was due to God, but that Premier Wran's victory was due to Neville Wran, not God. As Mr Wran and the A.L.P. Legislative Council team gained more votes than Mr Nile and his team, can we assume that Mr Wran is now more persuasive than God?

JOHN KERIN
Labor MP for
Werriwa, NSW
24/9/81

Christians

The Christian work ethic

IN answer to A. F. Parkinson, of Coogee (26/12), who requested my views on the above subject.

When I have travelled through the nations that are predominantly Christian, Moslem, Buddhist, Hindu or the atheistic communist countries, it becomes apparent that different civilisations and societies are produced by the spiritual doctrines of the people — or by the lack of spiritual doctrines.

Man is basically the product of his thinking and so he produces the environment that is the product of his thoughts.

Man can either be motivated from within or driven from behind.

If he is motivated from within, he is then fired by the desire to protect, support and defend his family, his freedom and his country.

If he is driven from behind, as it is in the case of atheistic communist countries, he then loses his precious freedoms and also his personal liberty. He becomes a slave of the State monopoly.

Man's personal power is multiplied when he is motivated by spiritual forces and ideals.

The miracle of Australia's growth over the past 200 years is evidence of this.

The Christian work ethic rejects laziness and encourages each individual to work for his family, and the welfare of society.

It teaches that work gives dignity to all people, irrespective of the kind of work they do.

Receiving something for nothing can be both destructive and degrading. Saint Paul to Thessalonians, Ch. 3, V 10: "Whoever does not WANT to work is not allowed to eat."

That is the Judaeo-Christian work ethic.

REUBEN F. SCARF
Vaucluse, NSW
6/1/78

Distasteful lampooning

AS a regular reader of *The Australian*, I am amazed that the editor of such a good paper can allow himself to take part in the publication of cartoons such as those perpetrated by your so-called "funny man" in issues over the Easter weekend.

I appreciate that Christians are in a minority in this country and that minorities never count for much in any country, but I feel that the miserable lampooning of Christ in the shape of Mr Peacock on the Cross and the blasphemous words made to be spoken by Mr Fraser are most distasteful, show a very sick mind and are quite unfair to the gentlemen involved, and to Christians who love Christ and believe He is the savior of all people, even editors and cartoonists.

**(The Venerable)
D. STUART-FOX**
Goulburn, NSW
25/4/81

It's more than pulpiteering

THE Queensland Premier, Mr Bjelke-Petersen, is reported to have remarked that clergymen involved in the recent anti-uranium demonstration in Brisbane performed a disservice to their calling and should restrict themselves to preaching the Gospel.

As one of those clergymen, allow me to respond by pointing out that the task of the clergy extends far beyond Sunday pulpiteering. Rather, as servants of Jesus Christ, they should be involved in similar acts and actions as He was.

And Jesus was certainly more than a comfortable Sunday preacher. He drove the money-changers out of the temple, associated with the poor and dispossessed, confronted the existing order and was crucified as a criminal.

While Christianity has long been submerged in comfortable middle-class mediocrity, it is increasingly breaking away from this crippling association to rediscover its more radical roots in the person and actions of Jesus.

Christians may well at times be co-belligerents with "the right" or "the left," but they refuse to serve as the handmaiden of either.

(Rev) CHARLES RINGMA
Paddington, NSW
14/11/77

Henry Lawson

Henry's sober side

GEOFFREY Hutton's theatre review of Leonard Teale's Henry Lawson presentation, While The Billy Boils (5/9), does not raise any doubts about Teale's acting ability (he is one of the best), but it does raise questions about his and Mr Hutton's sense of the appropriate.

For Teale to present Lawson "turning to the bottle at each pause and gulping down another swallow" is hardly "what might have been if Lawson had given the one-man show himself in 1917," nor is it much in the way of entertainment.

For an actor to pretend intoxication is not difficult nor, in this case, "an ingenious idea." The stage drunk is amusing only when the drunk is fictional and the situation humorous.

To present "old Henry Lawson" as such (and he was only 55 when he died) is simply not true. It is also to those who think about it,

remembering that two of his children are still with us, somewhat embarrassing, if not actually distressing.

Lawson, as Judith Wright points out in her Great Australians biography, "never drank much, as hard drinkers understand the term; but very little upset him." His brother-in-law, J. T. Lang, gave the same testimony.

If we are going to present Lawson with "all his faults observed, set in a notebook, learned and conned by rote," let it be a fair picture. After all, a man is entitled to be judged by his best moments. Leonard Teale is accomplished enough to present Lawson with that dignity which was part of the man.

W. PORTER-YOUNG
Walgett, NSW

(The writer is president of the Henry Lawson Society of NSW).

22/9/77

Henry Lawson

Lawson — warts and all

MAY I, through your columns, point out to Mr Porter-Young, president of the Henry Lawson Society of NSW (Letters, 22/9), that to criticise a performance he has not seen is at best unwise.

The simple fact is that Lawson was an alcoholic. We have as evidence his arrests for drunkenness, his frequent treatment in hospital, his attempted suicide while under the influence, the

banishment to Leeton (a "dry" area), the evidence of his friends and contemporaries and, most important of all, his own writings and letters.

In fact, my play is set in September 1917, the night before he went off on a monumental drunk after which he wrote to George Robertson (of Angus and Robertson): "The spree is over — and also the recovery. Have **Continued next page**

Leonard Teale as Henry Lawson

Henry Lawson

Lawson — warts and all

From previous page

sent ALL my clothes out to the cleaner, because they needed it."

Lawson's alchoholism was central to his life, therefore central to an understanding of the man and, therefore, central to my presentation of him. It is treated with compassion, dignity and, yes, humor.

My feelings are those of Denton Prout, who wrote the definitive biography of Lawson: "Tom Mutch, a true mate of Lawson's to the end, said: 'We want no sham biography of the greatest literary genius Australia has produced. We want no half lies or legends about him'."

By all means, let us venerate Lawson, but let us be sure it is the real Henry Lawson, not some fake figure prettied up for the purposes of respectability.

LEONARD TEALE
Melbourne
6/10/77

A personal experience

LEONARD Teale (Letters, 6/10) may be interested in a personal experience of my mother.

As a young woman, she purchased a book in Angus and Robertson in Sydney. The wrapped book and her change were left on a counter while she browsed nearby. A cadaverous man passed the counter and when she looked her change was gone.

She was about to pursue the man into the street, but was restrained by the shop assistant who reimbursed her change. He explained that Mr Henry Lawson was an alchoholic and did not have much longer to live. Within a year, he was dead.

EDYTHE BROOK PICKSTONE
The Gap, Qld
18/10/77

He was hardly a petty thief

THE incident described by your correspondent, Edythe Brook Pickstone (Letters, 18/10), casts a shadow on Henry Lawson's name and might more charitably have been left unrevealed.

My father had an experience which shows quite a different aspect of Lawson's attitude to money.

My father, a lifelong admirer of Lawson's, was approached by the poet at Circular Quay and asked if he could spare a florin — to buy drink, perhaps, but what does it matter?

As he was rummaging in his pocket for some money, my father remarked sincerely what an irony it was that Australia's greatest son should need to ask for money from such an ordinary citizen.

Lawson's attitude was abrupt and perhaps more characteristic than his behavior in Angus and Robertson's on that other day.

"Spare me your homilies — and keep your money," he said sharply as he stalked away.

It was hardly the attitude to be expected of a "petty thief."

W. S. SULLIVAN
Cremorne, NSW
20/10/77

A little charity

LEONARD Teale (Letters, 6/10) does an excellent job of defending himself against my criticism (22/9) of his Henry Lawson presentation.

However, he writes: "The simple fact is that Lawson was an alcoholic" and my point is that Mr Teale, with his outstanding ability, could do better by Lawson and be more acceptable if he did not present him as such on the stage.

We could cover acres of paper with gallons of ink disputing the various emphases and interpretations of Lawson's life and character and the value of such writers as the pseudonymous "Denton Prout," but some aspects could be left to the biographers and literary societies to argue about.

Of course, as Mr Teale writes, we don't want "some fake figure prettied up for the purposes of respectability," but I think an application of that charity which covers a multitude of sins would be in order. After all, it is at the heart of that Australian mateship which was at the heart of Henry Lawson. He gave Australia his gifts with both hands and he deserves some privacy in the weakness he had to carry.

W. PORTER-YOUNG
Walgett, NSW
(The writer is president of the Henry Lawson Society of NSW).
27/10/77

Bicentenary

Chance to atone for injustices

IN response to Mr Frank Everingham's statement (Letters, 9-10/6) that Aborigines have not made a contribution to the history and development of Australia since 1788 and that the bicentennial presents an occasion to make it possible for the Aboriginal population to make a contribution, I should like to point out that this line of thought is false and misleading, doing more to perpetuate injustice than to alleviate it.

Our admitted unwilling contribution of our entire country, which now forms the basis of the white population's economy, means we have contributed more than any other sector of the Australian population towards the country's wealth.

Without our initial "investment," which is all the land now known as Australia, there would be no Gross National Product, nor any other gains which have been responsible for the settlers' high standard of living, regardless of where they may have come from.

Only the Aborigine, who has made the greatest contribution of all, has been forced to remain in social and political poverty, while all other sectors divide up the gains.

The bicentennial celebration presents for white Australia the opportunity to recognise our major contribution, to redress historical injustice by acknowledging land rights in a meaningful way and to create within their system the means whereby we can claim compensation for land theft as well as historical and current injustice.

The bicentennial celebration certainly creates an ideal opportunity for settlers from wherever to straighten up their thinking regarding what they are doing here in our country.

They are picking up the booty of the historical theft of our country and this is a wrong which must be righted.

Assigning any other role to the bicentennial celebration will be hypocrisy and Aborigines will be, once again, denied acknowledgment and justice.

BOBBI SYKES
Editor
Aboriginal Islander Message
Glebe, NSW
14/6/79

Why not resettle the Harbor?

AS we enter a new decade there is in the community an unparalleled degree of optimism about the future of Australia. I believe we can build on this optimism and at the same time pay tribute to our past.

The year 1988 marks the 200th anniversary of the first settlement by Europeans in Australia. The importance of the bicentenary as a symbol of our development and the dawning of a new age for Australia should not be let go unheralded.

To date, planning for the bicentenary has been fairly low key. No doubt there will be a series of parties and festivals, but I think that for 1988 our plans should extend beyond celebration and fanfare. It would be a worthy and highly symbolic tribute to our 200th anniversary if we embarked now on a new plan of settlement in Sydney, the place where it all began.

My idea is to give back to the people their heritage as descendants of all those who have contributed to Australia as a colony and as a nation. The best way to do this is to bring people back to live in the areas which surround what Arthur Phillip described as "the finest harbor in the world."

The land is available. Between Woolloomooloo and Balmain, the foreshores can be reclaimed and used for housing and parkland.

Let us plan to build a future in our cities for the working people, the low-income earners and the pensioners. These people have their roots in that first settlement and are part of the heart and soul of our country. Let them also enjoy what those first settlers came, saw and marvelled at.

I have approached the Federal Minister for Housing on this matter. I hope that he will share my vision for the future of our fine city.

LES McMAHON, MP
Federal Member for
Sydney
9/1/80

The Bicentenary

What price national pride?

THE political hint that the 1988 Olympic bid might be abandoned is disturbing for Australians in its implications because the attitudes that such a decision would be based on are all negative.

If such an attitude had been followed by Cook, he would not have left England. A pride in Australia is based on achievements, our explorers, our pioneers, our overland telegraph, our Harbor Bridge, our Snowy scheme — achievements that were only possible by overcoming huge odds. All are the results of positive attitudes.

There is nothing wrong with an Australian city wishing to establish facilities for all sports. In fact, if they don't, it is a sorry indictment.

What better way of celebrating our 200th year than by hosting the Olympics to show the world our progress. The spin-off benefits in employment and permanent facilities for coming generations would be a fitting tribute to our pioneers and another step in our development.

Most negative arguments are based on cost (the rest on fear), with Munich and Montreal quoted as examples.

Munich used the Games to advance the development program for the city. It obtained facilities geared to the city's size; it obtained the inner-ring road, the outer-ring road and the extension of the underground, together with many other benefits including massive landscaping. The Games centre was a building rubble dump before they started. All of this to a time deadline. This meant they had to sit down and think positively about what they were going to do.

On the positive side of the ledger — what value does one place on national pride?

DAVID N. HILLAN
Bolivar, SA
23/2/81

A 200th show for the world

THE Olympic Games for Melbourne controversy is missing the real point. In 1988 Australia's bicentennial celebrations can focus the eyes of the world upon Australia. At that time we can be host to the world, or we can demonstrate that vision of a future and pride in our heritage has given way yet again to the knockers.

Let us join together at all levels to show the world not only that we are a great sporting nation: let every sporting organisation seek the best in their field, e.g. world soccer, an international horse race, a world quarter-horse championship, basketball, bowls, perhaps a cycling championship from Perth to the Gold Coast and how about The America's Cup for Australia? Already the Government has agreed to my request to explore the possibility.

What of our history? Our arts, the services, medicine, law. Surely each field could and should already be organising world conventions. Our film industry should be producing a film of the past 200 years. Television, too, can demonstrate the achievements of today.

What of the United Nations? Will they contribute to our greatest budget day when Australia reports to the world on whether we have been good stewards of the great natural resources with which we have been blessed?

Time is short at every level of our community: in every town, city and home, in the schools, in government, we should already be making plans to contribute to our 200th birthday.

May I suggest one theme could be "One Nation One People: One People One Nation."

R. F. M. HOLLOW
Frankston, Vic
29/9/80

PS

NOW that the electors have shown what they think of New England, how about an Australian referendum so we can show what we think of Old England?

JOHN McNAMARA
Bega, NSW
5/5/67

Towards the Republic

We're still just old colonial boys

THERE can be no doubt that Australia still labors under a colonial mentality.

Not only do we lack an Australian chief of state, we don't even have a national anthem. The High Court of Australia is not the nation's highest tribunal and when we wish to honor one of our citizens, we get the head of a foreign country to bestow some medal of an empire that is as dead as a dodo.

Australia is backward in this respect, even when compared with other nations of the Commonwealth. Patriotism in Australia consists of an almost superstitious regard for "ties with Britain." As a result of this, we have a sovereign nation of 11 million people promoting intolerable anachronisms to virtually the status of a religion.

Australia should not only be independent, it should also seem independent.

I am all in favor of a republic and, therefore, a little disappointed to see the president of the Republican Party advocating inconsistent half measures.

Australia should declare itself a republic and elect a president. In this way, Australia would obtain an identity and become a nation to which both its youth and new settlers could feel committed.

ALBERT NIEUWHOF
West Hobart, Tas
10/9/64

The Republic

Sit down to protest

I HAVE been troubled lately as to what Australia really is.

By this I mean what form of government rules Australia? Is Australia a kingdom?

This must be so, since we are still under the subjection of a monarch.

Every few years, a royal visitor will arrive on our shores, seemingly to refresh our memories as to this very fact.

Australia has no real independence of spirit. We are still tied to Britain's apron-strings of tradition.

Indeed, God Save the Queen is broadcast ad nauseam, almost in propaganda fashion, at sporting fixtures, public gatherings, dances, theatres.

We have no real "national" anthem, nothing to stir Australian sentiment. Even our flag has the Union Jack dominating.

The term "commonwealth" is defined as "independent community," yet Australia can never be really independent till it has thrown off the last vestiges of British rule.

I am one of the increasing number of people who sit down for God Save the Queen.

It is not our national anthem, it belongs to Britain, so it would be a farce to stand for it.

A republican form of government must come to Australia; it can only be hoped that the day is not far distant.

(Miss) CLARE PETRE
Engadine, NSW
6/10/66

Stand and be counted

MUCH as I agree with Miss Clare Petre's republican aspirations (Letters, 6/10), I feel obliged to raise several objections to her sedentary protest.

Refusing to stand during the playing of the national anthem ("it belongs to Britain") is a particularly puerile form of dissent which is matched by Miss Petre's childish justification for her act.

To reason that Australia is under the subjection of a monarch because the anthem "is broadcast ad nauseam" is exceptionally naive.

To illustrate Australia's lack of "real independence of spirit" by referrring to the Union Jack "dominating" our flag is mere ignorance.

Fortunately, the Australian ethos is a separate entity transcending the presence of Union Jack or monarch.

My desire to be rid of "Britain's" ubiquitous dirge is equal to Miss Petre's, but I would suggest that, insofar as it is representative of our own country, it is surely worthy of our respect.

To sit during its playing may express a dissatisfaction with the monarchy, but it also shows an irresponsible disregard of Australian embellishments to the British tradition.

Republicanism will come as a course of history, not as a result of Miss Petre's particular style of protest.

I therefore exhort her to accept the anthem for the present, to stand up and be counted as a patriot.

MICHAEL S. DALTON
Ashburton, Vic
14/10/66

Dinkum party

HANGMEN and footmen are two occupations which Australians regard with the utmost contempt, so that it has always been necessary to import these fellows from the UK.

Now that English footmen are again required for Canberra, vigorous demonstration by Australians against this much overdone Edwardian nonsense are in order.

In fact, the whole question of a non-Australian governor-general cries out for review, a situation which, at the moment, only the Australian Republican Party is firmly resolved to do.

This infant political group has many such stimulating aims and because it represents "the dinkum Aussie" idea so well, it will be most interesting to see how much resistance is forthcoming from the "Establishment" and the colonial-minded die-hards.

B. C. CLENNETT
Rokeby, Tas
3/5/65

PS

CONSIDER this letter a panicky gasp on my part for clean air and what every red-blooded Australian wants — a republic. This will not be achieved while we have a Prime Minister who belongs in the House of Lords, an ex-House of Lords Governor-General, who wants to keep singing Britain's National Anthem, and members of our Parliament bucking for knighthoods.

G. H. CRAIG
Enfield, SA
18/9/64

The Republic

Great destiny

HOORAY for Mr Whitlam!

One can only hope that his suggestion on the establishment of an Australian national awards system (*The Australian,* 19/5) will indeed be acted upon by the Prime Minister.

For too long has Australia showed its national immaturity — even adolescence — in causing its distinguished citizens to be honored only by the motherland.

Australia is emerging from the hangover of its colonial past and the sooner this transformation is achieved the better.

Australia is destined for great things — as an Australian identity, not a British schizophrenic.

J. G. DICKINSON
Victorian organiser
Australian Republican Party
Melbourne
29/5/67

Strong poll

IF the Prime Minister genuinely placed prime importance on the development of this great country in the interest of its people whom he represents, how is it he can openly state that he sees no signs towards a desire by his fellow Australians for the development of a republic?

Particularly when a recent Gallup poll in 1968 indicated a strong and growing interest in republicanism.

Australia as a republic would grant us the true right of final decision in all matters pertaining to future economic and national developments.

G. J. SCHILLANI
Croydon, Vic
(Mr Schillani is national organiser of the Australian Republican Party.)
2/4/69

Be thankful for our colonial cringe

AUSTRALIANS have been building it for more than a decade, have lavished $100 million on its construction and some even have the wistful hope that it may become a centre for an indigenous theatre.

Still I would not dare to voice the disloyal thought that a mere Australian might be worthy of opening it. Indeed, I was relieved to read (*The Australian,* 21/9) that our noble Prime Minister, Mr Willie McMahon, has saved us from this embarrassing possibility by stating:

"The opening of the Sydney Opera House will be a great national and international occasion and it is fitting that Her Majesty will be here to perform the ceremony."

It is fitting indeed. Just as it was fitting that Australian medal winners at the recent Olympic Games were hailed on the victory dais with the British national anthem.

What could be more fitting of a country that after 70 years of unity under a "national" Constitution, it still directs its loyalty to London, buys its foreign policy in Washington and in the finest Christian tradition disposes of its worldly goods, its bothersome national resources, by giving them at bargain rates to foreign corporations?

Let us thank the Lord that in this age of flaunting nationalism, when every Iceland, Chile and Tanzania has the temerity to trumpet its independence to the world, we Australians remain so modest and self-effacing that we don't even have our own flag, but are content with a little colonial banner with a Union Jack in the corner, that we could never support the scandalous idea of having our own head of State or Australian heads on our coinage, that we remain forever and always a nice humble little bunch of cringing colonial suckers.

Let us be thankful, too, that next year's royal visit will allow us to demonstrate yet again to the world our proficiency in the one sport in which we are undoubtedly supreme: conducting a grovelling Olympics of unsurpassable brilliance.

J. EEGAN
Granville, NSW
26/9/72

PS

THE Royal Australian Navy has at long last dispensed with the British naval white ensign and secured a flag of its very own. For a young go-ahead Australia, the next step is to gain a national flag and also to have its own national anthem. Advance Australia Fair will then perhaps have some real meaning for us all.

ROY POTTER
North Clayton, Vic
31/12/66

The Republic

Nationalism or chauvinism?

THE new nationalism, or the new brashness? The new spirit of purpose, or the new chauvinism?

Your ecstatic Robert Drewe, in his proud series on Australia's new aspirations, says we have found a certain rare feeling of national respect.

Not only the sun but the light of reason shines out of Mr Whitlam and overnight we have become a great and perfectionist people. And so say Ron Barassi, Paul Hogan, Jack Lang et al. Hallelujah.

Your columnist Harry M. Miller says that for once he can look foreigners in the eye without feeling inferior. Poor, cringing Harry Miller, how wonderful to be liberated.

Some of your other writers (Max Harris, Phillip Adams and company) and some of your own editorials show the same streak of exhilaration (or complacency?). Anything that Canberra produces to encourage Australians to look in on themselves and love it is welcomed without quibble.

The ABC is more blatant. Its excruciating double entendre. "The good-looking Australia," as sickening as it is repetitive, gets by without remark. Could this really be the national mood!

The Whitlam Government sets the style. Political nationalism, just for the kicks. Economic nationalism and to hell with industrial progress. Artistic and literary nationalism: if its Australian it's good. And a lot of bloody nonsense about flags and anthems and images.

Am I alone in finding much of this cheap and nasty and potentially dangerous. No powerful voice is raised against it. Through fear of facile accusation?

Nationalism has been and remains the curse of our age. Pride in one's country is a different matter. But when it is deliberately projected as a matter of policy it becomes harmful insularity.

Australia will not become great just through keeping on saying so. The growth of greatness at heart is something that cannot be easily articulated.

DOUGLAS BRASS
Elizabeth Bay, NSW
13/4/73

Time to live dangerously

AS a self-confessed Australian nationalist chauvinist pig, I have to admit that I prefer the new self-identification in Australia whatever the potential dangers suggested by Douglas Brass (Letters, 13/4).

I prefer an honest awareness of who we are to the cultural cringe of the past, or to the gutlessness of some Australians travelling or living overseas who pose as North Americans or English in order to pass critical inspection.

Let them now live dangerously, I say, explaining to Americans in particular: "When I left Oz it was in the bloody Pacific. Wadderyermean Austria bloody Europe?"

On second thoughts, perhaps before long they won't even have to explain.

JOHN HAY
Wollongong, NSW
20/4/73

We must become a republic

I AGREE with Edsel B. Ford II's plea for Australians to show more pride in their country. (*The Weekend Australian*, 15-16/11). But first we must become a republic.

Australian children are more familiar with the words of the British national anthem than they are with the words or tune of Advance Australia Fair. Many migrants haven't even heard of our national song.

At a recent athletics carnival for independent girls' schools, I was appalled when the school band chosen to perform at the event marched into the Perth Stadium playing The Stars And Stripes Forever.

Every year during the Christmas season, thousands of West Australians who attend open-air concerts on the Perth Esplanade stand to sing Land of Hope And Glory, not just once but often twice. It's still all the way with Britain and the United States.

No wonder Australians become confused at the sound of their own national anthem. I haven't heard Advance Australia Fair sung in Perth for years.

SUZANNE WELBORN
Nedlands, WA
25/11/80

Migrants

Record flow from Britain

I WISH to correct the impression created by Mr M. R. Sheehan (Letters, 6/1), particularly as it reflects on the current success of Australia's immigration program.

Our migrant intake in 1964 was the highest for any year except 1950, when the influx of displaced persons from Europe was at its height.

When final figures are available for 1965, they will be even higher than in 1964 and will include a record number of assisted migrants from Britain.

It must be recognised that these results have been achieved notwithstanding today's unparalleled prosperity and intense competition in Europe compared with the depressing economic conditions and political pressures which forced many people out of Europe in the early post-war years.

Following precedent, the statistics quoted by the Government for the years 1949-53 were based on total movements in and out of Australia.

They covered the arrival and departure of a significant number of people other than migrants.

The Commonwealth Statistician pointed out that these figures did not give an accurate position of the arrivals and departures of migrants.

Therefore, with him, my department has gone to some trouble to record specifically the arrivals and departures of migrants as such and it is now on these figures that the results of the Immigration Department should be judged. We will continue to seek the highest number of migrants we can absorb under conditions which are satisfactory to both Australia and to them.

HUBERT OPPERMAN
Minister for Immigration
Canberra
10/1/66

It's preposterous!

THE case of the family who came to Australia from a slum area in England and then disparaged everything they saw here gives one seriously to think. The fact that they were reported to have "demanded" their fare back seems utterly preposterous.

I know of many young Australian families who have one or two children and would gladly have four but simply cannot afford it. Take income tax relief, for instance: £90 for the first child and £65 for the next and so on. It just does not make sense. Child enowment is the merest pittance and so it goes on.

Practically nothing is done to help and encourage Australians to populate their own country, despite lip service to the contrary.

Yet we have the position of British immigrants coming out here at our expense (how many hard-working young Australian mothers would appreciate a free trip to England and back!) — and acting as though they were doing us a favor!

(Mrs) H. H. WILSON
Dalkeith, WA
29/7/65

BYO milk, honey

IF migrants observed the following rules, Australia would be the only country for them:

1. Never be sick.
2. Never be unemployed.
3. Always remember that Australian Rules Football is the best game in the world.
4. Soccer is a sissy game.
5. Realise that the six o'clock swill is a good training ground for footy.
6. Never tell the boss the better way to do a job.
7. Don't be a Red: that means never complain that it's too hot to work when it's 100 degrees.
8. Admire Sir Bob. Your son's future is in his hands.
9. Read only the right books; the police will tell you the ones not to read.
10. Take an interest in television (except Channel 2) and admire the biggest dills that call themselves artists.

Do these things and Australia will be a land flowing with milk and honey (bring your own milk and honey).

H. NAMWICK
Pascoe Vale, Vic
22/7/65

Migrants

Where are ethnics among our MPs?

I DOUBT whether the fact that 180,000 migrants had left Australia in seven years (*The Australian*, 13/10) will induce Australian mini-brains to draw proper conclusions from the debacle of your immigration program.

I attribute the main cause of this situation to virtual disenfranchisement of migrants.

On a population basis, there should be 4 non-British migrants in Federal Cabinet, 20 in the House of Representatives and 10 in the Senate.

There are, of course, none. I recommend that naturalised migrants, irrespective of their places of residence in Australia, should vote on a separate electoral list.

While the spectrum of migrants' political opinions approximately parallels the trends apparent in Australian politics, migrants have many interests in common and strongly at variance with Australian short-term interests.

A block of migrant mem-bers of Parliament would exert decisive influence, because no government could remain in office without its support.

History has often proved that a substantial minority of second-class citizens plays a disruptive role in a society which denies it justice.

Nominal equality of legal rights is worthless, unless these rights can be exercised in practice.

(For instance: the right to apply for an executive or academic post does not entail a guarantee that the best qualified candidate will be appointed).

It really boils down to the vital question of power.

If Australians persist in their refusal to grant migrants a fair share of power, Australia will become progressively weaker and isolated among enemies, until Australians lose all power themselves.

ANDRE CORVIN-ROMANSKI
St Kilda, Vic
23/10/67

Some are more equal

FOR once I am in complete agreement with Mr Whitlam when he says that Australia has to rid itself of the comfortable illusion that it had achieved a classless society.

Before migrating here some years ago, I was told this by a third-generation dinkum Aussie:

"You will be handed a lot of poppycock about all men being equal in Australia, but you will find that some people there are more equal than others.

"For instance, if you obtain a government job in Canberra, you will be classified and pigeon-holed according to the department which employs you and your grade therein.

"Should, however, you decide on Adelaide, one of the first questions put to you will be, 'Which church do you attend?' after which dis-

Continued next page

Warning on colored migrants

I WISH to make some personal comment concerning Australia's current immigration policy.

Australia would place herself in a most unhappy position if she accepted an "open door" immigration policy and allowed unrestricted colored migrants into the country.

I say this for two reasons, based on my personal racial experience in Australia and overseas.

Reasons are:

1. Australia has already an indigenous population which, although small in numbers and most compatible, has yet to be integrated into Australian society. This must be Australia's first concern.

2. Australia is uneducated in race relations and unrestricted entry by colored migrants would have disastrous results.

I agree with the current Australian immigration policy. It is realistic and well thought out.

Australia should elevate the Aboriginal people to their rightful place as equal citizens in the economic, political and social sense before she so benevolently opens her arms to other people.

Restrictions should also apply to "unbalanced" white migrants — they are as much a danger to our great way of life in Australia as an "open-door policy" towards colored people overseas.

CHARLES PERKINS
Hughes, A.C.T.
5/5/71

Migrants

We can't afford Australia

I KNOW the power of the press, having spent nearly 17 years on the advertising side of publishing, and I simply can't let the remarks by Mr Lynch, the Minister for Immigration (26/9), pass without replying.

On July 19, I arrived from America with my wife and three of my four children. Based upon the information I received from the Australian Consulate office in New York (from literature through the Immigration Department and in a personal interview which cost me $150 in fares to New York to be sure I got the correct information), I was quite content to accept a job with a weekly magazine at 50 per cent less than my income in America. Content, because I was assured that "yes, wages are much lower in Australia, but the cost of living is comparatively as low," as I had heard and read many times before coming here.

I wanted a few acres of ground about 20 miles out so I could get a horse for my 14-year-old daughter and a small animal for each of the two younger girls, something they could care for and love, a place where we might all be able to grow a little stronger spiritually in the quietness. I expected to have enough net income to be able to buy shoes when necessary, go to the dentist, keep the insurance policies current and even invest in a few stocks in this big growing country. Is this asking too much?

My family and I are now returning to America. This fiasco will have cost us about $9000 when it's all over and that was hard-earned wages. We have nothing waiting for us in America when we get off the boat, but with God's help we'll be right.

Mr Lynch, I say your statement is a lot of plain unadulterated garbage. We're returning because we're just plain dissatisfied. We were misled about the economic conditions here and the system stinks if you have to mislead people or misrepresent a country to get people to migrate here.

And how about the great number of people who can't return home? The low wages/high cost of living has them trapped. There are more people in this situation than the Immigration Department cares to hear about I'm sure, but it's true. They are included in the percentage of immigrants who stay here, distorting the true picture. Actually, most important of all is the quality of person who doesn't stay. Could that person or that family have contributed something of value to this country?

Me? I can't afford to keep my family here. Housing and land is extremely high; food is just as expensive; for the value, clothing and appliances are greatly overpriced. With four dependants, I'm allowed $802 deductible against my annual income tax, but was allowed $2000 in America. Weekly income tax deducted is 22½ per cent of gross, while in America it was 13 per cent. Prices here aren't low — they're very high compared with wages.

After I return to America, I'm going to start my own campaign. I won't have near the budget your Immigration Department has, but I hope to keep a few fellow-Americans from making the same mistake I did and they should be told the truth. This country is behind in many ways that are good ways, but advanced in many ways that are bad.

Be sure, I will have only good things to say about my fellow human beings, the Australians, but the system leaves a lot to be desired. Goodbye and God bless you!

ROBERT STEVENSON
Ex-Sydney
9/10/70

Some are more equal

From previous page
creet inquiries will be made to find out whether you occupy a pew up in front or have been relegated to the lesser fry at the back.

"In Melbourne, on the other hand, you will soon be asked what school you attended.

"If it happens to be one of the more fashionable schools in Victoria, you will go immediately to the front of the social rat-race.

"For a Pommy like yourself, if you have a title, or can claim relationship, however distant, with some titled family in the Old Dart, you will do very well.

"But Sydney is the easiest of the lot. All they want to know there is how much money or property you own.

"It does not matter a hoot how or where you got it, so long as you have plenty. No further questions will be asked."

Now, I did not make this statement; but I have learned since that most of it is true, especially as regards Sydney.

H. F. DAVIES
Harbord, NSW
23/5/67

Migrants

Why some migrants hesitate

MR A. J. Grassby states that ". . . would be disappointed if anyone remained in Australia for 20 years and didn't feel it worthwhile to become an Australian citizen," adding that "the invitation to join the family of the nation is warm and sincere . . ."

What Mr Grassby omits to mention is the fact that by becoming Australian citizens, most migrants cut themselves adrift from the country in which they were born; should they wish to visit it and to spend some time with their relatives and friends, they would have to register as aliens, apply for a residential permit and they are prevented from obtaining employment.

That is the main reason why migrants hesitate before applying for Australian citizenship.

Australia, of course, cannot grant double citizenship in connection with other coun-tries, but she is known to be against it, so that many countries where the migrants come from hesitate in granting it because they do not wish to offend the Australian Government.

Yet all that is asked is that an Australian passport should be stamped showing the holder to have citizenship rights — he should apply for them and they should be granted only at his request — while visiting the country of his birth.

He would then not feel a foreigner among his own people and the knowledge would induce many more to become Australian citizens.

Mr Grassby was asked if he had anything against this at a press conference in Rome last January, which I attended. He declared himself unequivocally opposed to such a move, stating that "it would be like having two wives."

I pointed out to him after-wards that it was more like not being cast off by your own mother when you married into somebody's else's family and still being treated as a son when visiting her. Mr Grassby then gave me the impression of seeing my point and perhaps even agreeing with me!

Incidentally, I am an Italian national, a British subject and an Australian citizen, and I am proud of each of those attributes. I have lived in this country for more than half a century and I have been an Australian citizen for some 30 years.

Yet when I visit Italy, as I try to do every year, I still feel that I am at home; I still feel I am among my own people and I still would like to be treated as one of them, and not as a foreigner. Anything wrong in that, Mr Grassby?

ANTONIO GIORDANO
Mile End, SA
30/12/74

We don't recognise dual nationality

I NOTED the letter by Mr A. Giordano in which he expressed the opinion that by becoming Australian citizens most migrants cut themselves adrift from the country in which they were born.

It is important to understand that Australian citizenship laws, which I was able to reform with the unanimous support of the Parliament last year, are based on the authority that can be exercised by Australian governments.

In other words, it is not possible for Australia to legislate in relation to the policies and practices of other governments.

To be specific, an Australian citizen who takes on an-other citizenship, whether it be British, New Zealand or Italian, automatically ceases to be an Australian. That has been the state of the Australian law from the time of the first Australian Citizenship Act. We don't recognise dual nationality.

At the same time, other countries, including Britain, Greece, France and Italy, do recognise dual nationality.

They make the laws in respect of their citizens and in respect of their continuing rights as citizens of those countries no matter what action is taken by someone who migrated from them.

In the great majority of cases, Australian citizens born in other countries can return to them for visits without let or hindrance, but the conditions of their entry depends not on the Australian Government but on the administrations in those countries.

As an Australian, I don't find it a hardship or offensive to seek permission when I visit other countries, even those I am linked with by language and heritage.

After all, when I visit my mother, who lives alongside me, I always knock before entering.

A. J. GRASSBY
Special Consultant to the Government on Community Relations
Canberra
8/1/75

Anzacs

Too ashamed to march

YESTERDAY was Anzac Day, a day of memories to most of us; a day to renew old friendships, born of respect and mutual trust with old comrades.

Anzac Day is a day on which the establishment and the speech-makers endeavor to rekindle the spark of national pride and unity of purpose, born of personal courage in the face of adversity with particualar reference to a military operation which, let us be honest, was in the end a dismal failure and an example of incredible bungling and ineptitude on the part of its planners.

It may also be a day to take a cold, hard, analytical look at ourselves and our present attitudes in our brave new Australia that we fought for so long ago.

In 1939-45 — when, completely united, we were fighting for national survival — we did not think it necessary to introduce total military conscription except for certain limited objectives. Yet today we conscript our youth without any li-

mitations whatsoever, only by the spin of a lottery barrel, to fight in a military operation in which the immediate military objectives, or the end political aims, are most obscure, to say the least. Why?

In 1945, as the indignant and righteous victors, we put on trial many members of the armed services of our defeated enemies for crimes against humanity and yet today we remain discreetly silent in the face of ever-increasing evidence of similar acts of inhuman behavior, committed or condoned in the name of freedom and democracy on a vast and shocking scale, some of which can be proved to contravene an international agreement of which Australia is a signatory. Why?

Some of us belong to an ex-servicemen's organisation that not so long ago endeavored to revise its rules to restrict the freedom of speech of its members and has now become a political football rapidly losing the respect of the younger gen-

eration — a far cry from the intentions and ideals of its original founder. Why?

Australia may well need strong and efficient defence forces backed up by some form of compulsory military service for our own security, but surely it must now be apparent to all of us, irrespective of our shades of political opinion, that our continued military involvement in Vietnam can no longer serve any useful purpose.

Yesterday when you marched with your comrades, so proud in your old regimental traditions to listen to Land of Hope and Glory, you should have spared a thought for "Joe" the conscript who may have died in Vietnam at that very moment, only because his name came up in a lottery barrel.

Sorry I couldn't join you — I was too ashamed.

A. D. HOLDER
(Ex WX3940)
Mount Pleasant, WA
26/4/71

Stop glorifying wars of the past

ON Monday at my school and I presume most other schools, a ceremony was held as part of the Anzac celebrations. Lessons were suspended to enable pupils to take part in a special service being conducted at the Shrine of Remembrance, students were asked to sing, recite and observe a minute of silence in order to remember the men and women who died at Gallipoli a half-century ago.

During the ceremony, my thoughts were not of those who died two generations ago, but of those who, at that very moment, were suffering untold pain, to the point of death, in Vietnam. I thought also of the recent statements of our own Prime Minister, praising the courage of the American stand in Vietnam, pledging support for the struggle against the Viet Cong and as if that were not enough,

claiming that he is prepared to stand alone against the world in his refusal to promote negotiations.

Isn't it about time we stopped glorifying wars of the past and made a positive step towards peaceful settlement of the present conflicts?

ROD LEAVOLD
Baxter, Vic
28/4/65

Anzacs

Lest we forget . . .

ON January 14, with seven colleagues from our Federal Parliament, I visited the historic shores of the Gallipoli peninsula.

We had just completed a 500-mile trip by road through snow, rain and slush from Izmir, Turkey's third largest city on her western coast, to Istanbul, her largest, in order to make our pilgrimage.

We placed our wreath on the Australian Memorial at Lone Pine and we visited the New Zealand memorial at Twelve Tree Copse.

As those veterans who were there will know, the place is so isolated that very few are able to visit it.

Therefore, it is with great pleasure that I convey the news to those interested thousands in our country that the graves and memorials to their relations are being extremely well cared for. Their memory liveth.

Although I was not born until 16 years after the fateful operation, I found the occasion most moving.

This was not only because I knew my father was there in very different circumstances almost 56 years ago. It was not only because I discovered on one of the memorials the name of one of my three great-uncles who died there.

It was because I realised that, for all our faults and even though other great mistakes are being made, such an operation would not be undertaken today. The 35,000 have not died in vain.

CHRIS HURFORD
Istanbul, Turkey
(The writer is MHR for Adelaide.)

28/1/71

. . . best we forget

I WRITE to object to the celebration of Anzac Day as a public holiday and propose its abolition, and in its stead the introduction of a replacement holiday. I do so as I believe too many Anzac Days, American war films and RSL clubs romanticise war and do nothing to educate our children to live in peace with their fellow man.

It should not be forgotten that the present generation, having been raised in this atmosphere, were duped by hysterical propaganda into supporting the tragic folly of Australia's involvement in Vietnam.

I don't believe that militaristic parades have done anything to assist those directly affected. Having been brought up fatherless as one of three children on a war widow's pittance, my personal experience has been that thousands of men marching and making jingoistic speeches have not assisted in any way.

My proposal for a replacement holiday would be the first day of spring to be celebrated as National Peace Day, as flowers are always associated with peace.

War is death; best we forget.

BOB PRINGLE
Waverley, NSW
(The writer is president of the NSW Builders Laborers Federation and a member of the Waverley branch of the A.L.P.)

15/4/74

True mateship

THE private approval and public shame apparent in the Cooktown RSL storm over the Anzac Day march leader, who happened to be on the German side in a world war, poses a question — just what purpose does Anzac Day serve?

Does it perpetuate war and international enmity? Or can we only feel a strong mateship in memory of the worst days of our lives in terms of killing and destruction?

What a reflection on the double thinking in our society.

Instead, is it not time we had a holiday and a Holy Day for peace, when each one of us thinks, talks and acts only ways and means of international mateship?

E. LOWNDES
Randwick, NSW
24/4/68

PS

WHY march with medals? As an ex-member of the AIF and the RSL, I would like the Anzac Day marchers to explain why, in order to honor fallen comrades, they have to march with all their own medals on?
JACK RANDALL
Glen Iris, Vic
3/5/66

I INVITE anyone who cares about either the Anzacs or Sydney to stand in Hyde Park with a view of the north side of the war memorial and witness the way in which its dignity has been completely destroyed by the erection of an office block in Liverpool Street immediately behind it.
G. C. DAWSON
St Ives, NSW
29/11/73

Anzacs

The uglier side of the glories

AS a compulsive participant in Anzac Day ceremonies over many years, I wish to express my concern about the future of what has become our National Day before we lay it aside for another year.

The sight of the faltering footsteps of the few remaining World War I veterans touched us all deeply as they marched past on April 25. Anzac Day will never be quite the same when they can no longer march.

The dilemma which faces the RSL is that of maintaining the significance and the dignity of Anzac Day while the number of ex-servicemen and women willing and able to march declines each year.

To date, the answer in Canberra appears to have been to let the young people participate. The presence of groups such as scouts, cubs, girl guides and marching girls certainly adds color and numbers to the march, and to the Dawn Service.

I applaud this decision, provided that young people are given an opportunity to gain an understanding of the ugly side of war: the legacy of broken families, ill health and so on, and not just the glorious sacrifice, the glamor of military bands, colorful uniforms and service medals.

The Australian War Memorial, to its credit, has done excellent work in this respect with the Nolan exhibition and the Japanese prisoner-of-war camp display.

Other groups in the community may wish to participate in the march to present a view which reflects more contemporary attitudes towards war.

I am concerned that a group of women was prevented from marching on April 25 to remind us that another ugly side of war, which many prefer to forget, is that many women are the victims of rape and murder in wartime.

I had an interesting discussion on Anzac Day with a senior RSL official about the comparative relevance to Anzac Day marches of the many groups of young people who were welcomed to participate and the group of young women which was refused.

As another example of the problem, after viewing the ABC's excellent segment on East Timor on Nationwide on Anzac Day eve, I am left wondering what the reaction would be to a group of people seeking permission to march under the banner of "Lest We Forget — East Timor."

No doubt the RSL, of which I am a member, will give some thought to these questions before next Anzac Day.

KEN FRY
Member for Fraser
Canberra
3/5/80

Cockney Anzacs

THE Anzacs reviewed in *The Weekend Australian* (7/11) is a splendid tribute to splendid men. But stripped of the image which has accrued since, just who were the Anzacs?

The fact that Private Simpson, remembered for his donkey rescues as "the Spirit of Anzac," was an Englishman who enlisted hoping to be posted home, might be dismissed an an ironic quirk.

But what of the published Gallipoli recollections of that most Australian of all war correspondents, A. B. "Banjo" Patterson?

Referring to that initial and immortal Anzac convoy which sailed from Australia in November 1914, he wrote:

"The ranks were full of English ex-servicemen, wearing as many ribbons as prize bulls.

"These English ex-servicemen, by the way, volunteered to a man when war broke out and the Australian ranks were full of Yorkshiremen, Cockneys and Cousin Jacks. Every one of them had the fixed idea of rejoining his old regiment when he got back to England.

"Fortunately, this expedition was halted in Egypt for training, so they had to stick to the show whether they liked it or not.

"When we talk about the glories of Gallipoli, we should give credit to the 50 per cent or so of Yorkshiremen, Cousin Jacks, Cockneys etc who did their share in it."

Hard luck, Banjo. History has not been as generous as you were.

J. SHERWOOD
Leederville, WA
18/10/78

In brief

Order of the stinkpots

HOW appropriate that the Queen's most medieval-minded minister should have had bestowed upon him that medieval honor, Lord Warden of the Cinque Ports.

The ABC's newsreader on Thursday morning seemed to pronounce this: "stink-pots" — or so wishfully deceptive are my ageing ears.
BADEN BACKUS
Mittagong, NSW
13/10/65

I REFER to the comments and cartoon in *The Australian* on Sir Robert Menzies' comment, "I do not happen to be a reader of that paper (*The Australian*)."

Well, I have been a reader of "that paper" since its first edition and I will gladly donate a year's subscription of *The Australian* for Sir Robert if he will read it.
JOHN P. HAMMOND JR
Mt Waverley, Vic
14/12/65

AS an American citizen, I would like to remind Anthony R. Gillingham and Co that had we minded our business some years ago, Collins Street would have now been called The Rising Sun Street.
W. R. CONWAY
Melbourne
21/2/66

AFTER reading a Scot's impression of Aussie Rules

I SEE a new name (extra-nuptials) has been invented for children born out of wedlock (report, 10/3). How silly! Why not call them what they are — just "children," or perhaps "kids."
C. W. ELDER
Toowong, Qld
17/3/76

football (*The Australian*, 21/4), I'm glad it's not only the people of NSW who think it's a form of glorified basketball with a lot of drop kicks, Mr Barassi!
J. B. WALKER
Elanora, NSW
12/5/67

THE British yachtsman, Francis Chichester, will arrive in Sydney Harbor later this week after an epic solo voyage in his ketch, Gypsy

Moth IV, from England.

It would be a fine gesture on Australia's part if the Queen, through either the Governor-General, or the Governor of NSW, could suitably honor him on arrival.

Aviators, sportsmen, the Beatles and the like have received honors — why not Francis Chichester?
W. D. MARGERISON
Kingston, A.C.T.
9/12/66

In brief

The end of the 20th century

IN spite of what is being written, we are NOT approaching the end of a decade. The decade finishes on December 31, 1970. A person reaches his 10th birthday only after having lived 10 full years and there is no reason to believe Our Lord was any different. There never was the year AD 0.

Similarly, the 20th century will end on December 31, 2000.

J. N. HANKS
Ivanhoe, Vic
1/1/70

I SUGGEST we sell our 24 F-111 aircraft to Israel. It would settle the controversy of whether we should accept or cancel the order and it would keep everybody guessing as to which side we are supporting in the Middle East conflict.

N. G. P. BIRCHALL
Everard Park, SA
20/1/70

THROUGH the medium of your paper, may I express the deep appreciation of my association to all those people and organisations, seen and unseen, who so magnificently threw their efforts into endeavoring to alleviate the tragedy of the West Gate Bridge disaster.

R. M. LUNDBERG
State Secretary
Federated Ironworkers
Association of Australia
Melbourne
27/10/70

NOW that Chou En-lai has told an American table tennis team that its visit opened a new page in Sino-U.S. relations and has prompted Nixon to break down the barriers, can we

POLITICS or tactics? South Africa's ban on Basil D'Oliveira could be the greatest left-handed compliment ever paid an international cricketer.
I think I, too, would be trying to squeeze him out of any side I had to play against!
J. T. NORMOYLE
Camp Hill, Qld
1/10/68

please never again hear or read that dreadful, hackneyed phrase about keeping politics out of sport?

W. McKEOWN
Darling Point, NSW
21/4/71

THE argument within the Liberal Party as to whether their energies should be devoted more to advancing policies rather than personalities is irrelevant. The presentation and substance of the current Prime Minister's speech indicates they have neither.

WILLIAM BALMAIN
North Adelaide, SA
10/12/71

MURRAY Hedgcock (11/3) writes about the discrimination against black South Africans in the selection of Rhodes scholars.

Quite apart from this, Rhodes scholarships discriminate against half of any population, since they can be awarded only to men.

SUSAN DONATH
Kew, Vic
17/3/72

I WAS surprised when Mr Whitlam said on the Frost TV interview that he consumed French champagne.

Someone should let him know about the lamentations of the local wine industry over the past few months and perhaps the recent bans and condemnation of anything French, so strongly enunciated by his union supporters.

M. BROWN
Ridgehaven, SA
7/9/72

IN reference to Mr Whitlam's statement that Australia will one day be a republic, if we must have a head of state I for one would rather have our Queen than some paunchy politician. At least there's never any need to doubt the Queen's integrity.

MARION HOULDSWORTH
Darwin.
15/6/73

SHOULDN'T a word as long as "deinstitutionalisation" (Henry Schoenheimer, 11/9) be avoided?

I write because I am anti-deinstitutionalisationally inclined.

HARRY LINDGREN
Narrabunda, A.C.T.
20/9/73

In brief

So what's new about sausages?

SO the Hawkesbury Agricultural College is "well on the way" to producing a no-meat sausage (*The Australian*, 15/2).

It's news to me that there is any other type in Australia.

E. S. ROBERTSON
Cabarita, NSW
22/1/74

SINCE the Liberal Party "didn't lose the election, but merely has fewer seats in the new Parliament," might we not be entitled to think that Mr Snedden wasn't "refused equal time on the ABC, but merely didn't get it?"

M. HARRIS
Palm Beach, NSW
11/6/74

I NOTE (news report, 4/3) that Mr Whitlam considers medicine to be too serious a matter to leave to the doctors.

I suggest that the next time he is ill he attends an economist.

(Dr) PETER G. PETTY
Fitzroy, Vic
18/3/75

WHAT a sad day it is when the one Liberal member with a social conscience is forced to retire when so many older members cling to their seats.

I just hope that the Liberal Party is thoroughly ashamed of the shabby way John Gorton has been treated. He is going to be a loss to this electorate as well as the country.

I. WATSON
Malvern, Vic
11/3/75

THE death toll on the roads will decrease if we start a campaign to cut out

Excitement in the arts

I PUBLICLY supported the Labor Party in the 1972 election. Because of my criticism of the Council for the Arts, I have been approached by an opposition party to make comments opposing the Government.

I want it to be publicly known that I support the present Government. The progress it has made in its brief period has been exciting, particularly in the areas in which I am most concerned, those of the environment and the arts.

I am looking forward to voting Labor so that proper and serious consideration of both these areas will continue.

CLIFTON PUGH
Hurstbridge, Vic
15/5/74

the old Australian custom of shouting drinks. It will assist the economy by reducing the number of sickies taken at work, improve the family budget and reduce cirrhosis of the liver (as found in England during the war when shouting drinks was forbidden).

I would not suggest they be forbidden, but made taboo.

(Mrs) C. L. BUTLER
Castle Hill, NSW
8/8/75

FAREWELL to the Spirit of '72. We won't see its like again for many a long hard year. Oh but wasn't the honeymoon glorious?

How miserable the prospect of returning to live with

Mum and Dad for another 23 years.

JAN MARSH
Avalon, NSW
8/7/75

THE trouble with economists is surely their marginal propensity to confuse.

JOHN REID
Elwood, Vic
6/8/75

SO it's to be the OA (Order of Australia)! I'd go along with Max Harris on that one: Order of Australia, or the Ocker Award — they're synonymous, really.

BERNARD OSBORNE
Paddington, NSW
18/2/75

PROFESSOR Ian Turner's theories of the origin of Australian Rules football (22/4) are at variance with my own research which suggests that the "game" was invented by a couple of Poms in a moment of drunken revelry in the early days of the colony and many Australians still haven't seen the joke.

JOHN KELLY
Mount Osmond, SA
2/5/78

AS at some time in the future I am going to depart this life, it would be appreciated if Mr Howard could please let me know where I might pay my $10 departure tax?

LEONARD BROOKE
Darling Point, NSW
16/11/78

DOES the Repco Round-Australia Reliability Trial prove that our fuel crisis is just a farce?

ANDREW KAVANAGH
Roseworthy, SA
20/8/79

In brief

Bitter irony

THERE is a bitter irony connected with the murder of Lord Mountbatten in the name of Irish nationalism. Lord Louis, like the Queen, is directly descended from Brian Borce, the last great king of Ireland.

Viking blood, too, is in that line and by a strange twist of fate, those fanatical killers gave Lord Louis a Viking funeral by fire and sea.

(Mrs) KATHLEEN FISHER
Taringa East, Qld
7/9/79

YOUR item The Last Laugh in Spot On (*The Australian*, 5/3) states Woods Desk Calendar as showing Mr Fraser as the author of "Life is not meant to be easy."

I draw your attention to James A. Michener's The Source which contains the line, "Life isn't meant to be easy," written in 1965. Someone should correct the impression that Mr Fraser coined the phrase. Like most things, it turns out that an American got there first.

JIM COTTON
Alice Springs, NT
12/3/80

SURELY Friday May 23 was Australia's day of infamy. How can the Australian Olympic Federation in all sincerity, have voted to attend the Moscow Olympics?

JACQUES HOCHSTADT
Sydney
21/6/80

I WISH to congratulate the new TV Channel O on its inception. Thanks to it, the wishes of deaf people are answered. Besides this group, our language teaching and students of language will greatly benefit.

MICHAEL J. CIGLER
Hawthorn, Vic
6/11/80

RON Livingston (Letters, 2/2) rues the lack of national pride that results in the pronunciation "Austraya." Perhaps it's because so many people think our country's had the "L" knocked out of it.

DAVID RICE
Coogee, NSW
5/2/81

THE passing of legislation relating to their own superannuation entitlements in less than 10 minutes by both Houses of Federal Parliament is a disgrace.

J. B. NICHOLSON
Lindfield, NSW
20/4/81

I AGREE with B. R. Hardy (Letters, 10/7) that we must pay for the best. I would go further and suggest that we now have in Parliament some of the best men that money can buy.

NEVILLE COHEN
Randwick, NSW
15/7/81

OUR leaders are said to be dying prematurely because of overwork and stress. In fact, since Federation, Australian Prime Ministers have done consistently better than the rest of the population, dying on average at the age of 74.

J. R. JOHNSTONE
Nedlands, WA
9/9/81

HOW sad to walk the streets of Sydney last Monday and see so many flags at full mast. A great Australian had died and it was time to show our respect. Each flag at full mast was a blatant insult to Sir Robert Askin. I know we are a young nation, but judging from Monday's example, we have still to cut our teeth.

JOHN COWPER PRATT
East Sydney, NSW
17/9/81

A fair dinkum welcome

I NOTICE that 84 Vietnamese refugees were whisked off to Villawood Migrant Hostel where, of all things, a meal of spaghetti bolognaise awaited them!

Spaghetti bolognaise! Now there's thinking for you!

While they were about it, it's a wonder they didn't serve them up a pie or two and a pint of beer, and have the band playing Waltzing Matilda and really make them feel dinkum Aussies!

E. O. STANTON
Birmingham Gardens, NSW
24/2/77

TO us sailing-mad Australians, the epic cross-ocean journey of the Vietnamese refugees must have more than proven their suitability for citizenship. Perhaps we should reimburse them assisted passages.

SALLY TAN
Enfield, NSW
7/7/77

And to end on a high note

DAME Joan Sutherland, as Suor Angelica, offers a heartfelt prayer during Puccini's opera . . . and, as herself, makes a plaintive appeal to Australians to see their nation as the rest of the world views Australia, as a young, vibrant country with an exciting future.

DURING my travels around the world, I have become conscious of the warmth with which Australians are welcomed by people in other countries.

They see us as coming from a young and vital country with a limitless future. And Australians respond to the interest in a vital and exciting way.

Yet not at home. Too many of us wander about this Promised Land with anything but the hope that others see for us.

So I am especially encouraged by Project Australia. I see it as a very definite chance for Australians to espouse with pride national attributes that would be claimed the land over were they bestowed with similar good fortune on, say, the French, the Germans, the Spaniards or whoever.

Apart from the physical contrasts of this sprawling, beautiful continent, we have personal freedoms and lifestyles which are so tragically denied to millions and millions of others.

Project Australia must succeed. And it must be only the start of a new awakening by every one of us.

It can lead to a new national awareness, new enlightened thinking by industry, families, farmers, entertainers, perhaps even the tax man!

As the advertisement says, Let's Advance Australia. We'll all be a lot better off when we do.

JOAN SUTHERLAND
Sydney
23/8/79

Index